BUD LE

ROAD
OF A
Boat Builder

— VOLUME TWO —

START TO END

outskirts
press

Table of Contents

Foreword

TIME HAS A way of moving quickly and catching you unaware of the passing years. It seems it was just yesterday that I was young, just married, and embarking on my new life with my mate. Yet in a way, it seems like eons ago, and I wonder where all the years went. I know I lived them all. I have glimpses of how it was back then with all my hopes and dreams. But here I am in the winter of my life, and it catches me by surprise. How did I get here so fast? Where did the years go, and where did my youth go? When I look in the mirror, I sometimes still see a younger man staring back at me. A man that is still full of life with ambitious dreams of new adventures. Other times I see the real image looking back at me telling me it is now time to start slowing down and enjoying life's moments a bit more. I have been appreciating the beauty of the Pacific Northwest where I live a lot more, taking it less for granite and more for the beauty of what it really is. I also want to explore a bit more of this wonderful country with my longtime partner. I plan on taking our land yacht and touring all the National Parks on this side of this great Nation.

My friends are retired and getting gray, and some friends are in better and some in worse shape than me. I see the changes and like me, their age is beginning to show, and we are now those older folks we used to see and never thought we would be. I also read the obituaries every Sunday morning, first to make sure that I am not in them and secondly to see who I had known that is no longer with us and then wish them well in their new journey. I look back at my life and hope the road I went down was the right road and was not just me trying to hide from the reality of life. I learned a long time ago that you cannot get any more out of life than what you are willing to put into it. You can sit along the sideline and watch life pass you by or you can jump right in and become a big part of it. Right or wrong, I always jumped in with both feet. One of my pet sayings was "go big or go home". This may not always be smart, but it was for sure a real motivational tool for me.

And so now I enter this new season of my life unprepared for all the aches, pains and the loss of strength, agility, and ability to go and do things I did in the past. But at least I know that though the winter has come—and I am not sure how long it will last—when it is over on this earth, it is over. I have been reminded that this is not a "dress rehearsal". We do not get to go back and have a "do over" at the end. I have also been reminded that the time will come when I will be looking up at that bright light and I do not want to be telling myself that I wish I would have when I could have.

If you are not in your winter yet, let me remind you that it will be here faster than you think. So, whatever you would like to accomplish in your life, please do it quickly. Do not put things off too long. Life goes by quickly, so do what you can today as you can never be sure whether this is your winter or not! You have no promise that you will see all the seasons of your life, so live for today, say all the things you want your loved ones to remember, and hope that they appreciate and love you for all the things you have done for them in all the years past. The only thing of real value and what will be remembered the most when you leave this earth is your reputation, make it something worth leaving for your future generations.

Introduction

I WROTE THIS book for several reasons. First, I wrote it because several people asked me to after hearing parts of the story. Second, I wrote this book to hopefully entertain the reader. Third, and most importantly, I wrote this as an inspiration to others who want to venture out. I want people to know that with the right amount of inspiration and perspiration, anybody can achieve his or her goals—if the goals are in fact achievable. That is usually all that separates the entrepreneur from the rest of the people. It is not the knowledge as much as it is the drive, even though knowledge of what you want to do always helps, drive is what will get you there. If only one person can be inspired to follow their dreams and work with the focus required to make the dreams come true, I will be greatly rewarded.

As I write this book, the memories of the past become truly clear, and even some of the smallest details come back extremely clear. I realize how supportive my parents must have been to have this crazy kid who was always working and not out just playing with the other kids. Sure, I had my times with the other kids, but my rush was in creating something, not destroying something. I was never able to just stand around and shoot the breeze when I was younger. I got over that later in life but not until I was well into middle age. I am now capable of standing around and shooting the breeze, in fact my wife tells me that I am at the top of my game at telling stories. The stories are a by-product of a life that was full of adventure. I learned a new saying when I was in my early thirties, "it isn't worth doing unless it's worth talking about first". Sometimes it is just talking to myself in my quite voice, but it is still discussing what I will be doing. That is probably about the same time that I overcame some of my shyness and was more at ease talking with unfamiliar people. Yes, I was a very shy person and pretty much kept to myself during most of my formative years. This may have been what kept me out of trouble. Trouble happens when you get a group of young people together and everybody must challenge the others. It is usually a challenge that requires one to do things that he would not normally do. This is quite common in the wild animal kingdom. We are all wild animals. Being a hunter, I have witnessed this on several occasions. The male deer or elk is always challenging the other males to a fight. This is usually for the attraction of a female. If you do not think that we are like this, than I challenge you to go to a bar on a Friday night and watch the same thing in action. In the wild kingdom this challenging the others for the female only happens once a year during the "rut", which is when the women will put out a pheromone that attracts the males and excites them to their fighting frenzy. The only difference in the human animal world is that women can buy that pheromone across the counter anywhere cosmetics are sold. We call it perfume but it does the same thing. In the wild kingdom the girls are walking around in their birthday suite. In the human kingdom the females that the men fight for are walking around with little covering their birthday suite. We do not know if males in the wild kingdom are attracted to females by visual stimulus, but we do know that it works in the human kingdom. And that is what starts all of the trouble. So being extremely shy, I stayed away from the females and therefore never got into trouble as a younger man. I did get in trouble from being challenged by other kids to do stupid things, such as throwing a rock to see if I could hit the streetlight. My aim and strength in grade school was much greater than I thought. The one throw hit the lite at the same time my mom was coming to find me for dinner. The explosion of the light got her attention and the other kids running away leaving me behind was all that she needed to place the entire blame square on me. That led to yet another spanking.

Shyness is also the reason that people become comedians. Most of the great comedians were very shy people younger in life and the comedy was nothing more than words becoming a bit mixed up or misused while talking with strangers. I have experienced this first-hand. As a student in Washington State History class in ninth grade I, along with the entire class, had to research an occupation in the State of Washington and then get up in front of the class and describe that occupation. I did my homework and when it was my turn to give my speech, I was scared to do it in front of the class. I walked to the front of the class and gave my description of a particular job in the state. The teacher, who was the toughest teacher in the school, sat in the back of the class while everybody gave their speech. During my speech, I would notice him making faces and trying to not make fun of me. Not being able to see him while others gave their speech, I did not know if that was what he did to everybody or not. I finished my speech and went back to my desk and sat down still nervous. Others got up and gave their little speech and finally the bell rang, and it was time to go to my second class of the day. The teacher called my name for me to come to his desk before leaving. I shyly went to his desk to see what I did wrong. He said that he had never laughed so hard in his life and that he would give me an A for the last quarter if I would get up in the front of the class every morning and give another career speech. I did, and he kept his word. The best I would have done was a weak C so the A for the final quarter brought my average up a bit. Luckily, it was close to the end of the school year, so I only had to "preform" for a couple of weeks.

It is always interesting to sit back in the winter of one's life and reflect on one's past. I have enjoyed the first portion of my life, even though all the bumps in the rough and windy road. Now I must look forward to the final quarter of my life. There was a bit of poetry I was required to learn back in grade school that I never forgot. The author was Robert Frost, and the part I have always remembered went something like this:

Two roads diverged in a wood, and I—
I took the one less traveled by,
And that has made all the difference.

That was how I lived my life—not just the boat-building portion but almost everything I did. From the first house that I built with my wife, my hunting and fishing expeditions and the processing of a six hundred–year-old log that I dug up out of the ground during an ecology clean-up in 2012 on a piece of waterfront property in Anacortes, Washington. The property was once the largest plywood mill west of the Mississippi. The mill received two sections of a five-foot-diameter Spruce tree that were twenty-four feet long each. My theory was that in 1937 when the tree was cut down and towed to the mill, the mill did not have the capability to pull that large of a log out of the water and into the mill where it could be processed. They were just too big to deal with, so they left them in the water, and during their expansion projects, they eventually built the mill over the log sections. I picked one of the sections up with a twenty-two-ton crane and weighed it at twenty-four thousand pounds. I would have to assume that they were a bit heavier when they were green and wet. The mill was built at least one hundred feet past where I dug the sections up. The log, being cut down around 1937, was over 150 years old when Christopher Columbus discovered America in 1492. A retired scientist that lived in the area saw the log sections sitting on the property and became interested in their history. I borrowed a large chain saw from a friend and cut the end of one of the sections off so that John could actually count all of the growth rings. After counting them he would study the different rings and with a lot of research determined that the tree was cut down around 1937. He used the size of the rings and compared them to the weather patterns around that period of time and determined the approximate year. That information along with the history of the mill placed the logs there about 1937.

Dr. John McMillan, measuring the growth rings, a 2-day process

Unlike most people, who would "slab" the log to make tables, which would only yield about six "great" slabs, I split the log in half lengthwise and then cut the pieces at a bias so each piece would have all the grain from the tree. As you can see from the image, the logs halves were sitting in my driveway at my house, where I started to cut the slabs off them. You can see in the picture that the tree survived at least one forest fire. That is evident by the black scorched area that is seen in both halves of the log. The fire only damaged one side of the tree, so the tree survived the fire.

The log is fifty-six inches in diameter and has been sliced down the middle

As I sit here and look back, I realize I always worked hard. My motto was to work hard so I could afford to play hard. It was not until I was in my early twenties that I decided, probably after some sound advice from my dad, to start to work smart. I took on every project with full on focus using my best assets—my splendid work ethic and my imagination—to help drive the projects and complete the task, from building our first house, where my wife and I literally pounded every nail in ourselves with some help from my dad on certain weekends (when he wanted something to do or felt guilty), to starting and running an underfunded start-up Boat Building company and turning it into a mega-yacht builder in just a handful of years. This is when I really started down that less-traveled road. I knew it was going to be tougher than working for a big company like the Boeing Airplane Co., where I was making great money and had all the benefits. I guess it just was not in my DNA to be just a small cog in a big machine.

I enjoyed my life as I believed I lived it almost to the fullest. I met some great people who have touched my life in a positive way, none of whom I could have met without traveling down that less-traveled road. The people I met along the road all were traveling down the same less-traveled roads in pursuit of their own happiness and success. Success, in my mind, is not always measured by how much money you make. Money is important because it relieves you of some of the stresses in life, but actual success is the knowledge that you did something you were proud of at the end of the day. My success came from my knowledge that I did the best I could in almost everything that I did. If the project was not the best, it was not because I didn't put in my best effort, it was because I didn't have the knowledge or ability to get it to that next level.

When I look back at the backyard boats I built, I am proud of what I accomplished. I had to come up with the design for most of the inventions I put into my boats. From my keel-cooling systems to the steering systems, none of these were anyplace to be read about or on somebody's boat that I knew about to steal the idea from, and I didn't have the time to spend in a library trying to read about something. I would enjoy the challenge of figuring the problem out. Besides that, reading was the best way to put me to sleep, and in the 60's there was no Internet to look up designs or ideas from. The plans for most of the boats cost less than one dollar and were nothing but one page of information that left a lot for creativity or imagination. I never bought full-size templates or books of instructions. You could send for drawings and instructions for building the same-size projects, but they were not in my budget. Creating these boats did not make me much money, but they greatly added to my lessons learned, which would become a great part of my future success.

I have always given back as I traveled down this road. I have always helped others when and where I could. I have even helped my competition with their problems. My phone is always on and I always answer it. My latest and probably my most-rewarding gift is the Boat

Building School in Anacortes, Washington. Most people do not know what I did to help get the school off the ground. I was one of the few people behind the scenes helping get the grants to make the school the success that it is today. I actually did it for a bit of a selfish reason because I wanted a local supply of new talent for my boat building business. I am on the advisory board for the school and I still on occasion give little lectures (talks about the career opportunities) to the students to try to help motivate them to look deep into themselves to try to get further ahead in the success department.

The long and winding road I started meandering down over fifty years ago has now ended. As I start down this next road of quasi-retirement, I see yet another fork in the road, and I am considering which fork to take. I have always been drawn to the road less traveled, but I am considerably older and hopefully wiser and pray that I can head down the right road going forward.

These forks are the same challenges that the first explorers had to face. When George Vancouver explored the Inland Passage to Alaska, there were many forks in the road. Some would lead to great areas with beautiful waterfalls where they could replenish their fresh water supplies, and others would be dead ends with nothing but mud flats where the boats could become stuck, thus ending the trip. Life's roads are the same, with not every road leading to where you want to end up. There is the main road that most people travel down that is safe, but it is those side roads that always intrigue the entrepreneur.

The following pages describe some of the thought processes that went into the designing and building my hobby boats as well as some of the thoughts and ideas that set me apart from others during my boat-building career.

The Road of a Boatbuilder Start to End

HOW DID I GET HERE?

I am standing on the fly bridge of the 57′ Northern Marine Long-Range Expedition Yacht *SARAVA (this was the second vessel of this series that I built after starting my own business.)* in Tracey Harbor just off Wells Passage in the Broughton Archipelagos which is to the east of the top end of Vancouver Island in British Columbia Canada.

We have been using boats that I have built years ago when I owned a boat building company, Northern Marine. I always thought that the people liked me so they would let me use their boat for our month-long summer vacation. Than I thought that maybe it was be-cause they liked Sherrie, my lovely wife, but then I just figured that who better to loan your boat to than somebody that could fix a lot of the problems on the boat. It does not take much repair or maintenance work on a boat at ninety to one hundred dollars an hour to justify loaning the boat to

SARAVA at anchor in Tracey Harbor

1

somebody that can fix it. I would pay for the fuel and supplies that I used as well as give the boat some well-deserved exercise and they would not have to pay moorage that month, so it was a win-win for everybody.

It is mid-August 2014 and the weather is warm even at 6:15 in the morning. As I look around, I see a small family of seals still sleeping on a log boom by the southern shore. There is a sow bear and her two cubs foraging on the beach to the north and a hand full of ducks looking for their morning meal. It is amazing to watch them as they casually walk the beach turning huge boulders over to look for their meal. I went to the beach after they left to see exactly how heavy some of the boulders were. There was no way that I could turn over the boulders that she could turn over with just one paw as she casually walked by it.

Two bears searching for breakfast

Off in the east corner of the bay there is an occasional splash of a salmon that is getting ready to head upstream to spawn. I am wondering if the salmon knows that this will be the last act of its life. Once they spawn, they usually die which is one huge reason that I want to be a human and not a salmon. With the salmon, this is all part of the master plan. Their bodies will feed countless birds and animals, from the bears to the eagles as well as all other species in between. As I look towards the east, I see the teal colored 95' Northern Marine Long-Range Expedition Yacht ATLAS at anchor.

The owner has brought some of his friends in from Idaho Falls to enjoy the serenity of the area. Once up and fed the men will be heading out into Wells Passage by James Point Lighthouse to catch salmon and bottom fish. It will be a contest between the two fishing boats, me in my 21' Hydra Sports that I towed behind SARAVA and the owner of ATLAS and his friends in his 21' Trophy that his captain towed behind ATLAS. Once on the fishing grounds the owner of the ATLAS will usually jump on board with me to help even the body count between boats. As I look towards the west, I see the forest green 80' Northern Marine *MEANDER* anchored. The guest that Tim brought has the bad reputation of catching more fish than anybody. If he touches the pole it will catch a fish. They are welcomed to fish near us but by no means will they be allowed to be part of any wager regarding today's fishing.

As I stand on the fly bridge looking around, I cannot help but wonder how I got here. What road did I take that put me in this magical place with these special people at this time? Sherrie, my wife of 40 plus years, is still sleeping in the king size bed in the master stateroom. She will be rising in about a half an hour. Her morning will start with a hot cup of coffee and will either come to the fly bridge or sit in the cockpit taking in the beauty of the area. She loves to watch the wildlife as it plays and feeds along the beaches or in the water. She especially loves to watch the bears. She is terrified of them and will not approach an area that has bears but she still loves to watch them from the safety of the boat. I have launched one of the smaller tenders from the upper deck of the *SARAVA* so Sherrie will have a means of transportation to visit the *ATLAS* where the women play cards during the day while the men are out slaving away at getting the winters supply of sea food.

As people start to wake in the other boats, the morning activities start to unfold. The people on the *ATLAS* are busy preparing a breakfast of "garbage can eggs" which include most of what was left over from dinner last night. If it can go into the pan with the eggs and taste good, it goes in. I have to start to get my 21' fishing boat, *WHITE CAP,* ready for today's fishing challenge. Before I leave the fly bridge, I ask myself again, how did I get here?

IT ALL STARTED A LONG TIME AGO.

I started my life like most others, or at least in my mind I did, going down that familiar road with the possible exception that I believe I worked a bit harder. We have all heard the stories from our parents about how tough it was to be a kid in the old days. "We had to walk a mile to school in the winter snow storms uphill both directions." My childhood was not much different. The grade school that we went to was thirteen blocks from home, although it was not uphill both directions. We did have the occasional snowstorm in the winter back then. We did not have any school busses either and back in those days not too many moms drove a car. Most of the families were one car families and dad took that one to work every day. There was a school closer to the house, but my parents did not like it as much, so they had us walk the extra distance to go to the "better" school.

I was born into what I considered a middle-class family. Everybody in the neighborhood was about the same. Everybody had just one car, and mom stayed home to keep the house and the yard in decent shape while the dads went off to work making just enough money to get by. Every time dad made some extra money on the side fixing somebody's truck or bulldozer, something at home would break and need to be replaced. First the furnace and then a dryer. We never took any vacations camping, in fact we never even owned a tent till I was in high school. We did take occasional fishing trips in dad's boat. All the kids had to get their daily chores done before any playtime. We did get a small allowance for the work.

DOWN ON THE FARM

While in grade school, after about the fourth grade, I spent my summers at my grandparents' farm just outside of Vader Washington where my job was helping with bringing in the hay, logging pulp, cutting and splitting the years firewood and working the garden, which cured me of ever wanting to have a garden or doing gardening later in life. Working in the garden in those days meant pushing a small hand powered tiller that would weed between the rows of whatever crops grandpa planted. The garden usually consisted of a large crop of corn (mostly for the beef cows that he raised), a crop of carrots that I liked, some squash, beets, strawberries (which I loved), raspberries and a small patch of rhubarb. The rhubarb was made into a sauce that was great for breakfast. I would also be required to get on my hands and knees and do a lot of hand work in the tight places where the tiller could not get. After a few hours of weeding in the morning, grandpa and I would go over to the "wood lot" where he had about a twenty-acre tract of alder that he would harvest and sale for pulp (a main product for making paper products). The work included me driving the Ford tractor dragging the logs out of the woods that grandpa would fall, remove the limbs and buck into the proper lengths. After we had several logs drug alongside the large pile, we would than change the rigging on the tractor and I would pull the logs up onto the pile with a cable that ran through a block hanging under a large "A" frame that grandpa erected for the job. Once the pile got big enough grandpa would call for a logging truck to come and pick up the logs. The truck would be a "self-loader" which meant that it had a crane mounted on the truck, so the driver could reach out and pick the logs up and stack them on the logging truck's trailer.

I used the axe to fall one small tree just to say that I fell a tree. Grandpa would not let me run the chainsaw, so the axe was my only option. It was not a big tree, but it was "my" tree.

When we were not plowing the weeds in the garden or logging, we were out in the fields haying. The community was sort of a co-op where different farmers owned different equipment. Grandpa owned a mower (which was a big sickle bar sticking out the side of the Ford 8-N tractor. The mower had teeth that went back and forth, like a giant set of hair trimmers), while the neighbor owned a rake and Alan, the rich farmer, owned the bailer. Grandpa was retired, so he and I did almost all the mowing and raking of the fields. I would be mowing a field while Grandpa raked a field, or I would rake a field while he mowed one. The rake was a device that would pick the hay up and put into rows. This process turned the hay over and put it into what looked like fluffy rows of hay which would help it dry. We usually worked on adjacent fields, so grandpa could keep a watchful eye on me. On the hot days, after a long day in the dry and dusty fields, Grandpa would get a bit thirsty. Just outside the small retirement town of Ryderwood was a small bar where grandpa could go in and have a beer with some of his friends. Even though everybody knew me as a "hard working ranch hand" I was still not allowed inside the bar because I was considered a minor. I was almost 11 by then. Grandpa would go inside and buy me a Byerly's orange soda to quench my thirst while I sat in the car and waited for him to finish his beer. He would usually finish his one beer about the time I was finished with my soda. We would than head for home to see what grandma was preparing for dinner. It would usually be a meal fit for any hard-working men.

After the rows of hay were dry than Alan would bring the bailer to the field and bale the hay. The bales of hay weighed about ninety pounds each. I was not strong enough to lift a bale of hay, so I was the one who drove the old Ford tractor pulling the trailer. I was not heavy enough to be able to sit in the seat of the tractor and depress the clutch so I could stop. Every time I tried to depress the pedal I would just raise up off the seat, so I would have to stand up to drive the tractor. That allowed me to put all my weight on the pedal and depress the clutch so I could shift gears, usually just from forward to reverse. That is also when I learned how to back up a trailer. It was a four-wheeled trailer with a forward-steering axel and a back-fixed axel. To back it up, you had to learn how to anticipate what the trailer would do and get one step ahead of it. It was a real challenge, but with some coaching from Grandpa, I was finally able to master it by the end of summer. (This lesson helped me a lot later in life when I had to move large vessels to the launch site.)

When it was time to bale and stack the hay, all the farmers would help as I pulled the tractor and trailer and Grandpa drove the big flatbed truck while all the farmers with their helpers loaded the bales of hay onto the truck or trailer. We would then drive the loads to the owner's barn, where we would all pitch in and put the hay in the barn. This would require people on the ground placing the bales onto a conveyor belt that would lift the bales of hay from the ground through an upper opening in the barn where the hay would drop onto a pile where the workers inside would move the hay to form the stack of bales. The stacks of hay could reach 35 feet in height in the barns.

My free time at the farm was spent fishing for trout on Stillwater Creek that ran through my Grandparents' property. Grandma would love fresh trout. It was my job to go out behind the barn and rummage through the manure pile to find the best worms for fishing. One-time Grandpa snuck up behind me and he reached out and grabbed the electric fence that went around the barn to keep the cows out and grabbed my right ear at the same time. If anybody has been in this situation, they would realize that I was acting as the ground, so the electricity passed through Grandpa and into me via my right ear. I screamed like a little girl and he ran away laughing his ass off. He took a bit of the jolt but to him it was well worth it.

The creek had a good run of cutthroat trout. My favorite fish getting combination was a two bladed Colorado spinner with a worm. I knew all the good fishing holes, so I could always get a couple of trout for grandma whenever she wanted them. If she were not hungry for trout, I would play catch and release. I would start at the upstream portion of the creek and work my way down stream working all the potential fishing holes. Occasionally I would find some crawdads in some of the shallow holes. They would make excellent bait. I would only take one for the days fishing. That one crawdad would almost always guarantee me a trout for grandma.

On one occasion while heading down to the creek, I turned the last corner in the cow path leading to the creek to run face to face into a large buck deer. I dropped my fishing gear and ran back up the hill to the farmhouse. I was in full panic when I encountered this buck, but by the time I reached the farmhouse, I had calmed down a bit and told grandpa that he needed to come down to the creek and see the big deer. He returned to the creek with me, but the deer was probably just as surprised to see me, so he had left. When grandpa saw my prized fishing gear strewn all across the trial, it did not take him long to conclude that I panicked. He gave me a bit of a tough time about that little incident for a while.

BAD AIR

Every year my grandparents would host the family reunion. On one year as we were cleaning up around the house Friday in preparation for all the relatives to come down to the big event on Saturday, grandpa saw a skunk coming out from under the work shed. Not wanting to have a problem with a skunk on the property during the reunion, grandpa went and got his 22-caliber rifle to eliminate the potential problem. Grandpa was a great shot with a rifle. The skunk was a bit faster than he anticipated and he got a bad shot. The skunk ran off but was able to leave a huge reminder of his presence before doing so. It was so bad and the little breeze that was in the air was blowing in our direction, which was also towards the house. I could not stand the smell without almost gagging. I ran into the basement and buried my head in the laundry basket. Even the dirty laundry smelled better than the surrounding fresh air. The smell seamed to just linger there forever. It was Friday and that was the night that we went to the dance at Ryderwood, which was a retirement community that was once a logging town.

We cleaned up and got out of the house to where it was a lot fresher smelling. Grandma and grandpa had to explain to everybody why we had a bit of a strange order on our clothes. Grandpa loved to dance. He was still dancing twice a week at age 95. The smell was still there, but greatly diminished, the next day when everybody arrived for the family reunion. Grandpa went from hero to zero with one shot from his 22-caliber rifle.

FISHING THE CREEK

One year while at the family reunion my dad decided he wanted to go fishing. We went to the manure pile behind the barn to get the worms for the fishing. I was now always on the lookout whenever grandpa was around and there was an electric fence within arm's reach. I felt something coming and ducked as he grabbed the fence and then tried to grab my ear, this time he missed and took the full charge himself. Revenge was always a wonderful thing. My dad just laughed but when he heard the rest of the story about how grandpa got me then he really had a good laugh. I took dad down to a couple of spots that I knew he should be able to catch a trout. We made several casts but with all the overhanging trees in that area we ended out losing all the spinners that we brought with us that day and we never caught a fish. We were laughing as we walked back across the pasture and up to the house with our fishing rods. As we neared the house, we were met by a man that was just stepping out of his car. He asked what we were doing, and my dad said walking back to the party. He then introduced himself as a Game Warden and proceeded to tell us that the creek was closed in the area that we were fishing in. He then asked to see our fishing licensees. Well we never thought of getting licenses to fish on grandpa's creek, so my dad told him that we did not have any licenses. He said that we did not need licenses to fish closed waters, but the fine is the same. He said that he was going to confiscate our fishing poles also. That is when dad spoke up and said that he never actually saw us fishing only walking across the pasture with two fishing poles with not a single hook or fishing lure. Dad said he would pay the fine as a lesson to me, but we were going to keep the poles. The warden agreed, then opened the trunk of his car and showed us all the poles that he had seized that day. We went back to the party a lot wiser than when we left. That was also the last time we fished the river without checking the closure status or having a license. We had fished the creek for several years with no thought or concern, so I guess that we were lucky in the past.

BEAR IN THE PASTURE

At another one of the family reunions, while sitting in the covered yard swing, my aunt asked grandpa when he started raising Black Agnus cows. He had only had Herford cows for all the years. Grandpa said that he did not have any Black Agnus cows. He looked across the creek towards the far pasture and there was a bear in the heard of cows. The men all took off in the truck to head off the bear to get it out of the pasture and away from the cows. My uncle had grabbed one of grandpa's rifles for protection. It was not long that we heard a shot. I took the tractor to the other pasture where I met the men cleaning the bear. My grandpa took all the meat and processed it. He said that a bear is part of the pig family. He made a lot of hams and bacon. He set up a smoke house to cure all the meat. It was actually good. I became a really good hunter later in life but to this day have never had the desire to shoot a bear.

Another one of my jobs while staying at the farmhouse was mowing the lawn. I would mow the lawn with an old reel type mower with a Clinton engine on it. At full speed, I would have to run to keep up with the mower which helped get the job finished quicker. To this day, I have never seen a "walk behind" lawn that you would have to run behind to keep up with it.

FISHING WITH JACK

When I was not at the farm, my free time was spent with my friends where I lived in North Tacoma. One of my friends, Jack, and I would walk the two miles to Point Defiance Park in Tacoma, Washington, where they had a pier that was about 15 to 25 feet above the water depending on the tide. There was deep water under the edge of the pier and there were always piling perch hanging around the pilings just waiting for us to catch them. We would go down on the beach and walk under the dock during low tide and get some of the piling worms that lived on the pilings. As the tide came up, we would lay at the edge of the pier and drop our lines in front of the perch to get them to take our bait. The challenge was to get the perch to take the bait and then get the fish away from the pilings. If the hooked fish could get around the pilings you would usually break the line trying to get the fish out. The pilings were covered with mussels and other sea life that would cut the line if the fish could get around the piling. It was a fun fish to catch because you could watch the fish and try to plan the catch. Neither one of our parents liked perch so any that we caught we would give to other people fishing from the pier.

We were regulars at the dock, so the men in the bait shop would make us exclusive deals on the bait whenever we wanted to try our luck on salmon. They all knew that we were giving our catch away to the needy, so I am sure that is why they would make us a good deal. We would pay for a dozen herring and they would usually give us two dozen. Back than the herring were alive, so it was great bait. We could catch a salmon during the salmon runs from the pier. We would remove the lead weight and just put the hearing onto the hooks. We would cast as far out as we could without much weight and let the current, which was quite strong on days with large tide changes, carry the line down the bay as far as we could without running out of line. We would than slowly reel the line back in giving the bait the action it needed to entice a hungry salmon to attack it for a quick meal. We caught several small salmon, but we seldom got them in because the pier was over fifteen feet off the water, so the fish would usually flop free before getting to the top. On occasion, we would be lucky enough to have a fisherman that was returning to the pier, where they rented out small fishing boats and had an elevator that they could drive the boat onto and be raised out of the water, see our dilemma and stop and net the fish for us. Jack's parents did not go fishing like my parents did, so I would always give Jack the salmon to take home to his parents, who thought that it was an awesome treat.

One fall day after school, Jack and I were walking down the beach from the boathouse towards Point Defiance Lighthouse. The tide was coming in and was already high. There is usually a good current along the stretch of beach before you get to the lighthouse. A large tree had fallen and was sticking out over the water. I thought that I could get on a big log that was floating along the beach and using the branches of the tree I could pull myself around the end of the tree. This was almost a good plan. If it was not for the current it may have been and excellent plan, but instead the current was winning the battle as it was pushing me under the tree instead out around the end of the tree. I could not fight against the current and was finally swept under the tree where I was swept off the log. I was dressed in heavy clothes and had my rubber boots on, so I became waterlogged quick. I could fight my way to the shore, but I was on the wrong side of the tree. There was no way back because of the steep bank so I had to go back into the water and using the branches near shore I pulled my way back to the other side of the tree where Jack was waiting for me. We walked as fast as we could to get back to the boathouse which was more than half a mile away. When we got there, I got in front of a heater and, after taking a lot of my clothes off, warmed up and dried out the best that I could. I knew that it would be dark before we made it home and I was already going to be in trouble, but if I did not dry out, I would be grounded forever. I was not all dry by the time I walked into the house. I went straight to my room and changed my clothes, so nobody could tell I was wet. Jack and I continued our trips to the dock, but we learned a valuable lesson and never tried navigating around down trees on our walks down the beach. We would go at low tide, so we had lots of dry beach to walk on.

STEALING PEARS

One afternoon, while I was waiting for my friend Jack to get his chores finished so he could come out and play, I went on a walk-about into a neighborhood that was past his house in an area that I had never ventured into before. I noticed some ripe pears that had recently fallen off a tree and were lying on the ground. I snuck into the yard and grabbed two of them and started to leave when an elderly lady came outside and started to yell at me for taking her pears. She told me to just wait there a second and went back inside her house. I was sure that she was going to get the man of the house, and I was in for some sort of punishment. I never ran from trouble, so I just stood there waiting to take the punishment. I figured it would be mostly verbal and I could handle that. She returned with a bag and instructed me to start picking up the pares that had fallen on the ground and take them home where I could enjoy them. This came as a huge surprise to me. I picked up a bag full of the ripe fruit and then asked if I could pick up some for her. She said no thank you, that she got hers from the tree. I thanked her and headed down the road back towards Jack's house. I arrived at his house about the time I had finished my first pear. Jack's mom was outside when I arrived, so I offered her some of my new-found fruit. She gladly accepted my offer for half of my bag of pears and she must have seen this as a bribe to allow Jack to stop his chores and come play. We walked back to my house where I gave mom the rest of the pears and Jack and I started to plan our next adventure.

THE NEIGHBORHOOD COOKOUT

There was the time while in grade school when all the kids in the neighborhood built their buddy burners. If you do not know, a buddy burner was an old coffee can with a little opening cut into the side near the top and a series of small holes poked into the side near the bottom, usually with a simple can opener. When you turned it upside down, you would have a flat top (the bottom of the can) where you could place the food you wanted to cook. The small openings that are now on the side near the top would let out the smoke from that fire that you would make inside the can. The little opening in the side near the bottom is where you would insert small pieces of wood for the fire. The fire was never very big, but it was enough to make the top hot enough to cook on. The food of choice to cook was thin slices of potatoes sprinkled with salt and pepper. My problem was that everybody had a coffee-can buddy burner, but nobody had a five-gallon can for a buddy burner. Having a five-gallon buddy burner only meant you could have a bigger/hotter fire and cook more things at one time. Our supply of wood was from the treed lot across the alley, so wood was never an issue.

The buddy burners as they were built. Note the holes around the top that were installed with a can opener and the door on the bottom for placing the wood inside for the heat. This was just a simple coffee can that everybody had plenty of back before the new pod systems or the coffee shops were invented

My thought was to have the cooker near the wood supply for more efficiency, which worked great. There was an ample supply of dry wood lying on the ground from all the dead limbs that had fallen off the trees during storms. I would make the fire and get the top to a hot enough temperature to be able to cook anything that I could scrounge up from the refrigerator. Hamburgers were always a hit. While my buddies were cooking their potatoes, which were good, I would be frying up MEAT. We would have great lunches whenever we got to-gether to have a "cookout". I would cook the hamburgers that mom would reluctantly provide for the cookout. They would have some American cheese on the ones for the kids that wanted cheeseburgers. I could even toast the buns on my big cook surface. The cookouts became a weekly event. The parents would donate some of the items to make the event a special event for us kids. Not all the parents would allow their kids to play with fire. I think that they still believed in the theory that if you play with fire you will wet the bed at night. That helped keep the group to a small manageable size with regards to food.

The other thing I learned at an early age is that during a problem, such as a forest fire, most people seem to run and hide and do not stay to help. Staying around and helping is always a terrific way to learn new things. In this particular incident I learned that a small forest fire, possibly caused by a 5-gallon buddy burner being set too close to a pile of wood to be used in the buddy burner, only requires a small fire truck to extinguish the flames. I also learned that if one has a water hose or even a hand-held fire extinguisher close to the fire source, one can extinguish the fire one's self. Noting that there are no warn-ing labels on home-made buddy burners warning of the possible fire danger or even that a fire extinguisher should be handy when using one of these devices. It only took a small fire truck to put the fire out, so I really did not think I deserved as big of a spanking as I got that night. I think experiences such as this made me react in a helpful way during a crisis and not just stand around and watch or go hide from a crisis. This was also the last we saw of our buddy burners. It seemed like the parents had their own little secret meeting place where they could discuss the issues that the kids were having, and they would all become unified on making and enforcing the neighborhood rules. They obviously did not know about the three-strike rule at that point in our lives. One strike and we were out.

HELPING DELIVER PAPERS

Another memorable incident that may have had long lasting psychological impact on me was when I used to help my friend deliver his papers. One evening in the winter when the sun had already gone down, and we were finished delivering the papers and heading back towards home, Mike saw a fire hydrant along the side of the road. Mike was always challenging me to do things and I would always surprise him with my willingness to do almost anything. He taught me how to roll the paper and tuck in the end so it would stay together when you tossed it onto the porch as you walked by the house. This eliminated a lot of the walking time. He would challenge me to do the long-distance tosses to see if I could land the paper on the porch and still stay tucked together. The rule was that whoever tossed it would have to retrieve it and place it on the porch if it did not land on the porch or came apart when it landed. I did not really understand this at the time, I thought that he was just challenging me to see if I could make it. He just needed a runner for the long-distance porches. On this particular dark evening while heading home, Mike asked if I could go next to the fire hydrant and then kneel down next to it. He asked if I could raise my right leg high enough to reach the top of the hydrant. I struggled a bit but was able to reach the top of the hydrant. Just about the time I did that the lady that lived in the house closest to the hydrant came outside to see what was going on. She yelled something at Mike just about the same time I realized what he was having me do. I was supposed to be looking like a dog peeing on the hydrant. All would have been OK if the lady didn't come out at about the same time, I was completing the challenge. She knew who we were, and that rumor got through the neighborhood really quick. She embellished the story a bit. I was not actually peeing on the hydrant like she said I was.

Another one of my jobs was to help drive his car on the days that it would be rainy. He would go to a neighborhood and deliver the papers and then move to the next neighborhood. The area was fairly wooded, so the different housing projects were a bit spread out. While driving his old Mercury car from area to area, my job was to hold the stick shift lever in place in the floorboards. It had a bad habit of popping out of place while driving and the car would pop out of gear. The body of the car was so rusted that the normal attachments were about gone.

RELOCATION

After I finished grade school, my parents moved to a new housing development, on the west hill of Kent Washington in South Seattle, so there were a lot of opportunities for a young strong boy to work to make a few bucks. There was not a single lawn around any of the houses when we moved in. Besides removing all the rocks from my parent's yard and helping with getting the grass planted and the flow-ers planted, I also helped others rake and plant their yards. I believed that the builder of this development removed all of the topsoil and sold it to make extra money leaving only the rocky soil in all of the yards which made the job a lot tougher. That was one of the reasons that I was able to get work because nobody wanted to rake up all the rocks and put them into a wheelbarrow and take them to a location where the particular owner wanted them for fill. Some of the yards that I did required me to move the rocks in the wheelbarrow almost 2 blocks to get to the dump site. My motivation for working so hard was twofold: I liked helping people, and I also wanted the money for my projects and toys—toys being a good bicycle and some good fishing gear. At about twenty-five cents per hour, it would take a lot of work to get enough money to get what I wanted. The one good thing about the twenty-five cents was that back then you could buy candy bars for a nickel each. I remember that in those days, we would build our own fishing poles from a rod blank, reel seat, and guides. You would get the pole you wanted for not a lot of money. My free time, which was really limited, was spent fishing on Star Lake, which was about 5 blocks away. I had to fish from shore which made it almost impossible to catch a trout. I realized that I needed a boat if I was to be a successful fisherman on the lake. As soon as I could, I got a small paper route. The work was not that hard, but in those days the carrier was responsible for going door to door to get new customers as well as collecting money from the existing ones. This taught me some things about business. If they did not pay, I would have to stop delivering. I would try several times to collect, but being responsible for buying the papers, I had to collect from the customers, or it came out of my pocket. Today we do not even know who the paper boys are; they drive by delivering the papers and leave an envelope in the paper box for the payment. This "lesson learned" was helpful when I became a businessman and having to collect from the customers. If they did not pay when due I had to be smart enough to not continue investing my money into their project. I was fortunate that I only had to exercise that option a couple of times.

I thought I should spend a paragraph talking about the tools I had as a schoolboy to perform the backyard projects I would dream up. I had no real wood working tools yet, but my dad had a Skill saw, a jigsaw, and an electric hand drill, along with other basic hand tools. My dad had built himself a drill press and a band saw when he was a kid. The drill press was the forerunner of what is now known as the "Shop Smith". It was an upright drill press that was like any floor model drill press. It would lay down ninety degrees and the drill press part where the drills would go into the chuck would now become the power for the wood lathe. An adaptor that my dad made would mount into the drill chuck and would become the "face plate" to turn round objects such as bowls. If you wanted to make something like a spindle or a shaft out of the wood you could either just put the end into the drill chuck, if it was small enough, or mount it to the faceplate. Dad made a "steady rest" that he could mount on the main post that supported the motor. Unlike the Shop

Smiths of today this one did not have the table saw attachments just the drill press and the lathe portion. The lathe worked well enough for me to build the spokes for a steering wheel that I built for one of my "backyard" projects.

The two power tools that dad made were built using pipe fittings and pipe, with a few pieces of flat steel for some of the parts like the motor mount and the table. Anybody who lived back in the '60s knows that you could power up any device with a washing machine motor, which is what powered both tools that he built. We had no table saw until I built one, so I could build one of my projects a bit later in life. The ten-inch table saw had a tilt arbor and a maple top, which made it cheaper to build and easy on the finished wood surfaces.

The steering wheel that i built using the "Shop Smith" drill press.
this is still sitting in my man cave today

The Beginning

WHAT IS A BOAT BUILDER?

Over the centuries, boat builders were the inspired craftsmen, or dreamers, who took the raw materials of the surrounding land, and with not much more than a dream, an idea, and a sketch drawn in the sand with a stick of wood, they created the vessels that would venture out and discover the new lands around their villages or around the globe. From dugout canoes to the ocean-going vessels of the early explorers, they all had to be built with whatever was available in the adjacent land. There were no UPS deliveries or even a Sears's catalog where one could order the tools or parts to build vessels from. There was not even a library, let alone a web site, to visit to research boats that other people built or even designed. If you wanted to do your research, you had to go and physically look at the boat.

No matter how far back you go in history, boats were the essential tools to bring a civilization to the next level. With the world being about 70% water, it is easy to understand why boats were a necessity for every village along the water to own. It was the boat that took the people to neighboring civilizations, so they could learn innovative ways of existence, discover new food sources, and meet and trade with new people. If you look at the globe, you will note that unless you wanted to travel across a desert or a frozen wasteland, you would have to venture out across one of the major oceans of the world to get to the "unknown." Who was behind all this creativity? The boat builder of course. We all remember the stories of Christopher Columbus who took three ships and sailed off into the far reaches of the globe back in the days when the world was considered flat by some of the area's skeptics. By then there was a lot of people that knew the world was not flat but was in fact round. They knew that there was a lot to see and possibly a lot to acquire out beyond where one could no longer see but only imagine. It is easy to understand what they must have thought back in those days. All you must do is to go to the beach at any of the oceans of the world and look out across the horizon. If you remove the knowledge of what is out there and start to imagine what could be out there than you too can understand what went through the early explorer's minds. As you sit on the beach wondering what is out there, the explorers sit there trying to figure out how they are going to get there. That is what separates the entrepreneur from the rest of the people. The entrepreneur is not satisfied to sit there in awe and look at what may be there, they must get to wherever it is they want to be or at least think they want to be. They become obsessed with the mission. They focus their thoughts on a single goal, and they become successful or, as with some of the explorers, die trying. As I have gone through life, I can tell which startup businesses will become successful and which ones will fail or just poke along and not really go anywhere. It is all in the focus and desire to be great along with the full commitment to be the best at what you have chosen to do. This steadfast desire to explore is what drove the early explorers to discover new lands and that same desire is what drives the entrepreneur to become successful in his adventure.

In 2013, I was invited on a two-month boat trip to Southeast Alaska from Anacortes, Washington. During the trip, it became very apparent to me that the first explorers required a boat builder to ensure the success of their trip. As we were traveling along the Inside Passage heading north, we were planning our daily trips using paper charts that were developed years ago as well as books from previous explorers who have made the trip. As we traveled, we watched the Global Positioning System (GPS), which accurately tracked the location of the boat on an electronic real-time moving chart. This would constantly keep us updated as to where we were on the chart, showing all the unseen rocks as well as all the navigational information, we needed to make a safe voyage. Below is a picture of the chart plotter we used for the trip north. You can see all the information that is instantly available: the depth, the heading, as well as a real-time picture of exactly where we were at any scale that we wanted to see it in.

The chart plotter and depth sounder combination as used on the trip north. As you can see, we were stopped in 26.2 feet or water in a dead-end cove which made a grate safe anchorage for the night. Note: On the screen, it shows where the boat is and shows what direction the boat is traveling. Equipment such as this coupled with radar, which gives real-time data of what objects, such as other vessels, are around you, will allow you to travel during the dark of night or in a dense fog in safety.

None of the original explorers had any navigational charts, in fact, they were creating the charts as they traveled. They had to figure out the tides and currents as they went. If there was a "Y" in the road, they would have to either go down the channel to see where it went or send a small boat down. For anybody who has traveled the inside passage, you know there are hundreds of these "Ys" in the road. Some of the channels are just going around small islands and will meet up again with the main channel while others will go for up to fifty miles and become dead ends. I was fortunate to see some of the original charts of George Vancouver from his exploration of the inside passage. They were accurate except for areas like Princess Louisa Reach, where there is a magnetic disturbance. His chart is accurate as far as the description and the bends in the channel, it is just in the wrong direction with regards to true north.

Below is a sample chart that all navigators use in today's travels. You can see in the chart that there are several Ys in the road, none of which you can see from sea level. The chart is like an aerial view of the area

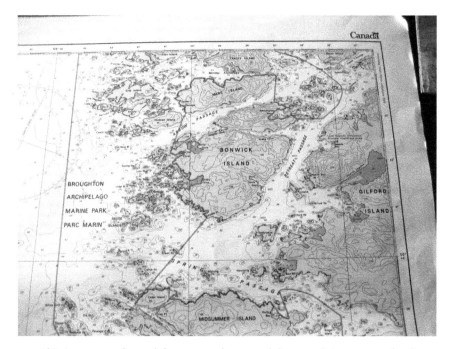

This is a paper chart of the area to the east of the top of Vancouver Island.

Note all the different passages that needed to be explored. Also note all the small rocks that had to be missed. It is hard to see on the chart, but there are several rocks that are just below the surface at high tide. All the dark areas near the shore are shallow areas, usually with subsurface obstructions. Also note all the "Y" s in the road. A lot of them are dead ends. As you get further north there are even more dead ends, some of them being a fifty-mile trip before you reach the end.

We also must remember that these early explorers had no mechanical propulsion, just sails or manpower via oars. If you have ever traveled the inside passage, you would also realize that there are not many inlets that do not have some navigational hazards in them. This is where the boat builder was an absolute asset to the voyage. He had to be ready to patch the holes that were put into the hulls after the impact with the structures. Remember that these were wooden boats, not metal or fiberglass, just wood. Whether you take the trip on a large cruise ship or in a small private boat, you will know exactly what I am talking about regarding all the barely submerged rocks that are in a lot of the Northwest Passage. Every summer there are several boats running aground with several of them sinking after hitting an underwater structure. Every one of these unfortunate boaters have the charts that will show the exact rock that they struck.

This trip has given me a lot more respect, even though I had a lot before, for the early explorers of this region. It is not uncommon to be traveling along at more than one thousand feet deep and pass rocks that are just barely under the surface. There are also large tides and fast currents flowing in these waters. They would have had to learn them just to make forward progress. It is a lot faster to travel with the currents instead of against them especially when your only source of propulsion is a sail that is totally dependent on the wind being in the right direction, or by human power.

There are some channels where the currents travel more than ten knots. Those early square riggers would have a tough time making ten knots on a good day with a following wind, let alone trying to sail against the current. If the current were not in a favorable direction, the early travelers, just like us of today, would have to wait for the tide to change before continuing their exploration.

The GPS system can overlay the current, letting you know the direction as well as velocity of the current. It can look forward in time, so you can plan your voyage in accordance with the currents.

HOW DOES ONE DECIDE THAT ONE IS GOING TO BECOME A BOAT BUILDER?

We all know the story of Noah. What made Noah become a boat builder? Did he fall on his head when he was just a lad? In every civilization that prospered, there was a boat builder. All the Indian civilizations had their boat builders. Whether living on the oceans of the world, a river, or just a lake, the boat builder was the revered one who everybody praised and gave inspiration to, so he would make the crafts that would allow them to harvest fish from the waters where they lived as well as explore further out. Where would we all be now if there were not the great explorers who ventured out to sea?

Who made all this possible? The boat builders, of course. To this day men buy boats to continue the explorations, even if only in their own minds. We all have a bit of Columbus in us, and the boat gives us those avenues to become an explorer, even if it is just for a long weekend. I have been told this by several of the people I have built pleasure yachts for during my forty-five years of building boats, "My boat is the only place I can go and be my own man." I know that this is true for me. I am a totally different person when on my boat. I can actually relax. It is the only place that I take a nap during the day.

What was it that inspired the early boat builders to become boat builders? For me it was partly the challenge of the build and partly the desire to get out onto the water and discover places not reachable by foot or by car. I have been fortunate enough to live with a view of the water ever since I got married and had to live in my own house. The significant difference from living with a splendid view of Puget Sound and boating on Puget Sound is that the view can always change when on a boat. If you do not like the view you have today, then all you need to do is move to the next harbor and you will get an entirely different view. I have lived on Puget Sound in the Pacific Northwest, and there are a lot of islands that can be explored that can only be reached by boat. The ferry system only goes to a few of the Islands, the rest have to be by private boat, and I plan on exploring all of them from the southern portions of Puget Sound to the Northern Portions of the Canadian Islands and on into South East Alaska.

I am sure the early boat builders were as inspired if not more inspired than I was. Imagine standing on the beach and looking out at a faraway land or even an island just a few short miles away and trying to figure out how you were going to get there. Paddling a log that floated into the beach was never the best way to get there, especially when the wind and the waves came up and you had to try to keep the log balanced and not rolling over as you paddled along. Even worse, imagine looking out on the ocean and wondering what lands may lay out in the vast horizon. This could be equated to people today laying outside and looking up at the stars and wondering if there is another planet out there with intelligent life.

WHY DID I CHOOSE TO BECOME A BOAT BUILDER?

Was it destiny? Fate? Were there different forces of nature at play? Or did boat building choose me? I never grew up dreaming about boats or travel. We all had our models of the hydroplanes, which were made from a scrap of wood with a basic hydroplane shape and with a scrap of wood nailed to the back to represent the tail fin, which we pulled behind our bicycles with playing cards clothes pined to the forks on the bikes so that they would hit the spokes in the wheels and make the sound of the engine as we raced down the streets during the hydroplane season, but other than that, boating wasn't on top on any of my lists. I, like most other kids of the era, built go-carts and worked hard and prayed until I got that cool bicycle. I had my model cars and airplanes to put together on the wet days when I could not go outside. Like most kids, I had my gas-powered model airplane that I could fly on a control line. I did crash it a few times, but it was one that the main parts were held together with rubber bands, so it would come apart instead of breaking into hundreds of pieces. My dad must have had an idea about my flying ability when he picked that plane out. My dad did own a boat, but I do not ever remember going out on it much as a child except for the occasional fishing trip in Puget

Sound. I saw pictures of it later in life, but again, it was not something I ever dreamed about.

I think the big turning point in my life, or destiny, as it is sometimes called, was when I was a young lad of about ten years of age. My best friend's dad was going to come home early from work and take the two of us boys to a lake, where he would rent a rowboat, so we could go fishing. I was looking forward to the trip all morning long; I even got ready by putting on my rubber boots in preparation for the adventure. While we were waiting for Robbie's dad to come home, we were killing time by climbing a large tree that was in the alley behind his house. I was climbing the tree in my rubber boots, and back in those days, there were no warning labels on most items you purchased. I am sure that today there would be a warning in every box of kids' rubber boots stating, "Warning; climbing trees in rubber boots could be hazardous to your health. Consult your parents before climbing trees in these boots." As you may have guessed by now, I did fall from the tree on that fateful, life-altering day. The fall was not that bad, but like we all know, "It isn't the fall that kills you; it's the sudden stop at the end."

I was fortunate; I landed on the only part of my body that could take such an impact. I landed on a sharp rock, and fortunately, the left side of my forehead took the brunt of the fall. I was rushed to the doctor's office, where I was stitched up and put back on the street. The biggest disappointment was that the fall canceled my fishing trip for that day. I never got to go out on a boat onto a lake that day. In fact, I never went out on a boat onto a lake until later in life, when I went on my own boat that I built.

NEIGHBORHOOD GO CARTS

All the kids in the neighborhood made their go-carts one summer. We teamed up with others to pool our resources to create the best go-cart that no money could produce. We all had about the same budget, which was practically nothing but what you could scrounge up around the neighborhood for materials. Somebody would have an old wagon lying in a heap someplace, so we could get the axles and wheels from it. Somebody would have a couple of scrap two-by-fours lying around that we could make the bodies from, and then the girls would decorate them. Tin-can headlights and plywood seats were all common in our neighborhood.

The only difference between my cart and the rest of the kids' carts was that I did not have any two-by-fours to work with. My mom did have a collapsible aluminum clothesline, that was sticking out of the ground in the back yard, that was like a big umbrella. It would fold down when not in use. Well, with the invention of the electric clothes dryer, which my dad bought mom to help her do the chores around the house, the clothesline wasn't needed any more, or so I thought, so I dug it out of the ground and used it as the frame for my go-cart, with the top being the front and the 4 arms angled back, 2 on each side, to form the wider rear section of the cart. I had an old wagon that I could cannibalize for the axels and the wheels. The seat was nothing more than a board sitting on the 4 arms and lashed with a bit of rope to help keep it in place. The cart worked ok but required a buddy to push it on the flat roads. We did have a bit of a hill in the neighborhood that we could pull our carts up and then ride back down. This sport lost its appeal quickly. The fun was in building the carts no dragging them around.

Looking back at it, the spanking I received for removing the clothesline would not have been as bad if I had not assumed that the clothesline was no longer needed before I dug it out of the ground. My argument for removing the clothesline seemed to fall on deaf ears. I still blame that spanking on that fall from the tree. That rearrangement of my brain may have been the start of my entrepreneurial spirit and the real reason I became a boat builder later in life.

I did sustain a second hit on the forehead, but that was after I actually started building boats in my parents' garage. The second hit was to continue the rearrangement process of my brain. We had the day off from school, so we could go to the Washington State Fair. While I was waiting for people to get ready to go, I went out to pick up the garden tools. Instead of bending down to pick up the shovel, I stepped on the metal shovel end so that the handle would come up off the ground. I did not realize it would come up at multiple of the speed you step down on the metal shovel end because of the pivot point. That would not have been a problem except that I had already picked up a couple of items, and my hands were a bit full. The shovel was one of those that had a real heavy-duty D-shaped handle that was held on with a metal fitting.

As I stepped down on the blade of the shovel, the handle came up at breakneck speed and collided with my head in about the same location that I impacted the rock. This required yet another trip to the emergency room for more stitches. Unlike the boating day, we did get to go to the fair that day.

This accident happened just after my friend Eric and I took a test run in a soap box derby type of cart we made. It was to be totally gravity powered, meaning we could go fast downhill but had to pull it back uphill after the run. Eric's dad brought a set of four soap box derby wheels home from work one day. These were the type of wheels that you could spin and then walk away for a couple of days and they would still be spinning when you returned. We made a simple cart out of scrap wood that Eric's dad, who made airplanes in his shop as a hobby, had lying around. It was a real basic design where the front axle was nothing more than a board with the axles sticking out of them and the wheels on the axels. To steer the cart the driver would put his feet on the front board that held the axels and push with the left foot to turn right and with the right foot to turn left, a very simple concept that has been used for centuries. The one improvement that this cart would have was a brake. The brake consisted of a piece of wood jammed between the rear axle and the ground. The harder the brakeman would pull back on the wood the more breaking force would be on the cart and the cart would come to a safe rest, at least this was our theory. The big morning came, and Eric and I were to take the cart for its maiden run. We lived on the west hill of Kent Washington. There was a back road that went down to the valley below, Star Lake Road, that was a bit windy and real steep as it got close to the bottom of the hill. There was an intersection at the bottom of the hill, south 272nd street, that was the main drive to the valley but was not a real popular street. We pulled the cart around the east end of Star Lake to Star Lake Road. We started down the gentle portion of the road. (The section before the steep hill was a bit windy but it was a nice ride. This is the area that several years later the bodies were found from the "Green River Killer"). We stopped before we got to the steep part and made the plan. Eric was the driver since the wheels were his, and I was the brakeman because that was the only other position on the cart. Being a safety minded person and knowing the steepness of the next leg of this trip, I picked up a larger stick from along the road. This was a wooded area back then and there was a lot of limbs on the ground to pick from' I wanted something of a bit more substantial mass, so I found one that was about three feet long and two inches in diameter. We started to go downhill. The cart started to accelerate a lot faster than I would have anticipated. I just figured out that these wheels were made to run, and run is what they were doing. About halfway to the intersection, which was at the bottom of the hill, I started to apply the brake. It did not seem to be making any difference, so I put all my strength into getting this runaway stopped. We were slowing down a bit but not enough to get stopped before the intersection. The break that I so carefully chosen for the job turned out to be rotten and was disintegrating as fast as I could apply it. The harder I pulled back on the break the faster it would disintegrate. We had enough time to discuss the next step. Do we bail off and take our lumps or do we shoot the intersection? We were both very quick witted and would be able to reason out any problem. We both came to the same conclusion and that was to shoot the intersection. We figured at the speed we were going our duration of time actually in the intersection would be so slight that we should be ok. The only part that we did not put into the equation was that there was a swamp on the other side of the road. At our speed calculated with the curvature of the earth and the momentum of the mass minus the drag of the wind and adding the run potential of the wheels we ended up in about the middle of the swamp. We towed the cart back up 272nd street to Eric's house never to lay an eye on it again. After I returned home, I started to clean up to go to the fair and, as they say, the rest is history.

These events seemed to continue to align themselves and point me down a road less traveled, not by choice but by some mysterious forces that kept pushing me in a direction in which I had no desire to go.

How It All Started

IN 1961 MY parents decided to move after I finished grade school. I do not really think they waited for me to finish sixth grade to relocate. I think it was their timing. When we relocated, my parents purchased a new house in a new housing project on the west hill of Kent Washington. Like all new things, the first thing you do is to modify or "improve" them. My dad, being a great mechanic, decided he was going to add some more wood details to the interior of the house, so he and I loaded up into his 1949 Dodge station wagon and headed to the nearest lumberyard, Frank Dunn Lumber in Kent Washington, to purchase the necessary wood to do his project. While at the lumberyard, I noticed a rack that had a lot of plans for home-built projects: how to build a new deck, how to build a fence, as well as anything else you could dream up. Next to the rack of home projects was a stand with boat plans published by the Douglas Fir Plywood Association (DFPA). I looked them all over and found a set of plans for an eight-foot pram.

The eight-foot pram after completion and ready for the water.

Now having a real allowance to work from, I purchased the seventy-five-cent plans as well as the one sheet of three-quarter inch and the two sheets of quarter-inch plywood—Douglas fir, of course—so I could build the boat. Living in a neighborhood of new homes with several more under construction, it was easy to beg the workers for some scraps of wood for some small projects. I could scrape up enough scraps to build the set-up jig to build the boat on. This was a winter project that I would work on after my schoolwork and chores were finished. Some of the simple details that I put into my boats all started here. I, like everybody else, used the Weldwood Plastic Resin Wood Glue that came in powdered form and you mix with cold water. The different thing I did was to lay a strip of cheesecloth on the chine and keel before applying the glue and nail the plywood skins on, forming a strong joint. The nailing process required two people because I was using silicone bronze boat nails that were ring shanked, so they were tough to drive in.

This required somebody to lie on his or her back under the hull with a heavy hammer used as a bucking bar while somebody else drove the nails in. Being the youngest, and possibly the dumbest, I was always the one who got elected to lie under the hull, with the excess glue dripping down, holding the heavy bucking bar while my dad drove in the nails. This was a small price to pay to get somebody to help with the task. Like most boats, the hull did not take much time to build. After the hull was completed and I sanded all the seams smooth and fair, I painted the boat with whatever color my dad had lying around. Once the paint was dry, I rolled the boat over with some help from Dad and removed the set-up jig. After cleaning up the inside, I made and installed the seats, sheer clamp (extra cedar rail on the exterior of the hull skin), oar locks, and many intricate details I thought were necessary to work the boat.

By the time spring of 1962 came along, my boat was completed and ready for its first sea trial. I loaded it sideways across a wheelbarrow to transport it to Star Lake, which was just five blocks away. The public boat launch was on the opposite side of the lake, but again my entrepreneurial spirit kicked in. I had started mowing a widow's lawn on the near side of the lake, so she would let me launch my boat from her property. She would eventually let me keep it there, so I would not have to haul it back home when I was done for the day. I spent the first part of the spring after school rowing the lake and fishing with good success. I would sometimes take my dad fishing when he got home from work. This was the first time in my life I was ever on a lake in a boat. I swam in several lakes but was never on a lake in a boat.

After school ended for the year, I, like all the previous other years, was shipped down to my grandparents' farm both to help them with the haying as well as get out of my parents' way. While I was at the farm, which was in southwest Washington, I did some stream fishing. They had a creek running through their property, which provided several good fishing holes where I could go down, after digging some fresh worms from the manure pile behind the barn, and get Grandma some fresh trout, which she loved. The creek was named Stillwater Creek and was probably named that because it had several sections that ran slow and deep. My dad made sure that I had a fishing license and that the creek was open for trout fishing.

I could not help but dream about my boat, so I had to call my parents and have that tough conversation with them. They thought I was homesick, but in fact I was just "boat sick." After a bit of persuading, my mom was convinced to borrow a car-top carrier from a neighbor, get the boat loaded on top of the car, and transport it down to the farm, where I could use it on the river, both for fishing as well as taking people on a quiet river ride up to the next set of rapids about three-quarters of a mile upstream. My grandparents lived near Ryderwood which was an old logging town in South West Washington that was converted into a retirement community complete with a dance hall and saloon. We would attend the dance social every week especially since my grandpa loved to dance. There was always tasty food there for me to eat. When have you ever gone to grandmas without getting some great food? Now imagine about forty grandmas making their favorite dishes to share with their friends and being a Friday night event, they would mostly bring deserts such as peaches and cream, and of course every kids favorite, thick and gooey chocolate brownies. I was just the lucky kid that got to take advantage of the situation. My grandparents would invite some of the people to their farm to take a ride on the "kids" boat up the river. This was a novelty to most of the people there so several would take them up on their offer. I would take the ladies for a little boat ride up the serene portion of the river which they genuinely enjoyed, and they would bring me great brownies to eat.

I returned home before summer was over, so I could get back onto the lake with my boat. As summer drew out with the long days, it became tiring to row all day, so I noticed there was a breeze on the lake in the afternoons. I took a bed sheet off my bed—never did know why you need two of them anyway—and with the aid of two C-clamps, I clamped two sticks up in the air along each side of the boat, tied the bed sheet to them, sat in the back of the pram and sailed downwind while I fished using one of the oars as the tiller to help keep the pram on course. The only problem was that I had no control of the speed because I was totally at the mercy of the wind. This did not work well for fishing, not just because of the speed but also because I would have to row back upwind to continue fishing.

My dad had a second 1949 Dodge station wagon that he used as a parts car, so when something failed or fell off his car, he would have all the parts from the other car to fix it with. One day while I was out on the boat, I was thinking about how to solve my dilemma on powering the boat. When I got home that evening, I saw the 1949 Dodge parts car, so I got to thinking about that during the evening. Using my better judgment, I asked my dad if I could take the heater motor out of the car and make a project with it. I remembered the spanking from my last project with the clothesline and did not want a repeat of that, so this time I asked first. To my surprise, he thought it would be an innovative idea and allowed me to remove the fan motor for my project.

The very next day I had the fan motor out and was trying to figure out the next step when I noticed standing in a corner of the garage was a Wash and Suds car-washing device that was never used. Nobody washed their cars in the old days, or at least not at our house. It was a long handle with a brush on one end and a place to hook up the garden hose on the other end. It also had a red knob on the end where you could remove the cap, put some soap in the handle, and turn the knob to either get soap or only plain water.

As my mind conjured up a plan, as all previous boat builders throughout history, I could envision this being attached to the motor with the power cord going down the tube where the water once flowed, and the red knob would somehow control the speed of the motor. I started by removing the brush, and with a scrap of aluminum, I formed a band around the motor, and with some rivets found in Dad's toolbox, I riveted the bracket around the motor and onto the shaft of the cleaner. I pulled a piece of wire, from an old drill motor that did not work anymore, down the shaft and reconnected it to the electric motor. I cut a propeller from a scrap of aluminum and pounded it onto the shaft of the electric motor. To hold the motor to the back of the boat, I found two pipe clamps that were a bit oversized for the diameter of the shaft and screwed them to the back of the pram. This way I could turn the motor 360 degrees, so I had a reverse, and I could also lift it straight up in shallow water.

The next and most difficult part was the electrical hookup. I could not figure out how to make the red knob change the speed of the motor, so I had to go to a higher source of knowledge: my dad. He explained how a battery is designed as a series of two-volt cells placed in a sealed box, and each cell is connected to the other with lead straps. The straps are covered in the black goop that they put over the batteries, but in those days the straps were very noticeable protrusions on the top of the case. He said that the easy solution to my problem was to insert wood screws into each of the straps between the individual cells and then put

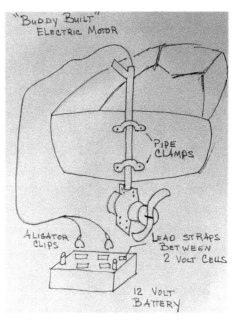

This was my first electric outboard design

some alligator clips on the ends of the cables and just clamp them to the screws. This would give several different speeds on the motor. The motor was a six-volt motor, and with a twelve-volt battery, I could have anything from two-volt to a twelve-volt power to my motor with any combination in two-volt increments. This system worked great. It turned out that it only required two volts to fish on a calm day. As that two-volt cell became weak, I would just move the alligator clip to the next two-volt cell and continue.

I became the talk of the lake. Nobody had seen an electric outboard before. Some of the people were real concerned that the motor would "short out" being in the water. The fan motor had openings for cooling air to get into the motor to help it run cooler, so the water also had a direct passage inside the motor. I went to my mentor and asked about the water issue and he explained about electricity and water. Fresh water is a non-conductor of electricity, so the motor would only run cool not short out. This design would not work in the saltwater just the fresh water. People were also concerned because this lake had a sign at the public launch stating in big bold letters No MOTORS ALLOWED, so I was looked at as somebody breaking the law. My mom, who was the secretary/treasurer of the Star Lake Community Club, was asked to have me stay off the lake with my motor. This upset my dad, who went to the next meeting and told the people that I was not doing any damage to the lake. If they wanted to play games about the semantics of a motor, he would bring an engine to the lake and stir it up so bad it would take weeks to clean back up. They did eventually back off and allow me to continue.

Toward the end of the summer when the weather was the warmest and a lot more people were playing on the lake, I was constantly being challenged by somebody who wanted to beat me in a race, them with conventional oars and me with my motor. Most of the people could beat me at the start of the race, but I could get them in the long run as long as I started with a fully charged battery. It was the classic tortoise and the hare race, with me being the tortoise.

There was one boy who could always beat me, so one day I went back to the old 49 Dodge, crawled under, and removed the starter motor. Knowing that the car really was only used for parts, I did not think it required permission. In fact, I thought that if Dad needed the starter for his driver, I would already have it out for him. I fashioned a simple mount, knowing this motor had a lot more power. It was obvious just by temporarily hooking it up to the battery and watching the torque it developed. Like before, I fabricated a propeller and mounted it on the shaft. I used some heavy-duty jumper cables for the wires and took the boat to the lake early one morning for the test trial.

I was astonished by the horsepower this motor had. I had to tweak the propeller to get the full use the power. After recharging the battery, I returned to the lake in the afternoon and laid in wait for my rival. He did show when he saw me out there, so we set the rules. The race was from the west end of the lake to the launch ramp, which was only about eight hundred yards. When the race started, I put the cables on the six-volt stud, and the boat took off. He was keeping up, so I moved the cables to the twelve-volt terminal, and the boat just about came up on plane. I shot past him with amazing speed. The battery was about dead by the time I got to the end of the racecourse. I won the race and earned the respect of the competition on the lake. That was the one and only time I used that motor. After I told Dad about it, he said that on twelve volts with the six-volt starter motor, I probably had about seven horsepower, which was a lot more than I anticipated. I think my dad was proud of the fact that I took it upon myself to develop the electric outboard motor which is common today on all the lakes and even in the bays.

NOW THE BUG BITES

In the winter of 1962, I went back to the lumberyard with Dad, and now I just focused on the rack with the boat plans while he was getting the wood for his next project. (The lumberyard, Frank Dunn Lumber in Kent, Washington, would come to know me quite well as the years progressed. I became a familiar face with my yearly boat projects as well as the thirty-six hundred–square-foot house I built later in life using materials from their lumberyard.) This time I found a set of plans for a thirteen-foot, four-inch Ed Monk Sr. designed runabout. With the sale of the 8' pram, Dad also was my "Boat Broker" selling every boat that I built, and my now expanded paper route, I now had some extra spending money to add to the lawn-mowing money and my allowance, so I could get the lumber for the bigger boat.

That winter was spent building the boat with technical advice and some significant help from Dad. It was a fun project that brought Dad and me closer together because I think he was getting a bit of the bug also. He had his own projects, and I also think he wanted me to take ownership in my boat projects, so he let me make a lot of the decisions as well as do a lot of the work, except for the nailing part. He did let me nail once or twice while he did the bucking under the hull.

The build was like the eight-foot pram, just a bit bigger. It had some exterior decks, which were more of a challenge. This boat started an innovative design idea that I dreamed up. Because of my "low-budget Bud" philosophy, I devised a way to use one size thinner plywood than what the plans called for by installing more longitudinal stringers. This would reduce the effective panel size, which would keep the panel, or "skin", strong enough. This method would not only build a stronger hull but would also build a lighter hull. The lesser cost was a bonus even though that is what started the design change in the first place.

Dad had an old ten horsepower Martin outboard motor that he had as a kicker on an old boat he had used for fishing before we relocated. I made sure it would still run so I knew I had dependable power before the boat was finished.

Once the boat was complete, I had a bigger problem. I had no trailer (and no car or driver's license), it didn't really fit on the wheelbarrow, and it was a long five-mile walk and about five hundred feet in elevation, which meant a big hill to climb to get home from Puget Sound, where I wanted to go boating. I had to find some other way to get the boat to Puget Sound, so I could go fishing.

We had met a friend who lived on the other side of Star Lake who had a flatbed truck. John also liked to go fishing, as well as eating my mom's cooking (I am sure he liked the cooking a lot more than the boating), so he and I would load the boat onto the back of his truck and take the boat to the public launch ramp at Saltwater State Park in Des Moines, Washington. We would slide the boat off the back of the truck and then push the boat bow first into the water. We would place the motor onto the boat and put the gas cans as well as all the fishing gear inside and head out to fish. I had a spare outboard motor that I would through up into the bow of the boat in case we had an engine failure. I believe in Murphy's Law. (Murphy's Law is an adage or epigram that is typically stated as: Anything that can go wrong will go wrong). My theory was that if I had a spare motor the main motor had no reason to fail. (I did experience this phenomenon much later in life. I bought a new 9.9 trolling motor for my 21' fish boat because I was going to take the boat along for the two-month trip north. I wanted a "take home" motor incase the big motor should fail. A few weeks before the trip and just 2 days after I installed the trolling motor, the kids wanted me to take them out to get some prawns. I put all the gear into boat and headed to the launch ramp, so we could get our supply of prawns. We got out onto the prawning area and tried out the new trolling motor which worked great. The big motor looked over at the small motor and knew that the main reason that I bought the small motor was in case the big motor failed. So that is exactly what it did. It waited until we were out on the fishing grounds with the 4 prawn traps down on the bottom in about 300 feet of water. The motor died and would not start when we tried. I had a good mechanic along with me, so we tried everything that we knew to get it started again but we could not get any spark. We determined that the computer was gone so we had to give up while we still had some battery left. Pulling the prawn traps requires an electric powered puller which requires the big engine to be running so that it would keep the batteries charged with its charging alternator. Now that the engine won't run, and we depleted a lot of the battery trying to start the big motor we didn't have enough battery power to pull the four prawn traps from the 300 feet of water that they were in. This required pulling them by hand, so I made teams of two people to pull the traps. With five of us on the boat that would allow one person to sit out. That was usually one of the girls. I do believe in equal rights and had to continue to remind both of my daughters that they had to take their fair turn. We got the four traps in and started to head back to the launch ramp that was not more than one and a half miles away. The only issue was that we had to go through Deception Pass. Anybody knows that the current can move pretty fast through the pass. I, being an expert boater, had a plan. We would travel in the back eddies which would help us get through the pass. Murphy's Law was now in full effect. We had the tide dead against us, and it was a day that had a large tide, so it was moving opposite us at about one knot faster than we were able to go. While in the back eddy we could make good speed, so my expert theory was to "shoot" out into the current with as much speed as we could get. It almost worked. Both daughters, because they love their dad, grabbed the paddles, and tried to give that extra boost that could get us through that one bad spot. It did not take long to come to the realization that it wasn't going to be. We had a choice, we could either bob around and wait for the tide to change or we could take the boat to another launch ramp about five miles away and have somebody come and meet us, so we could go and get the trailer. While the captain was considering the two options somebody came along in their 18' power boat and offered to tow us through. We sent them a line and were through the pass in less than five minutes. He continued to tow us to the launch ramp instead of letting us loose, so we could go in under our own power because he knew that it would hurt my pride the most by doing that.) This fishing kept John and I occupied during our spare time throughout the summer of '63, or at least when I could get John to take the boat to the water. Sometimes I would have to bribe him by letting him run the motor while fishing.

On one trip, we encountered stormy weather coming back, it took us a lot longer returning than anybody expected. My mother called the US Coast Guard, but there was nothing they could do, which was probably a good thing for me because I did not need my name on their books. This would not be the only time my mom called the USCG to have me found. Looking back on it, a simple VHF marine radio would have been a good thing. Remember that there were no cell phones back in those days, and neither were there any phone booths out on the water. If they were really concerned, they would have gotten me a VHF marine radio for Christmas or my birthday or even as a christening present for one of my boats. When I look back at it now, they probably never actually called the USCG; they just wanted me to believe they did. If I would somehow get "lost at sea," they would have gotten their garage space back, and there no longer would have been a boat stored in their driveway where they wanted to park their cars.

THE BITE BECOMES AN ITCH

The next winter, 1963, a bigger boat was on the table. My dad sold the thirteen-foot, four-inch Monk design to a friend, and I took the money and bought plans and the materials for a fifteen-foot open boat. I spent the winter building the boat. As in the last boat, I used one size thinner plywood and added more cedar longitudinal stringers, so the boat would stay light but strong. This time I realized sooner than later that I would need a trailer, so my dad and I searched for an axle to build a trailer on. While looking through the want ads in the Seattle Times, I was able to locate a rear axle from an old Flint car complete with brass hubcaps. I never was able to learn much about the Flint until somebody named Google made a device for the "magic box" that would allow me to learn more. I would have given almost anything for a computer when I was trying to figure out all of my systems for all of the boats I built. I guess not having easy access is what made me what I became. I had to figure it out on my own.

Dad and I fabricated the trailer when we were not building the boat. This is when dad taught me how to weld. He allowed me to do a lot of the work, so I could learn more. I would fit and weld most of the parts and dad would go back over any critical welds to make sure that they were going to be good, especially the ones that held the axel to the frame and the one that held the hitch coupler to the tongue.

I was going to use my paper route money to find a motor for the boat, but Dad came through by trading a small metal lathe that was collecting dust on the work bench for a two-cylinder, air-cooled Onan gas engine that was from a refrigeration unit mounted on a semitrailer. The engine was put into the boat, and I direct coupled it to a shaft and ran it through a homemade shaft log with a shaft packing gland (which is designed to keep the water out of the boat) and homemade support strut. The exhaust was run directly overboard through the hull side with no muffler. I fabricated a specially designed hull fitting to protect the plywood hull side from the heat of the exhaust (this was similar to what was used in canvas tents to keep the stovepipe from burning down the tent. All of the pieces that I had to fabricate are sitting on the shelves of the better marine hardware stores today. I probably did not have enough money to pay for them anyway, but I would have had an easy source to see what I needed instead of having to dream it up on my own. I did it the same way that the first boat builders had to do it, by using their imagination and just work out the solution to the problem. The downside of this setup was that there was no neutral or reverse. As soon as the engine started, you were moving forward. If you remember, there were a lot of old outboard motors that were the same way. My dad had a large four-cylinder opposed (two cylinders opposing each other with the spark plugs on the two sides of the engines, so it was easy to get a shock if you weren't careful) Johnson outboard motor lying around that had no neutral or reverses. You would wrap the rope around the exposed flywheel, pull like hell and hang on. If the motor started, you were off and running. You were smart to always have somebody else on the boat in case you fell over that way they could turn around and hopefully pick you up.

The steering was another "low-budget bud" system consisting of a steel shaft with a rudder blade welded to it. The top had a short tiller arm welded on facing aft. The shaft was secured to the transom with a similar method I used for the electric outboard on the pram but with a slight upgrade. I screwed a pipe nipple into the side branch of a one-inch pipe T and then screwed a pipe flange onto the nipple. I made two of these assemblies and then fastened them to the transom of the boat with the runs of the pipe Ts running vertical. The two Ts had to be placed onto the rudder shaft before the tiller arm was welded onto the rudder shaft. The steering itself consisted of the parts from any standard outboard boat and could be purchased from the Sears catalog. The parts consisted of some pulleys and a steering wheel with a grooved section that the tiller cable was wrapped around. Two big springs were installed to compensate for the tiller arm length during a turn.

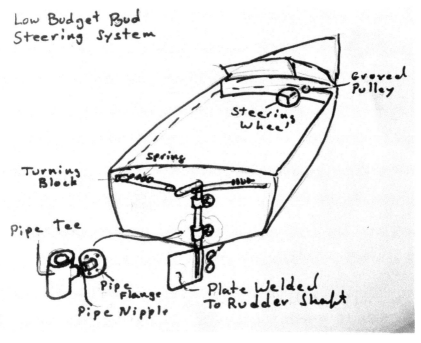

The steering system I used on several of the boats.

The boat ran well, with the biggest problems being no neutral or reverse and there was no muffler, making the boat sound like an airplane going across the water. The boat trolled well so Dad and I could go fishing. We would take some friends who would want to go fishing also. I remembered my almost fishing trip to a lake that I never had, so I wanted to make sure I always gave people the opportunity to get out onto the water. I do remember taking one friend out fishing with Dad. Steve brought some snacks that his mom put together for him. They consisted of a can of sardines and a bag of crackers. Steve's mom never knew that one of my dad's favorite snacks was crackers and sardines, so Steve lost out. I do believe he caught a fish, so Dad thought it was an even trade. Dad enjoyed fishing and being on the water almost as much as I did so it was not a problem convincing him to tow the boat to the launch ramp on the nice weekends, so we could use the boat. Being my boat, I usually got to run the boat. I was the CAPTAIN, he was just the Admiral.

The fifteen-foot boat took me through junior high school. My boat-building experience made shop class a breeze. The junior high shop teacher, Mr. Flairity, had me become his assistant helping the others with their projects. I had a good working knowledge of the tools that were in the Junior High shop class as well as how to sharpen and get the best work out of the tools. Mr. Flairity had a story that he always told in his shop class that always stuck with me. He told of a sign in Mr. Pools barber shop that read "we don't charge for the amount of hair that we remove; we charge for the knowledge of how to remove the hair". That has stuck with me for many years. In later life, when I had my own boat shop, I would tell the customers my own line, "the quality remains long after the price is forgotten".

THE ITCH GETS WORSE

In 1964 I entered high school, so the boat-building projects become more complicated. Since I had scratched the surface with inboard power, I decided to expand my process. It was the winter of 1964, and I had another set of DFPA plans and a small truckload of wood purchased from my now-expanded paper route and the sale of the fifteen-foot boat.

I was ready to start a new build. I spent all of my extra time building a seventeen-foot cabin cruiser complete with a stand-up helm station.

After the hull was built, I had my mom take me to a junkyard to find an engine for the boat. (I would get a job several years in the future at the exact location where the junkyard was located. It became the site of Delta Marine Inc in South Seattle.) mom had just got her driver's license and dad bought her an old Ford station wagon to drive us kids around. This time I picked out a four-cylinder Austin A-40 engine with a four-speed manual transmission. I picked the manual transmission because this boat was going to have a neutral and a reverse. The reason I picked this engine was that in my search at the junkyards, I would pull the engine and transmission out of the car, roll the engine over, and pull the oil pan off and inspect the crank shaft. This was the only engine that had a good crank shaft. I had helped my dad rebuild several engines as a boy and knew that the expensive part to fix was the lower end which consisted of the crank shaft, the connecting rods, and the pistons.

I need to note at this time that I did not have a driver's license. If it were not for my mom, I could never accomplish a lot of what I did. She was the one who would drive me to the store for parts, to the junkyards for parts, and to do most of my other scrounging around. Her reward was that this kept me off the streets, and she also liked being on the water and salmon fishing with the family.

After I purchased the engine and brought it home, I mounted the engine into the hull, at which time I realized this engine required water for cooling. Marine heat exchangers were too costly and required a sea water pump, which was too much for low-budget Bud, so I built my own keel coolers. At the time I did not know that keel cooling was actually a way of cooling marine engines. I thought they were all heat-exchanger cooled.

The keel coolers I built consisted of galvanized pipe secured to the bottom of the hull with two flanges attached to the underside of the hull and bedded with a sealant to keep the seawater out. The pipes formed a long "U" so that the water would flow in from one pipe fitting and flow out from the other fitting located close to the first fitting. That kept the plumbing on the inside simple. The two hoses would go to the same fittings on the engine that went to the radiator. My dad made the couplings, so I could attach hoses to the inside and run to the cooling ports on the engine. The water pump on the engine is enough to circulate the water though the keel coolers just like it must circulate the water through the radiator on a car. I had to mount a small expansion tank to contain the extra water that would result from the thermal expansion of the water as it became heated, just like in the cars.

I also wanted to have a bit quieter boat, so this time I ran the exhaust out the back of the boat. Knowing the exhaust would get hot when running hard, I had to design a way to keep the exhaust cool, so I made a scoop-shaped through-hull fitting that would pick up water once the boat got moving and spray it into the exhaust pipe, keeping the exhaust cool to the touch. The faster the boat went the more horsepower it used and the more water it would spray to cool the hot exhaust pipe. The system worked great. My dad always said that it was better to be lucky than smart. Most all of my systems worked the first time, and it was not because I did any engineering of math equations to figure the problem out. I just studied the problem and tried to "reason" the problem out. The keel cooler was a big example. It was not a big engine and the car did not have a big radiator. I knew from experience that if you set a can of warm pop in the refrigerator, it will get cold. If you set that same can of Warm pop in a bucket of icy water, it will get cold a lot faster. The radiator, being the pipes that were under water, would have no problem cooling the engine down.

I welded up a steel strut and installed a simple plastic bushing that I homemade using the drill press as a lathe. The forward end of the shaft was coupled to the engine using the original universal joints that were on the back of the transmission of the car.

To be able to put a propeller onto the shaft, I had to machine the shaft to fit the prop. The propeller I was using was an extra outboard propeller from previous boats. The normal inboard boats have tapered shafts which would have required a machinist to do which would have meant a considerable expense. I could not imagine how many newspapers I would have to sell to pay for the machinist or even a propeller to fit. The machining process was time consuming, but all that had to be done was to make the diameter smaller, so the propeller would slide onto the shaft. I had to start the engine, put the boat in gear, and work the shaft down using a series of metal files. To keep the engine cool, I put a lawn sprinkler under the boat to spray onto the keel coolers. The old-style outboard motor propellers had "shear pins" instead of keyways so all that was required was a hole in the shaft for the shear pin to fit into. I would thread the end of the shaft, so I could put a nut on to make sure I did not lose the prop if the shear pin broke. After the prop was fit to the shaft and my now-common outboard rudder system was installed, I was ready to go boating. The last task was to build a simple trailer to be able to transport the boat to the water. Dad was more excited about getting this boat out to see what this weird system would do so he did a lot of the work on the trailer to make it get finished in a weekend.

This time I had to do all my household chores, so Dad would tow the boat to the marina, where they had a lift system to launch the boats. The lift system consisted of a large elevator that would go from the water to the three floors of boats that the customers had stored inside, you would back up in front of the lift and they would pick the boat up with two overhead hoists and straps and then sit the boat on a cart that they had that they could push onto the elevator. You would put all your fishing gear into the boat, climb inside and they would lower you into the water. They could stop the lift when you got deep enough to start your engine and make sure that it would run. After you gave them the thumbs up, they would drop the boat the rest of the way into the water, so you could leave. When the boat was lowered into the water deep enough, I started the engine and checked for leaks. All looked good, so I gave them the thumbs up and they lowered the boat the rest of the way into the water. I pushed in the manual clutch, put the boat into reverse, and backed out of the hoist. I had to be beaming from ear to ear. In the summer of 1964, the marina people would watch as I paddled the boat off the hoist and paddled it back onto the hoist because of my direct drive system, but in the summer of 1965, it was all different. Reverse was a bit slow because I had no way to calculate the speed and reduction. After backing into the sound and clear of the docks, I put the boat in second gear and headed out.

As I ran the throttle up, I realized I was still in a lower gear than the power I had available with the propeller I had on, so I shifted all the way to fourth, and Dad and I went for the sea trial. The boat performed well, and as luck would have it (Dad always said it is better to have luck than skill, and I sure had the luck), the prop match was perfect for fourth gear and two people in the boat. When we came back to the dock to pick up Mom and my sister, fourth gear was a bit much, so we had to cruise in third gear. Fishing was easy because we could pick the gear that would have the perfect trolling speed at engine idle. The family spent a lot of time on this boat during the summer. As with the others, Dad sold the boat at the end of the season, which was when I had to go back to school anyway. And as with the previous boats, we went back to the lumberyard and again I bought a set of plans and the materials to start the next boat.

THE ITCH BECOMES DISEASE

In the fall of 1965, after looking at several boat plans, I opted for an eighteen-foot with a cabin, so I could sit inside and steer when the weather was bad. It was all the same scenarios as before with the hull building during the winter and a trailer to move the boat on. By this time Dad had taught me how to weld good enough so I could do a lot of the fabrication myself. To make extra money I took on a fabrication project to build a trailer for a neighbor. The neighbor was one that paid me to rake all the rocks out of his yard and plant his grass which helped on earlier boat projects. He knew that I was a hard worker and treated him fair and honestly with his projects, so he trusted me with the trailer project. He wanted the trailer to look somewhat like his camper that went onto the back of his pickup truck. There were no trailers available that looked like what he designed, so the only way to get it was to have it built. I would also assume that by now the entire neighborhood knew about this goofy kid that worked hard to earn some money so that he could build these crazy boats. He probably also knew that if I got to a difficult part on the build that I could consult with Dad and he would be there to help.

When the hull was completed and rolled over, the exterior painted, and the trailer readied, we dragged the boat out of the garage and winched it onto the trailer. It was left in the driveway, where I built an A-frame, so I could put the engine into the boat. The A-frame was from three trees that I borrowed from the wood lot behind the house. It was about twenty acres of undeveloped forest that was a wonderful place to restock the firewood supply for the winter. The three trees, after I was finished with them, helped keep the family warm during chilly winter nights, so I actually did a double service by felling the three trees. Below is a picture of the hull sitting on the trailer under the A-frame.

The A-frame with the boat backed under it and the engine in the boat.

I next had to come up with an engine. I had a friend named J. J. whose family owned their own junkyard. They had an old Studebaker with a straight six-cylinder engine and an automatic three-speed transmission. When I asked what he wanted for the engine and transmission, he said he wanted one of the outboard motors I had in my collection. I had a twenty-five horsepower Johnson that might have run at one time, so we made the trade. My dad, being an excellent mechanic and very knowledgeable about cars, told me that the transmission Studebaker used was built by Borg Warner transmission company (Borg Warner also built a lot of transmissions for boats), and they had a thrust bearing in the tail end of the transmission like what they would do for the marine transmissions even though there is no need for a thrust bearing in a car.

After removing the engine with the transmission as well as the complete dash panel, I proceeded to rig it up so I could, with the help of my dad and one other friend, hoist the engine into the boat. Dad hooked the boat trailer to his truck and moved it out of the way while we moved the engine under the A-frame and hoisted it into the air. Dad expertly backed the boat back under the now-hanging engine, and we lowered the engine into a close location, where we thought it could be positioned. The next step was to align the engine and fabricate the engine mounts, so it could be secured to the engine stringers. We always had enough scrap steel lying around to fabricate the different items with.

After building the Buddy-Built keel-cooler system, exhaust-cooling, and steering systems that are now my standard systems for inboard powered boats I could add the finishing touches. I had to install the dash, which was from the car, complete with the speedometer. I needed the speedometer because Dad said these cars had a built-in protection system in the transmission that would not let the transmission go into reverse if the car was traveling faster than about five miles per hour forward. The speedometer would let me know when the transmission went into reverse because the speedometer would fall below zero. I made a simple vertical lever that hooked to the transmission with a cable, so I could easily shift from forward to re-verse, and like the four-speed in last year's boat, I could select one of the three speeds. The transmission also had a vacuum module that would change the shift pattern if you pushed hard on the throttle. This was also part of the down-shift function of the transmission, so I disabled it, so the transmission would shift through the three speeds quickly. After the engine was installed, I pushed the hull back into the garage so I could complete the cabin structure. This boat had a short cabin with no standing room so to get to the steering station I had to crouch down and go alongside the engine box. The engine box was directly behind the seat, so it was a bit noisy at higher speeds. I did not know about or could even afford decent quality sound attenuat-ing materials to keep the engine noise out of the cabin. I need to add that my dad was one of the smartest people I have ever met. Not only was he a great sounding board to discuss my new inventions with, but he also knew the more I did myself, the more I would learn from the experience. He would help when the job required two people, but other than that, he had his own projects to keep himself busy. He was a self-made gunsmith as well as a mechanic, so a lot of his time was spent helping people with their problems.

Dad did have to help me on this project one night as he arrived home from work. The hull was built and turned right side up, the engine was installed, and I had finished the exterior decks with the cabin and the interior decks. He had gotten a lot of surplus cans of green spray paint, so he said I could use it on the boat. I took a case of the paint, went inside the hull, and started painting to see if I liked the color. He forgot to tell me that if I were going to paint, I would require a lot of ventilation. An eighteen-foot boat inside of a small two-car garage does not leave a lot of room for ventilation especially when the garage doors are closed. It was the wintertime, so I kept the doors closed to keep any heat in that I could. I was still spraying when he came home from work. He said I was singing, so that is what got him to come to the garage. He pulled me from the boat, opened the garage doors, and proceeded to give me a lecture that he had to repeat when he thought I could comprehend what he was telling me. Since it was surplus paint, there were no labels or warnings on the cans talking about proper ventilation—as if I would have read them anyway.

The day came for the sea trial, so Dad towed the boat to the water, and we launched at the same lift at Redondo. With the boat still sitting on the lift, I started the boat and made sure the engine would run and that there were no leaks. I then gave the thumbs up and they lowered the boat the rest of the way into the water. I put the boat into reverse, and the boat slowly slipped out of the elevator system. I backed out into the bay, turned, and faced toward open water, and put the boat in forward high on the three-speed transmission, and we started to accelerate. To my surprise the boat started in low, quickly shifted to second, and then went into high gear, and away we went, again being lucky with the size of the propeller for the horsepower and speed. The luck came from owning a lot of outboard propellers from different horsepower outboard motors. I would try to learn a system as I went, and it seemed to work.

Dad and I spent the day on the water fishing and doing some exploring along the waterfront. This time I believe he was more amazed than I was as to how good the boat worked. Dad and I had an unspoken respect for each other's talents and abilities that lasted forever. He was my best friend as well as my mentor. As you may have figured out if you kept up with the timeline, I was now in high school but still had no driver's license. I never had a desire to own a car or have a license, so I needed a good friend who would transport the boat to the water. The other strange fact of life is that the one with the biggest boat has the most friends. Everybody wants to be on the water on a lovely day, so it was easy to get the boat towed the 5 miles to the launch facility.

Our family spent all the nice weekends enjoying the water, fishing, and exploring. One weekend the engine started making a funny knocking sound, so we came back on a slow, easy speed so we would not destroy the engine. I lifted the engine up in the boat and removed the oil pan and saw that the bearings were all bad (the dreaded lower end). I guessed that you do not get much of an engine with a twenty-five horsepower Johnson outboard that probably doesn't run. I think it was my luck that kept the engine running as long as it did. With help from my dad, we rebuilt the engine, so we could finish the summer.

I do remember one incident while out fishing with my dad and a couple of other people on the boat. It got very windy and rough, so we decided to head back to the marina. After reeling in the fishing lines, I pushed the throttle forward. It went through all three gears like normal. As we increased speed, we encountered a large wave. As we started up the wave, the engine bogged down a bit, and the transmission downshifted down to second. When that happened, the engine speed went way up, and it scared the crap out of me. If you can imagine this eighteen-foot cabin boat with the engine sitting in a box next to you when it suddenly revs up to full rpm, it is quite scary. I quickly pulled the throttle back and started the process over with more care.

This was also the first boat I built that Sherrie, my future wife, went out on. We had become friends with their family through her brother John. We went to the same areas hunting as well as to the same parties. One Saturday I took my dad and John's dad Jack out fishing. John had gone off the be in the army, so Jack brought along his tom-boyish daughter Sherrie. The two of us sat up in the cabin where I would run the boat while the two men sat in the back fishing. Sherrie was easy to talk to. We talked about a lot of different subjects that day. She had a quick wit and I was not shy around her for some reason, we were not seeing each other at all just a boat ride with a nice junior high school girl, and her dad. I was not dating anybody at the time, mostly due to my shyness and that I was always busy. Mowing lawns, racking rocks and doing odd jobs to earn money to build boats makes for a tough life. Does not leave a lot of time for dating especially when you add school onto the list. Once school was out, I had to use the boat whenever I could.

The Last of My Winter School Projects

1966 AND NOW that it was my senior year of high school, I was looking for a different type of boat than what they had on the shelf in the lumber yard. This time I was looking for a boat design that would be a bit more challenging to construct as well as be a bit more stable platform for fishing. I sent for a catalog for boat plans from Glenn L Witt Design Co. After much consideration, I ordered the plans for their eighteen-foot Aqua Cat, which was a catamaran design with a cuddy cabin and a big cockpit for fishing. As before, dad sold the eighteen-foot inboard and I used the monies for the materials for the new build.

I enjoyed building this boat the most of all. It had a great hull shape and was a bit more complex structure wise. As with the other boats, I used lighter plywood than the plans called for, so I could keep the hull light. I would add a few more longitudinal stringers to keep the exposed panel size down. My reputation was for building light, fast, but strong boats. The frames were mahogany, and I handpicked them from the lumberyard. Each piece was of high quality and of a tighter grain than most of the boards. We used to call it Mountain Mahogany because we believed it was a bit harder because it grew higher up on the mountain and not in the lowlands like most of the Philippian mahogany that was in the lumberyards being used for interior house trim.

This was the first hull where I installed a layer of fiberglass over the entire hull exterior for added strength. All the build projects after the eight-foot pram required that a loft plan would have to be developed. The catamaran plans had a table of offsets that would allow me to lay out the loft plan onto a sheet of plywood without doing a lot of scaling and interpreting the drawings. I guess that was the difference from one-page plans that cost less than a buck to buying an actual set of plans. The way that the lofting would work is that there was a centerline and a waterline, which are the base lines for all the dimensions. The layout would have all the frames on the one sheet. After the loft was completed, then the trick I used was to pound some roofing nails (nails with big, thin heads) into the plywood loft plan with the heads halfway into the plywood. This would leave half of the head of the nail sticking up out of the plywood along the line for each of the individual frames. I would place the mahogany frame material over the nails and tap it down with a hammer. When I lifted the frame up, the heads of the nails would leave marks along the lines, so it was an uncomplicated way to transfer the lines. I would connect the dots and would have the layout transferred. After cutting one piece, all I had to do was to flip the frame over to make the opposite piece for the other side of the hull.

Below is what a typical set of plans would look like. From these plans you can obtain all dimensions for the frames, the angle the bevels have to be cut at, as well as any other information that may be required to build the hull shape. These were the actual set of plans for the eighteen-foot catamaran that I built at eighteen years old. There were three more pages, mostly for the cabin detail. This was the most information I ever received for building a boat until I paid bigger money for a sailboat design after this boat.

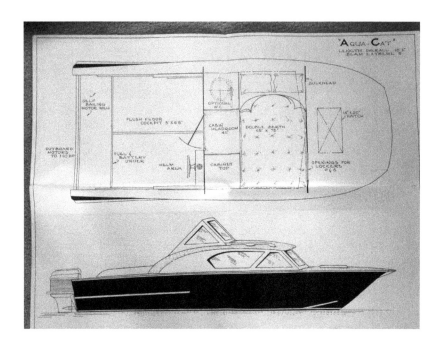

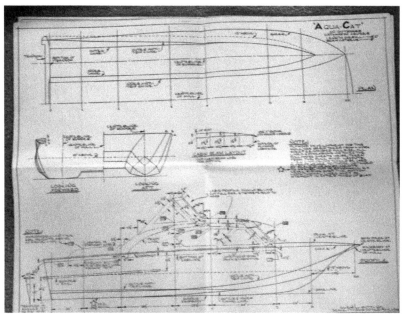

This was part of the design package that I purchased to build the boat.
the design was complete

After the hull was finished, I got a few friends together, so I could drag the hull outside and roll it over, so I could fiberglass the hull and build the cabin. The weekend came for the big move out, and we started dragging the hull outside when we realized the hull would not fit out of the door of the garage. The solution was simple: cut a notch in the main support beam for the garage. It was only a one-story house above the garage, and I was only cutting a notch about halfway through it, so I guessed it should have been OK. The boat came outside, and I preceded to fiberglass the hull.

After the hull was fiber glassed (Mom did not want the smell of resin in the house, probably because of my painting experience. I think that she thought I had lost enough brain cells during that epi-sode and could not afford to lose any more), I got a group of friends together to roll the hull over. It only took five people to roll the hull right side up proving that my "light weight" construction techniques worked.

I was successful in keeping the hull light, and four people could lift the hull off the ground. After the hull was turned over, Dad would not allow me to cut another notch into the door post. The one notch was near the ground and the new notch would have to be higher be-cause the widest part of the hull was at the sheer or upper edge of the hull, so I had to finish the rest of the boat outside. Dad helped with the cabin structure since it was a two-man job. I think that he started to dream of fishing out of this innovative design, so he wanted to help to make sure it was ready for the summer. We both enjoyed the build process on this boat.

Dad helped get the cabin built so we could get this one out on the water as quickly as we could. Note the station wagon sitting next to the boat. That was my mom's car that she would drive me around in to get my parts.

This boat was to be a twin-engine outboard model, so I spent some time looking through the paper's want ads or having Mom drive me around to the marinas, trying to find two equal-sized motors I could afford. I had extra money because of the sale of the last boat provided more than enough money for the building materials, the parts for a trailer, as well as some cheap motors and controls. The plans called out for two twenty-five-horsepower outboards, so I found two Mercury Mark 55s, which were rated about forty horsepower each. One engine was white and the other was green, but that did not seem to affect their performance. The motors came with controls that could be bolted together, so it looked somewhat professional. The steering system still used the same pulley system as before, but this time the cables were not exposed.

I mounted the outboards after finishing the interior and the painting, which I did with a brush this time, and the boat was ready for testing. The basic color scheme for all my boats was the same. If I got the paint for free, that was the color, but if I had to pay for the paint, it was going to be dark blue. (Also note that I never took any pictures. The pictures were from my parents. I later figured out that they were either proud of my accomplishments or were just wanting to document the disaster. I know they were happy with the catamaran because there are a lot of pictures of it, and they were out on it every weekend when the weather was nice.) I also needed a trailer for the boat so after scouring the want ads, I found another axel to start the project on. The design was simple with rollers located under the keels of each of the hulls. I had to put fenders on this trailer because I was going to be using it a bit more to transport the boat to various areas in Puget Sound.

The finished boat on its maiden voyage.
You can see the two-different colored outboard motors.

Dad and I took the finished boat to the same lift at Redondo, where we launched all the previous boats for their maiden cruise. The boat ran great. It was fast, about thirty mph, and handled superbly. The marina at Redondo had an interior storage section with its own lift, so I signed up to leave the boat in storage, so I could use the boat whenever I wanted without having to be at the mercy of somebody taking the boat to the water. I would use the boat any day the weather was good. At the time, pre-mixed gasoline at the docks was thirty-three cents per gallon, so it was not that expensive to run the boat. This boat was fast enough to pull skiers, so I borrowed a set of skis and tried that one weekend during an outing with the family. I did have one simple rule on the boat: if you wanted to come along, you had to put fuel in the tanks, which consisted of four six-gallon portable fuel tanks that sat in the back corners of the cockpit. This rule applied to everybody, even family, so I never had a problem taking the family out on weekends, with a queen-size bed forward for mom and dad and ample room in the cockpit for my sister and me to sleep on the deck. We would spend all the good weekends on the boat. We cruised the entire South Puget Sound area.

One of my excursions was to circumnavigate Vashon and Maury islands. The trip would take me from Redondo, where I kept the boat, south towards Tacoma and clockwise around the Islands. As I rounded the top of the Island, I headed towards Seattle to go by the oil company where my dad worked near the waterfront. As I was approaching Seattle, one motor made a funny noise and then died. I was just passing the mouth of the Duwamish river when the engine stopped. I turned and headed up the river to a dock that was close to a sports shop that I knew worked on outboards. Once I had the boat tied up, I started to work on the engine. Back in those days you would always take a toolbox with you to fix things. You could almost count on something requiring repairs on a long trip. I figured out that I did not have any spark in the spark plugs so I took the magneto off to test it. I had the wires laying in my lap and being the summer and warm outside, I only had a pair of shorts on, so my legs were bare. I manually spun the magneto, which is what makes the spark, and to my surprise it worked. Mercury was known for their great spark from their magneto and I was witness to that. I looked to see what the problem was, and I came to realize that the belt that drove the magneto was gone. I walked to the store and they luckily had one on the shelf. I took and replaced it and got the boat running and headed back home. I got home about dark, this tardiness prompted yet another call to the US Coast Guard from mom. Luckily, they are not in the practice of going out looking for lost boats the same day that they get lost, or I would have had the second mark on my boating career.

After Highschool

GETTING A JOB AND A CAR

I enjoyed this boat so much that I did not even plan on building a new boat that winter. Now that I had finished my senior year of school, I needed to get a job. I did get a job; in fact, I got two the week after school was out, so I could do some upgrades to the boat. The problem with getting the two jobs was that I still did not have a driver's license. I drove trucks while working on the farm during the summers and did move the cars around the block on occasion, but I never was excited about getting my license. It is now necessary to get my license, so I had to study the handbook, so I was ready to take the written driving test. Mom drove me around until she found a driver's license place that I could take my written and driving test that day. I had to start work the following Monday and this was Friday, so it was mandatory that I take and pass my test, so I could get my license. Mom found a place in Tacoma that could test me that day so away we went. I took the written test as well as the driving test and passed both. They handed me my temporary license and I was good to go.

Now that I had my license, I could make it to my two jobs, so I could make the extra money to do my upgrades to the boat. The other thing, and most important, was to put the starter back into dad's parts car so that I would have something to drive. Except for the missing fan motor, everything important was still on the car. I did not have the money to go buy a car and my parents were not going to go buy one when there was a perfectly good car sitting along the house. It was missing a fan motor, but I did not need heat for the summer anyway. I was sure that I would have something figured out before winter came along. I watched the want ads closely for a better car. I found a 1948 Ford four-wheel-drive pickup truck for sale for three-hundred dollars. It was close by so dad and I went to look at it. The body was in perfect shape and it all appeared to work, so I bought it and drove it home. Being an outdoors person, I liked the fact that this was a factory four-wheel-drive. That would be great for our hunting trips. The one issue with the truck was that it had the original Ford flat head V-8 engine. It barley had enough horsepower to spin the tires on ice. I drove that for a period that fall and then while washing cars at a dealership, I spotted a 1957 Jeep pickup truck that they took in on trade. They wanted six-hundred dollars for it, which was out of my budget. I watched it every day. being winter, people were looking for four-wheel drive vehicles. The owner put on a small Christmas party for the crew one Friday after work. I went to him when I thought that he was more in the Christmas spirit and told him that I would give him three hundred for the jeep. He looked at me and said that he would flip a coin and we would go double of nothing on the three hundred. If I won, I would get the Jeep for free and if he won, I would pay the six hundred. Not being a gambler, I said no. The Jeep went out on several test drives over the next few weeks, but nobody bought it. One day it came back from a test drive and I could hear the engine knocking. It sounded serious. I ask my dad how bad it could be, and he told me a strange fact about the Jeep engine. He said that if it were low on oil it would develop what they called a "dry knock". The next morning, I went straight to the jeep and opened the hood and pulled the dipstick. Sure enough, it was low on oil. I went to the owner and told him that the truck had a knock in the engine and that I would give him three hundred for it as is. He had his lead mechanic go start it and he also heard the knock. He told the boss that the engine was bad. I re-offered my three hundred dollars and he took it. Being young and not as intelligent as I should have been, I put the oil in the engine before I left the yard and sure enough the knock went away. The owner heard about this and was pissed at his service lead. How could he let a lot boy get the best of him? My dad sold the Ford just like he sold all the boats that I built. He sold it for enough to buy the jeep plus a bit for a used military winch that I could put on the front.

UPGRADING THE BOAT

Once I had extra money, the one thing I did was to trade up on the power. I met a person that had built a twelve-foot needle noised two-seat boat. It also had a Mercury Mark 55 outboard so by buying the boat I could put three motors across the back of the catamaran when I wanted that extra speed. The needle nose boat was fast. You sat in the back just in front of the motor on a bench seat. There was a long skinny deck in front that you would look over to see the water. When you hit the throttle from a dead stop the boat would almost stand on its tail and then once it picked up speed it would level out. The boat had a flat bottom with no keel so when you would turn the steering wheel the boat would change the direction that the bow was pointing but the direction of travel was still about the same. Sherrie, my kind of girlfriend now, hated the boat so we only used it a couple of times. I sold the boat and trailer as soon as I could find somebody to take it but kept the outboard motor for when I wanted more speed. Wanting more speed all the time and not wanting to deal with the third outboard motor I went back on the search for bigger outboard motors. I located two Mercury Mark 78A outboards, which were six-cylinder outboards that were direct reversing, so they had no gears. It took considerable coordination to run the boat because the motor had to stop and be restarted in reverse. The controls had a button on the top of the lever to make it easy to start when going from forward to reverse. This did increase the speed of the boat to fifty-five miles per hour, which was tested several times by pacing a car on a frontage road along the water. This is also when I noticed people exaggerating about their speed. My fifty-five miles per hour boat would pass a lot of seventy miles per hour boats. This new improvement extended the fishing range of the boat. Dad and I would fish from Tacoma to Seattle with no concerns. The catamaran design was a very stable platform to fish from even if it was a rough day.

The catamaran design made it very stable as well as fast and strong. One weekend, one of dad's cousins came for a visit. He wanted to try his luck fishing, so we went to the marina at Redondo, where the boat was stored, moved it onto the elevator and launched the boat and headed out to try our luck fishing for salmon. We only caught one salmon. It was the weekend, so there were several boats out fishing. As dad was playing the fish, he went to the fore deck and stood there fighting the fish. He finally brought the fish aboard and then turned to some of the other boats that were fishing close by and took a bow just to show off a bit. On the way back to the lift I saw some waves from a tugboat that went by. The waves were fairly big, so I thought I would show off a bit also and pushed the throttles to full power and headed towards the waves at 55 miles per hour. The waves were a bit bigger than I thought and when we hit the first wave the boat became completely air born. We flew over the second wave and hit the third wave a bit hard and flew up into the air again. The boat was built strong, so it survived the ride a bit better than the people. When we got home, I learned that my dad's cousin was a submarine officer onboard the submarine Snark. He said that he had traveled all over the world under water including the polar ice cap but has never been more scared than the trip in my power cat jumping those waves. He was impressed with the boat but was still scared.

A SLIGHT BEND IN THE ROAD

I started seeing Sherrie a bit more now that I was graduated from high school. I was their family "fix it man". If they had a problem with any piece of equipment, I was the go-to guy to get it fixed. I rebuilt two of the engines in their cars. Sherrie's brother John left her a Plymouth Valiant to drive when he was off on duty in the army. It was originally from the East coast where they used a lot of salt on the roads to melt the ice. It was about totally rusted out. It had a stick-shift that was mounted in the floor that would pop out on occasion. I would get a call to go rescue Sherrie so I would have to find out where she was and then go and put the shift system back together. One time when she was babysitting, she drove to close to the edge of one of the side roads that had loose gravel and a really deep ditch. Somehow, she ended up in the ditch. She said that the gravel pulled her into it. When I got to the car, it was almost totally below the level of the road. I drove a jeep Wagoneer that I built up a bit. It had an eight-thousand-pound military winch on the front. I proceeded to pull her out of the ditch and get her back on her merry way.

Now that I was seeing her more often, I would invite her out for boat rides across the sound to a nice sandy beach. She probably did not like the boat ride that much, but she did like the nice sandy beach. The more we saw of each other the more we wanted to see each other. I would start taking here to nice places for lunch and dinner. I was making good money with my two jobs just out of high school and even better money when I started working building test models for Boeing. I could afford to give her wonderful things, which I am sure was a bit of the draw to me. Our relationship was just friends for several years. Our relationship was going down a very unfamiliar road for me, but one that I looked forward to continuing to travel down.

I enjoyed this boat so much I kept it for three years before selling it.

MY FIRST 2 JOBS

To keep my projects funded, I always worked hard to earn money. I put in several of the yards around the neighborhood. This was hard-earned money because the soil was very rocky. It was a new development, and I was certain the builder must have scraped all of the topsoil off and sold it before he built any houses. My paper route expanded to over one hundred customers, and I mowed all the lawns people would pay me to mow.

Now that I was graduating from high school, I had to make a

career change. My reputation in the community as being a hard worker got me my first two jobs. The week after I graduated from school in 1967, I was forced to get my driver's license because I had one job as a lot boy in Kent working for Tom Matson Motors washing cars part time. I also got a job to build concrete casket liners for an individual at Washington Memorial Cemetery next to Seattle Tacoma Airport. The person that I would work for was the former Crew Chief for Ted Jones who was the unlimited hydroplane owner and builder that was famous during that period of my life. I had the pleasure of meeting Ted Jones while at work one day. He was a relative of the people that owned the cemetery. They had a large storage area under the main building where Ted could store his extra engines for the hydroplanes. Once that he learned that I was a bit of a boat nut he started talking a bit more about his designs and his new occupation at the time which was managing Lake X in Florida for Carl Kiekhaefer, who was the owner of Mercury outboards at that time. Once I learned that Ted Jones was a Mercury fan than I told him my history with the Mercury outboards. He must have been somewhat impressed because he gave me a lot of old Mercury parts, mostly controls and propellers.

The cemetery job was just for the summer months so by the time that job was up, I knew I had to find a new job. I became a full-time employee at the Dodge dealership, but I also did not want to be washing cars the rest of the winter.

NEXT CAREER CHANGE

The next job I got was selling, or at least trying to sell, for the Scott Fetzer Company, which as everybody knows is Kirby Vacuums. That job took up time, with not much success. Even though I did happen to sell a couple of vacuums, it became obvious that I was not cut out to sell something to somebody, especially something I was probably never going to use myself. Did you know that if you bought all the attachments with your new Kirby vacuum, you could actually paint your car with it? I learned several things about business while at the Kirby Company. They did an excellent job in helping each other out.

It was always a bit of competition as to who could sell the most units in a week, but they wanted everybody to succeed. That was smart on their part because when the salesman does well the company does well. They would start the morning with a song or two about Kirby, which I remember most of even today. After the morning song session than the salesman that sold the day before would get up and explain how he made the sale. If you sold a vacuum you would make about one hundred and twenty dollars, which was good money in the winter of 1967. The idea was to both inspire the others to get out and sale more and to also teach everybody any "tricks" to the sale. The one trick that they used the most was "contest close" this was done when you had a customer that was close to deciding but was on the fence. You would explain to him that you are in a companywide contest and if you make this sale you will be the winner and your prize is a paid trip to someplace like Hawaii. You would borrow their phone (not even a dream of a cell phone back than) and call the office and ask for CC (which meant contest close, so they would just coach you if you needed it). The call was to see if "Bill" had sold anything yet and if he had not you will be the winner. You had to show a bit of desperation with some excitement to get the people to buy the machine. I could not believe how well that worked. People want to help people. After the sales meeting was over, we were sent out into the neighborhoods with a box of Lady Bovina panty hose to give to the ladies that answered the door, so we could get the leads to come back in the evening to sell the machine to both of the adults. This made for an awfully long day with little results for people that would not push for the sale.

SEARCH FOR A BETTER CAREER

Because of my success level in the Kirby Vacuum sales I started scouring the help-wanted ads and found an opportunity to take a class to learn wind tunnel–model making. It was the spring of 1968 when I started the schooling. It was a nine-to-five class five days a week, so it was exactly like the working environment, complete with coffee breaks and lunch. My dad would take me to school on his way to work and pick me up every day on his way home. The instructor, who was employed by the Boeing Company, had a whole series of tasks for the students to perform, each designed to test the talent and thought process of the individual student. At the end of the course, they hired one person, from the eighteen who attended, to work at the Model Shop building wind tunnel test models. I was the fortunate one who was hired and was also fortunate to be placed in the Flutter Model section.

Because of my boat-building skills, I worked with wood, metal and fiber glass, which is what the flutter models are made of. The flutter model is comprised of several body and wing sections that are made from balsa wood covered with a very thin, .002-inch to .004-inch, layer of epoxy with reinforced fiber. The model flew in the tunnel. The only thing keeping it from going downstream was a rod going through the center of balance. One engineer would control the vertical attitude of the model while another would control the lateral stability, keeping it pointed into the wind.

TAKING PEOPLE OUT ON THE WATER

One of the best things about this job was the fact that most of the people were boat people. I worked in the same area as people who had built themselves a boat or two over the years, so we had a lot in common. On one occasion, I took a fellow worker on a boat trip to Mc Neil Island, an old penitentiary, in South Sound. The island was just South of Fox Island. The day was perfect with good sun and no wind. We were cruising and enjoying the view. The reason for my trip was not just to take somebody for a ride, it was also to test the Mark 78-A outboards that I had put on. Being "low budget Bud the two outboards were a bit different. The boat was built for the smaller motors which had short shafts. The two larger engines had one short shaft and one long shaft. The short shaft engine was not an issue, but the long shaft engine was a bit more of a challenge. The motors had the same type of clamping system as a normal ten horsepower engine and they also had holes, so they could be bolted onto the transom. I was still playing with the height adjustment of the long shaft motor, so I did not have the engine bolted on. As we came around Fox Island, we saw another small boat traveling in our direction. It was no big deal, so I ignored it. As we crossed its small wake, the boat bounced a bit pitching the long shaft motor off the transom. The only thing holding the engine from going to the bottom was the steel tie bar that I made for the steering and the battery and control cables. I headed straight for the beach. When we got to the beach I jumped into the water and with my adrenalin charged body put the engine back into the boat. We headed back to the launch ramp which was at least twenty-five miles away. I was surprised how fast the boat would go with just one engine. When we returned to the house, I put the boat in the back yard and put the motor back onto the transom, so I could work on it. We both worked second shift at the Model Shop, so I had a bit of time. My friend went to work, and I started flushing the engine out. Time got away from me and I realized that I was not going to make it to work on time, so I called the Model Shop to let them know. The shift had already started by the time I called so I was able to talk directly with my supervisor. When I told him that I had sunk a Mercury outboard engine he told me to not show up to work until that engine was running. He told me exactly what to do and what parts to remove so I could properly flush out the engine. I didn't take long to get the engine flushed and running again. I made it to work that night by about lunch time. When I showed up I was sure that I would be getting a lot of ribbing about my little mishap especially because the person that I took for the ride worked there also and I was sure that he had told everybody by then of my stupid mishap. When people saw me come in the word got out quick that I was there. The Model Shop where I worked was a small group of incredibly talented people, so everybody knew each other well. I was called to the office shortly after I walked in so I, with my tail between my legs, headed up stairs to the office to face the abuse of my stupidity but instead I was greeted by the supervisor who grilled me about what I did and how did the engine run. I could not believe that he, along with everybody else was concerned about the motor. Most of the people knew that I was a boat nut. I could not believe that they would pass up an opportunity to tease me about my mishap. After this event, I did bolt the engine onto the transom.

There was a worker in the wood shop area that wanted to take his son out on the water. He was from a foreign country and had never been on the water. I told him that I would take the two of them for a ride on the boat, so we set up a date. When the day came the weather was beautiful. We headed across the sound from Redondo and were cruising by Vashon Island when they wanted to explore the island a bit. I agreed. I knew a spot that people used for water skiing because the beach was all sand and was steep enough that you didn't have to tilt the outboards up when you landed on the beach, which was important because back in those days there was no such thing as power tilt or trim, you had to grab the handle on the top of the motor and pull hard to tilt the engine up. With twin engines, you would have to stop short of the beach, get the engines tilted and then paddle to shore otherwise you would hit the propeller on the bottom. I approached this beach fairly fast as I usually do. I put the boat in neutral, which was shutting off the direct reversing engines and, as usual expected the boat to settle back into the water and slide part way up the soft sandy beach and come to a secure rest. I guess I was going a bit faster than I expected or I shut the engines down a couple of seconds later that normal, but either way the boat slid up the beach just about the full length of the boat. I stepped out of the boat onto the sand as if this was a normal procedure. As we started to explore the beach, I continued to look back at the boat to see what way the tide was going. If it was going out, we were not going to make the start of the shift at work. To my surprise, and luck, the tide was coming in. All I had to do was to keep the exploration going until the tide came in enough to be able to slide the boat back into the water, so we could head home. The two of them were grateful for the trip and I learned yet another lesson learned.

UNEXPECTED CAREER CHANGE

I worked for the Boeing Model Shop until Boeing had a setback in about1969 and was forced to lay off most of the people in the Model Shop. This was the first time I ever experienced anything like this. The Model Shop had plenty of work to do and it was not a large operation, but it was 100% overhead in the eyes of top management. They did not make anything that could bring in any income. The shop was necessary because at that point in time the FAA required a model test for any aircraft that was going to be carrying paying passengers. All the designs were finalized, and they did not require a full team to do the scaled down workload, so the layoff was looked at as salvation for the company. Being a union shop the rules were simple, the last people to be hired were the first to be laid off. They printed out a sheet of paper with the names of all the employees with their hire dates and posted it on the wall by the tool room. The list was arranged with the most recent person hired on the bottom and the oldest seniority on the top. The shop was not that big, so it was only one page of names. As somebody got laid off, they would put a line through their name. My name was about a quarter of the way up the list. The lines through the names would happen on a weekly basis. Everybody would know about when they would be getting laid off. One day I was walking by the tool room knowing that it was getting close to my time to go and I noticed that my name did not have a line through it but the two people above me did. I went to the supervisor to let them know that they made a mistake. He had me sit down for a minute while he explained to me that the company can place a temporary retention on a small percentage of employees. The retention only lasts about ninety days and at the end of that period there is not a second chance. If the company does not start to rehire than they would have no choice but to lay me off. The ninety days came, and the supervisor called me back into his office and gave me a choice to either take a layoff or be transferred to 747 Production in Everett. I like to work so I took the transfer to 747 Production instead of taking a layoff. He also explained to me that they wanted me back as soon as the company started to rehire. To get me back I could not take any pay increase or that would change my status with the union, and I would have to go to the bottom of a different list. I was a single man and the Model Shop, not being production, had a different pay scale than production. I was already at a higher pay grade than most of the production workers anyway, so nobody thought that would be any issue. I needed to work because I had also just purchased a new Chevy K-5 Blazer. This was a new model for Chevrolet. A group in California was taking the four door Suburban and removing the section where the back doors were. This made a great SUV. I saw one on a Convoy truck and followed it to the dealership where I bought it. Being under twenty-one, I had to get dad to co-sign for it. He tried really hard to talk me out of it. He had never purchased a new vehicle in his life and thought that making the monthly payments would be tough on me. He did not know how much money that I was making at the time if he knew he would not have been concerned. I was making the same as people that had families and a house mortgage and probably a car loan too.

Starting Down A New Road

NOW THAT I had to work in Everett instead of South Seattle, I had to find a place to live. My parents were happy because they now were free from me and my projects, or at least they thought they were. I was always close to my parents. The day I moved out it was a bit of a tearful moment. It was not until years later that I realized it was not because I was moving out as much as it was that I was taking my boat with me. I searched the different neighborhoods in the area close to the Everett Production Facility and found a cheap place to call home. As long as I could rent a place that had parking space for my eighteen-foot catamaran I was happy. The rental place was also close to the launch ramp for launching my boat, so all was well in my world. It was a four-plex in a not so great neighborhood. You could hear through the walls, so it was difficult to sleep. I did not even stay the month. I looked around and found a small house in a better neighborhood that was just remodeled so I rented it.

My boating slowed down a bit because I was now about twenty years old, so those male mating urges took over and I had to find a mate, not just for boating either. Sherrie was neither a boater nor a fisherman, but I thought that I could change at least part of that with time. I was still seeing Sherrie on a more frequent occasion in fact we had become good friends. My buddies at the Model Shop were all introduced to her and also thought that she was a nice girl. I think that she got a bit of the explorer urge because she became the navigator on all our future voyages. I did not stop all my boating, I just had to slow it down a bit while I looked down this new fork in the road. Part of the problem was that I worked in Everett, which was North of Seattle and she lived in Federal Way which was South of Seattle. I would go meet her anytime that she would let me. That meant driving to South Seattle spending "quality time" with her and then driving back to Everett to go to work.

Right before Christmas break, my friend at the Everett facility brought in a bottle of Christmas cheer. I shared the bottle with him and became a bit tipsy. This was the very first alcoholic drink that I had ever consumed for pleasure. That evening my parents were hosting a party in their basement. Sherries family was invited as well as a few others. Still feeling a bit "brave" I waited for the opportune moment to catch Sherrie alone. She had gone upstairs to get something. The house was a split level so there was a one-hundred- and eighty-degree bend in the stairs. You walked from the upper level down to the entry landing or you could turn 180 degrees and head on down to the basement. I weighted just past the turn below the landing and carefully grabbed her and kissed her smack on the lips. This came as a complete shock to her as well as me. This was the first time that I had ever kissed a girl. Had a lot of dreams about it, but this was the first time for me. She did give me a funny look and I apologized a bit and we went back to the party. I could tell that she was thinking about it because of the way she looked at me the rest of the night. Either she liked it, or she thought that I was a really weird dude. I did, with her permission give her that polite goodbye hug as they were leaving. This seemed to open the door a bit more for a closer relationship between Sherrie and me.

My schedule was a bit messed up, so I went to my supervisor and told him that I wanted to go to third shift. That would give me time during the day or evening whenever it was convenient for Sherrie. I kept some blankets in the back of my 1969 Chevy Blazer so if I got too tired to drive home all I had to do was to pull over and park in a parking lot someplace and take a nap. I had an alarm clock to wake up by, so I could always make it to work on time. I finally decided that this arrangement was not that great and went back to see if I could move back into the house with my parents. I was making the commute anyway so I just as well live closer to where I played. They agreed if I would let them use the boat when I was not using it. This new plan gave me a lot more time with Sherrie. She was about to graduate high school when I made this move. After high school, I could spend a lot more time with her, boating as well as just hanging out. We became inseparable friends, and yes, we started to kiss on a more frequent basis. I learned along this road that man chases the woman. It is his instinct that is somehow bred into him. The woman catches the man that she wants. I learned that later in life when I heard a song and one of the lyrics was "a boy chases a girl until she catches him". This is a secret that the women keep close to their chest.

One day in early 1972, I got the nerve to ask her what her future plans looked like. Being a shy person, this was tough for me. My shyness was possible because I never liked rejection. I never got a lot of rejection in my early life because both of my parents encouraged me to do my projects and never criticized me about them. Well I did ask her what she thought about the future which led to a discussion about what she thought about marriage. She appeared to be ok with it so I thought that I might as well make it a real proposal. Before I could make it real, I had to ask her father for permission. This was the guy that really did not like me. I did ask and he did say that it would be OK as long as she thought that it would be OK with her. After we got engaged my dad sat me down and said that "marriage is a great institution, can you see spending the rest of your life in an institution?" And as he had told me on several occasions, "My free advice is worth every penny that it costs you". As of this day, my dad is still one of the smartest people that I have ever known. I am a huge believer in this country and the ability of the people in it. My belief is that there are a lot of smart people here. If you can dream up an idea, there is somebody in this country that can build it, he was one of them. We did get married. The only real issue is that I dressed myself and just before the big event, while all of the guests are being escorted to their seats, my best man's wife went to Sherrie and pointed out to her that I had lime green socks on. I did not see this as a big issue, but all had to stop until I went home, which was only a half mile away, and get the proper black socks. The event went well, and we were married. We spent our first night together in the cabin on the beach. The next day we boarded the sailboat and headed north.

This fork has run along without many potholes for more than forty plus years now, with Sherrie still navigating while out on the water on our power yacht or in our land yacht looking for a new place to explore. It may be a bit worthwhile at this point to say that Sherrie never did take up fishing, but she has done a wonderful job of preparing some fantastic meals from what I have harvested from the sea. From her macadamia-crusted halibut to her seafood jambalaya, she has taken the bounty from the sea and created spectacular dishes.

While my love was the saltwater with a bit of mountains, hers was the mountains with a bit of saltwater. We had to divide our time between the two. Since I was a true sportsman, we decided that the best mix was to go boating in the warm summer months and go camping in the woods in the fall months. That kept us out of the bug traffic. There are not many bugs on the water but there are a lot in the mountains in the warm months, especially if you are close to any water. My plan did happen to coincide with hunting season, so I was perfectly fine with that arrangement. Even though Sherrie never took a liking to fishing, she did enjoy the hunting part and became a great hunter. To this day she is still my best hunting partner, and it is not only because she is a great cook, she is actually a great hunter. The other advantage to taking your wife on the hunting trips is that it is a lot warmer sleeping at night. The other thing that happens to most men that must take a woman hunting is that the women are not as comfortable as men with sleeping in a tent on the ground. The mice can come and go as they please as well as other little critters. When the fire goes out in the wood stove in the tent it is instantly cold, or at least as cold as it is outside. These simple facts are usually the reason men starting to hunt out of large motor homes with large punch outs and generators to ensure that the heat will work. It has taking hunting to a whole new level. After the short hunting season, Sherrie felt a bit slighted because we would spend a lot of days on the boat, so we took up snowmobiling in 1981 to help even the time between water and mountains.

Paradigm Shift

IN 1970, WHILE I was doing all this work to earn money and perusing my mating urges, I still pursued my passion for my boat building hobby. After spending a lot of the summer on the water fishing with my catamaran, I took my younger sister and spent the weekend on the boat and went to Vashon Island, which was just across the bay from the lift at Redondo. It was a gorgeous weekend with hot weather with no wind or waves on the water. There was a sandy beach on the island in a slight cove where the slope of the beach was steep enough that I did not have to tilt the motors up to nose the boat onto the beach. In the old days, there was no such thing as a power tilt on the motors. I had to pull the engines up by hand to tilt them, so the prop did not hit the bottom. This particular beach was popular for the skiers. It made beach starting easy. The better skiers would like me to pull them skiing because of the speed I could reach. At 55 miles per hour they could reach incredible speeds when they cut across the back from side to side. The only problem with my boat was that at speed it did not have any wake, so there was nothing for them to jump. This particular weekend, I started out with sixty dollars in my pocket. Since they were using me to tow them around, they provided all of the food. My sister and I slept on the boat. She got the bed and I had to sleep in the cockpit on the floor. I would make occasional runs to Point Defiance marina in Tacoma when I was running low on fuel. They had a pump that had pre-mixed fuel (it had the oil already mixed into the fuel, so I did not have to do it myself). The fuel cost thirty-three cents per gallon. At the end of the weekend, the sixty dollars was gone and all I bought was gas. After that weekend, I put the boat back onto the trailer and decided to go a different direction in my boating. I told dad that he could do his magic and sell the boat, which is what he did. By then I had a reputation of building fast and strong boats. One of the boats he sold to one of his friends had a summer house on Whidbey Island in the Northern part of Puget Sound. He was heading back home from fishing one evening when he struck a huge log at full speed. He thought that he was sunk for sure. When he looked back, his motor was half gone but the boat was still dry. That was the story that made my boats easy to sell.

I decided I wanted to try sailing. The wind was a free source of propulsion, so after remembering the makeshift sailing I did back in my early boating days, I started my research for the type of sailboat I wanted. After a lot of researching—remember, there were no websites back in the early '70s that you could search for ideas so I would have to send for drawings and do my own independent analysis as to what boat I wanted. I was looking at several distinctive designs. One of the designs was a Douglass Fir Plywood Association twenty-six-foot Thunderbird. This boat was in the running except I could not figure out how I could get the cast keel cheap. I finally decided on a tri-hulled sailboat design because there was nothing on the boat that I could not build myself, except the sails.

I picked the tri-hull because of its ability to make speed as well as have some living space inside, and it was cheaper to build. The fixed keel of a mon-hulled sailboat would break my budget. I also decided on a Hortsman design because it was a more complex build, being of a molded plywood design. The molded plywood design meant the hull would be planked using strips of thin, eighth-inch plywood in a diagonal pattern, with one layer in one direction and the second layer in an opposite direction. My dad found a deal on the plywood from a lumberyard in north Seattle. The yard had purchased a train load of door skins, which are eighth-inch mahogany plywood but smaller than the standard four-foot by eight-foot sheets. When I went to the lumberyard, I was surprised that they actually made the purchase. They had the stuff stacked everywhere. They must have gotten a screaming deal on the stuff. The one thing I had to do was to make sure the glue was waterproof. They gave me a sheet as a sample, so I took it home and made the test. I was told that the test was to place the wood in boiling water, and if the glue did not fail, then it would work in a marine atmosphere. The sample passed the test, so I went to the yard and purchased several units of the material, each unit was about seventy sheets of plywood. The size did not concern me because I was going to be cutting it into strips anyway. They sold me the material at seventy-seven cents per sheet, which was almost three dollars less than anybody else at the time.

Now that I was building this "big" boat, I joined the Amateur Boat Building Society as well as the North West Multi-Hull Society, so I could get better deals on materials as well as meet people with the same passion for building these boats in their back yards. I was fortunate to be able to actually meet the designer, Mr. Hortsman, and have a discussion regarding the design and some ideas regarding making the boat a better boat. The people from the Boat Building Societies were always helpful, mostly with where to purchase the materials at the right price. They pooled some of their resources and bought fiberglass in bulk, so they could sell to the group at a greatly reduced price.

To build the boat I had to do all the rest of the normal boat building tasks. I had to create the loft floor, so I could lay out all the frames from the table of offsets. I had to transfer the information to the frame material and then cut out the frame sections and then put the frames together. I had three separate hulls to build this time, so I had to make three separate set up jugs to build the hulls on. I decided to make the Amas (Ama is the outrigger) first since they are smaller, and I could drag them out of the way when completed. After the three hulls were built and turned upright, I had to build a cradle system to hold the three hulls in perfect alignment, as per the design, and then attach them with the structural beams. I added some extra strength where I thought was necessary so that the hulls would never come apart.

This molded plywood design created an extraordinarily strong, rigid hull, especially when I finished it with a layer of fiberglass laminate. The design was also a flush deck, meaning it had a raised hull side where the main cabin was so there was more space on the interior and the deck was easy to walk over because there were no structures above the deck. This made for easy sailing as well as a great lounging space. The boat was twenty-seven feet long and had a beam of seventeen feet, six inches.

To build the three hulls I wanted to keep the water off the project, so I built a temporary shed along the side of Dad's house. I made it follow the same design elements, so it would look OK from the road. I also put some siding that was the same as the house, so it almost looked like an addition. This turned out to be a mistake. One of the neighbors up the street called the county to complain about the addition to the house with no building permit. Of course, this complaint came to my parents and not me, so my dad just handed the paperwork to me and said I had to handle it. I went to the county and had to post a bond to ensure that I would be taking the shed down when the project was completed. They also gave me a timeline when the shed had to come down. This put me in a bit of a bind time wise on the build so I did what any reasonable person would do and I quit my job at Boeing so I could concentrate on getting the boat put together to a point where I could remove the temporary shed.

ANOTHER CAREER CHANGE

After the shed was removed, I went out to Lake Union one Sunday to poke around at the different boat yards. I peeked into a window of a boatyard and saw a blueprint of a beautiful boat hanging on a wall. Monday morning, I was at their office applying for a job to be a boat builder. With all my experience how could they possibly refuse? I went in and filled out the application. They interviewed me as we walked through the boat shop where the boat in the drawing was being built. It was a sixty-foot Marlineer, which was a custom sport fishing yacht. They asked me some questions and I answered to the best of my shy ability. At the end of the interview they basically told me that building all those boats in my daddy's back yard was no recommendation. They would hire me because they needed a yard boy. My first job was to sweep the entire boat yard. I had to pull all the blackberry bushes from around the property and organize the yard space. By the end of the week the owner of the yard came to me and told me that I was the first yard boy that had broken two brooms in the first week of work, and it was not from just leaning on them. They promoted me to helping the outside repair people haul and block boats and prepare them for bottom painting. I was still required to clean the inside of the boat shop at the end of each day, so it would be clean and ready when the boat builders got there in the morning. The yard boss and I would haul out the boats, scrub the bottoms with brushes and Zep cleaner and apply a fresh coat of bottom paint. Today the bottoms are cleaned with a high-pressure power washer. I was also allowed to help install equipment to repair boats with the repair crew. I was small enough that I could get into tight places and work where they could not. The company started another new build and I was fortunate to be promoted to the planking crew. It was me and Eddy Olsen planking this new sixty-foot sport fish yacht. Eddie taught me several things about boat building. From how to extract more detailed information from the loft floor, which I knew the basics of from my projects, to the installation of the final plank on the hull exterior, I could get one hundred percent involved with every detail. Eddie Olsen was a great teacher that taught me a lot about wooden boat building. Eddie was not the only person there that would take the time to help educate me. They knew that I was extremely interested in learning and they wanted to help me learn.

FINISHING THE BOAT

Even with my new job I was still working every available moment to finish my boat building project. As with all my other builds, it had several of the low-budget Bud details. Complete with an inboard engine, which was a sixty horsepower (way too much power for the boat, but what I could get for twenty-five bucks) Scripts (which was a valuable antique the day I got it, like the Flint axle several boats before), homemade strut and rudder, as well as all the running rigging, including deck stays.

The mast was purchased from a member of the Amateur Boatbuilding Society who had built a forty-foot solid spruce mast that he no longer needed because he found an aluminum mast for his boat before he finished his build. To get the mast home, I hooked my dad's Jeep Wagoneer (which is a vehicle that I built from a Jeep pickup truck that I bought from my job as a lot boy and gave to Dad for Christmas the year before) behind my Blazer with a tow bar and then mounted roof racks on top of both vehicles. Both mounting sections had to pivot so I could make turns, and the mounting on the towed vehicle had to allow the mast to slide because the distance between the two points would shorten when I went around a corner. I went to the man's house to pick up the mast and started to bring it home when I passed a policeman, who instantly pulled off the side of the road and turned on his dash lights, which I was sure to see if there was anything he could pull me over for. He must not have found anything because he left me alone. The load was legal in almost all respects. I had the red flag on the back because of the overhanging load.

Note that the mast was forty feet long, so this is what I dreamed up to move it. As a side note, I was not always building boats. The 1957 Jeep Wagoner started as a Jeep truck that I purchased from the place where I was washing cars at for three hundred dollars. I found the Wagoneer body in a local junkyard for twenty-five dollars delivered to the house. The problem was that the truck had about a sixteen-inch longer frame, so I had to shorten the frame. (It was tapered, which made it a real challenge. I had to get advice from Dad on that part.) After I put the body on, I changed out the engine for a V-8 from a cheap car that I bought. About a year after that was all done, I purchased the 1969 Chevrolet K-5 Blazer, so I gave the Jeep to my dad for his hunting vehicle.

I finished the entire boat including installing the mast to make sure that all of the rigging was correct. I had to go up onto the roof of the neighbor's house to help lift the mast into the air. I even pulled the sails up to make sure everything worked as per plan. The mast was just a bare pole. I had to make all of the hardware that was attached to the mast as well as all of the hardware that was attached to the boat to hold the mast. I also had to make the boom that held the bottom of the main sail. I found a sail maker in Seattle that would make me the sales at a reasonable price. Barney Abrams must have liked me because he added some extra elements to the sails to make them better than I expected. The sails were the most expensive item that I bought for the boat, so I took a lot of precautions with them. They never stayed on the mast or even on the boat when we were finished sailing for the weekend. They went back into their sail bags and went into the house where they were kept safe and dry.

The mast installed while the boat was still sitting alongside dad's house. Mom looking out with anticipation for the first boat trip

LAUNCH DAY

Launch day was interesting. I borrowed a trailer, which was a frame for an old trailer house, from my junkyard buddy. I had the route totally planned. I do not remember getting any permits for this move; the boat was only seventeen and a half feet wide, so it only took up a couple of lanes of the two-lane road. We got the neighbors together to help. Some were going to be flagmen at different intersections to block traffic for the move. We had to go to a further launch ramp due to the beam of the boat, so it was going to be an interesting trip. We picked early Sunday morning to make the move because we thought the traffic would be the lightest. As we moved down the road, we realized that some of the flaggers were not to be seen. They were at a different location stopping the traffic on roads we were never going to be on. We got to the ramp with little issue and successfully launched the boat. Note the familiar dark blue hull color, which meant I had to pay for the paint. The red bottom paint was military surplus from a surplus yard in Seattle.

The best day of any boat builder's life—the launch day.

We already had a mooring spot for the boat in front of a friend's cabin on Puget Sound. We fired up the boat and headed for their location, with remarkable success. There was and always has been a great feeling of accomplishment after going through all the building process and finally being able to breathe life into the vessel and head off on the maiden voyage. This particular voyage was even more special for me because I had both my dad and my future bride onboard for the trip. Even though they did not do a lot of the build, they were a major part of my life and of my inspiration.

STEPPING THE MAST

Shortly after we launched the boat, we had to go someplace to step the mast. For a crew, I had my mom and dad as well as my future wife and her brother. I picked a location across the sound that had an abandoned pier we could use to get high enough to pull the mast up into place and get the rigging all hooked up. We fired the boat up and left the mooring buoy heading for the pier. I noticed that the alternator was not charging the battery but was not real concerned at the time. I had the mast set up in place prior to launching to make sure everything was OK So I knew that this should not take a lot of time and then we could head back to the mooring buoy.

Once we got to the pier, it did not take long to get the mast pulled up in place and get the rigging hooked up. After getting the rigging hooked up, we fired up the motor and headed back to the mooring. It was a beautiful evening. It was already dark, so I had to get the running lights working. Two of the lights were located on the mast so I had to get the wires ran and connected to the switch so we would have lights. To get to the switch I had to work above the engine which was located under the cockpit. I did not want to crawl over the engine while it was running so I shut it down to make the connections. After I was done, I tested the lights and they worked great, so it was time to get under way again. We were about halfway across the sound towards the mooring when I shut the engine down, now it would not start when I tried to restart it. I only had one small car battery on board. This was a sailboat not a power boat, we could always make it anywhere with the sails like all the previous explorers. The one problem was that it had gotten dark because of my exuberance in wanting this task completed before the weekend. We could not really see what we were doing, and we got two of the lower stays crossed up. We headed back toward the mooring when we lost engine power. It was no real issue because there was a bit of wind, so we could just put the sails up. That would not work because we had the lower lines crossed, so we were a bit screwed. Remember that in the early '70s, there were no cell phones, and neither did I want to waste money on a VHF marine radio. I never had a radio or even a depth sounder in any of my previous builds. Why start now?

I took an oar from the dinghy, which was another eight-foot pram I had built for this boat and pushed the mainsail partially up the mast, which would allow us to sail toward our moorage. After midnight, most of my crew had gone below to sleep—they all had to work the next day—leaving me and my future wife, Sherrie, to get the boat home. The early explorers had an advantage because they did not have a crew that had to be home, so they could go to work the next day. The wind totally quit after midnight, so I got into the pram, went to the front, and started rowing or towing the boat home. Sherrie sat on the bow singing, "Row, row, row your boat." Just before morning, the wind and the tide started against us, and we were making backward headway, so I threw out the anchor. When we got the anchor to hold, I got back into the pram and rowed the mile to the moorage, where we had a vehicle, and took the battery out of it so I could go back and get the boat started and brought back home.

As I was heading back to the boat, the wind continued to increase to a point that it became very rough for the pram. I got to the boat and put the battery in, and we were able to motor back to the moorage. We tied the boat up and went to shore with the battery, so I could take everybody back to their cars, so they could make it to work. Sherrie and I had already planned for the day off, so we did not have an issue as the others did. Our day was to be spent looking at wedding rings.

Later that afternoon I got a call from the friends who owned the house where we were mooring the boat, telling me that the mast had fallen. The crossed stays could not hold the mast up in the rough sea conditions caused by the wind. After the weather subsided, I went to the boat with Sherrie and my dad, and we took the boat over to the local marina, where I used to keep my catamaran, and had them lift the mast with their elevator so we could get the mast set properly during daylight hours, so we could see. It cost about five dollars to do this which went against my low budget mode of operation.

We spent the summer sailing around Southern Puget Sound enjoying the challenges of sailing. We learned a lot about sailing and totally enjoyed our time on board. Sherrie, who is now my full-time boating partner, was capable of bringing the boat back to the mooring buoy under full sail and having the boat stop facing upwind so I could get the mooring line hooked up. This was no easy task for most people, but she made it look really simple.

A Newly Married Man

FIRST REAL BOAT TRIP 1972

I am now a married man. Our late July honeying moon was spent on a cruise to the San Juan Islands on our new sailboat. As we started north, we had no real schedule as to where we wanted to anchor or be at any given day. We wanted to go to the San Juan Islands, because I had never been there by boat, except for the ferry boat that you have to take from Anacortes to get to the islands. I did go to San Juan Island twice to go rabbit hunting. Once with a couple of friends, my junk yard buddies that I got my parts from, and once with my future brother-in-law. The first day of our trip, we stopped just across from Seattle and dropped the hook. It was still early in the day, so we wanted to explore a small harbor that I was never in. We took off in the eight-foot pram with our five-horsepower motor and headed around the corner to explore the inlet. When we returned our new boat was gone. Why would somebody steal our boat? I knew exactly where we anchored, and it was only about twenty feet deep and I put out plenty of scope (the rule is that you put out anchor line to at least three to four times the depth which is the scope) to hold in this calm day with just a slight breeze. As we looked out towards Seattle, we see what looks like our boat heading towards the other side of the bay. We took off as fast as the pram would go with the five-horsepower outboard motor. We did catch up with the boat to learn that the anchor had dragged because we anchored on a steep slope and not a flat bottom.

After that mishap I made a depth sounder for the remainder this trip. It was a sixteen-ounce hammer with a string tied to it. I would through it overboard and when it hit bottom, I would pull it back in and measure the depth by counting how many armlengths the line was until it hit the hammer. We got back on board and decided that before we anchor again, we would do a better job of steadying the charts, which was no more than a plasticized place mat that we found in a gift store. It was a lot cheaper than an actual nautical chart and you could not ruin it if you spilled anything onto it.

We got the boat heading north again and pulled into Kingston Harbor on Bainbridge Island where we did a proper anchoring and spent the night. The next morning Sherrie and I awoke to a beautiful sunny morning. We pulled anchor and motored on north towards the San Juan Islands. We tried to put up the sails but somehow the halyard that pulls the sail up jammed and we were unable to pull up the sails. We continued to motor along with ease as we took in all the splendid views of the trip north. This was the furthest that I had ever traveled on water, so it was a new adventure for me as well as Sherrie. We had to cross the Straights of San Juan De Fuca, which can be a very treacherous stretch of water. Several large commercial vessels have put their nose out there to only turn back and wait for a better weather opportunity. This day was calm, so we headed across. Sherrie was a bit nervous because of the stories that she had heard so I wanted to make sure that I did not place her into any situation that would make her tense or scared. We passed a small pod of killer whales about a mile away. Sherrie wanted nothing to do with the whales, so I made sure that we kept a good distance from them. We had a great dinner as we traveled across the Straights. Sherrie put together some appetizers while I put a chicken on the barbeque. Just before the chicken was ready, we heard a spout from what we knew was sure to be a killer whale just behind the boat. The killer whales are about the same size of the twenty-seven-foot boat that we were on, so it would be real intimidating to have one come up to us and decide that it wanted the chicken dinner. Sherrie let out a scream and

I did the manly thing and yelled at the water to scare anything that was there away. When I regained my composure, I noticed a small porpoise following us. The panic subsided, and we continued across the straights. We pulled into a little bay called Fish Creek at the bottom of San Juan Island. We put down the anchor, after looking at the placemat and putting my new depth sounder over the side to check the bottom. This was the first depth sounder that I had that could accurately read the bottom and with a bit of experience I could tell if the bottom was rocky, muddy, or possibly even grassy. The device was a Craftsman sixteen once framing hammer attached to a fifty-foot line. As it hit the bottom I could try to feel if it hit hard or mushy indicating what the bottom was. If it came up with grass, I could assume that the bottom was grassy, very ingenious this invention of mine.

Now that we were safely anchored, I had to go up the mast to fix the stuck halyard, so we could sail around. To do this I had to have Sherrie pull me up with the halyard for the forward sail (jib). I am not afraid of heights but the top of a ladder and the top of a forty-foot mast is an enormous difference. I fixed the problem and returned down to the safety of the main deck where I could stop the slight tremor that my body was having aloft. When I was at the top of the mast, I came to realize that if our creator wanted us to climb to these heights and work on something, he would have given us two sets of arms and hands. One set to hold on with and the other to work with.

The next morning, we woke to another sunny day in the islands. We pulled anchor after a leisurely breakfast of cold cereal and milk. Sherrie always must have her cup of coffee in the morning, so she had to start the propane stove, so she could brew her coffee. I would have to stay out on deck because I never got used to the pungent odor of coffee brewing. As a child growing up both of my parents drank coffee and smoked cigarettes all day long. I never smoked a cigarette or drank coffee mostly because of the odor of both habits. My dad stopped smoking the day the Surgeon General announced on national TV that smoking was bad for your health. I am sure that he thought that it was not good for your health anyway, but when it was formally announced he had that additional push to help him stop. My mom was not able to fully stop but slowed down a lot.

After breakfast, we pulled anchor and motored out of the small anchorage and headed further into the islands. As soon as we got out into Cattle Pass, we pulled up the sails and had a great sail around San Juan Island. This was the first time I had ever been there by boat. I have been on San Juan Island as a younger boy with people rabbit hunting but never got to explore the island. By boat you can see all the shoreline including all the private locations that you cannot visit by car. We sailed into Roche Harbor and dropped anchor, so we could do a bit of exploring on the beach. Roche harbor is one of the most popular areas in the islands today, but back than it was mostly the remnant of the old lime kiln. We walked to the old mausoleum and past the old cemetery. In the cemetery, I looked at all the old headstones and was surprised to learn that most of the people did not live must past about forty-four years of age. There were also a high number of children in the cemetery which seemed to be an indication as to how tough life must have been back in the old days of the original settlers.

We left Roche harbor and continued with our little trip around the islands. We went to a bay across from Roche Harbor on Stewart Island called Reid Harbor where we anchored. This has become one of Sherrie's favorite anchorages in the islands. On one of our later trips we walked up the trail from the end of the harbor to learn that one of the last one room schoolhouses was still in existence there.

We woke up the next morning to yet another blue sky and warm sunny day, which is typical for the end of July. We pulled anchor, which is done by hand since my boat builder was too cheap to install an electric anchor windlass. In fact, he was even too cheap to install any halyard winches on the mast or deck so all the pulling up of the sails or adjusting the sails while sailing was done using Armstrong (mine) winches. We decided that we needed to head south, so we could get back to be at work the next week. It was now Friday, and we wanted to see a bit of the northern portion of Puget

Sound anyway. I have been all over the southern portion with my previous boats, but I have never been north of Seattle. We pulled the sails up and we headed around San Juan Island towards Port Townsend which is located on the mainland on the western side of Puget Sound. We sailed across the Straights of San Juan De Fuca again with Sherrie constantly on the lookout for killer whales. We did pass a pod of whales on the southern portion of San Juan Island (this is a popular location for whale watchers). The wind started to pick up as we continued across the straights and with the wind you get waves. With the wind, you also gain speed, so this became a bit of a nervous time for Sherrie. I was enjoying the sail. Being on a tri-hulled vessel it was very stable as well as fast. The wind and waves were more on our starboard (right) aft quarter which made for a great downwind sail. We rounded the point just before Port Townsend where we started to lose both the wind and the waves. This allowed Sherrie to calm down bit. We looked at our chart and decided to anchor just to the North of a small passage on the west side of Marrowstone Island. I used my new depth sounder to measure the depth and my recollection of what the tide was at about that time of day to judge the safety of the anchorage. The water was not very deep, but my recollection was that it was low tide and the depth would not be an issue. The wind had quit for the evening and we were anchored a safe distance out of what looked like the main channel. It was Friday evening and the temperature was warm. We watched the sun go down behind the Olympic Mountains and went to bed to have a great night's sleep after a bit of a stressful day crossing the straights. We woke up in the morning with our heads a bit downhill. I sprung out of bed thinking that we must have had a problem and we were sinking. I checked the bilges and found them dry. I went out on deck to find that my depth/tide calculations were a bit off. I was correct in reading the depth on my new depth sounder. I was almost correct in my recollection about it being low tide when I took the readings, but the one thing that I missed was that, which I knew, there are two low tides and two high tides every day.

The tides are not always the same. This day had a very slight evening low tide but had a huge minus tide in the morning. There was close to a thirteen-foot difference in tide. When you anchor in fifteen feet of water with a boat that only draws a couple of feet of water that should not be a problem. The rudder draws about four feet of water so that was my only issue. The only other problem was that it is now Saturday morning, and this appeared to be the main channel for all the people that wanted to go boating to or from Port Townsend. There was a steady line of boats passing us and wondering why we were a bit bow down. All we could do was to sit and patently wait for the tide to come up and free the muddy bottoms grasp on our rudder. Luckily, that was not my normal cruising grounds, and nobody recognized me. There is an old saying, if you are a boater it is not whether you will hit bottom but when. I was lucky that I hit early in my boating career and got that out of the way. No damage was done except my ego got a bit hurt. There is another little saying and that is that you can have hundreds of dockings or anchoring in this case, but nobody remembers them, they only remember the one bad one. She still brings that up when she has the urge to cut me down a bit.

We headed back south and pulled into our anchorage later that evening. We spent the night on the boat to finish up our little trip. We have been up to the San Juan Islands hundreds of times since then with no major problems. We now live on one of the first of the San Juan Islands, Fidalgo Island.

NEIGHBORS

Sherrie and I moved into the cabin on the beach where we moored the boat as soon as we got married. It was on medium bank property with a nice sandy beach. We could get gooey ducks (a large clam mostly found only in the Pacific NW) on the extreme low tides.

A typical gooey duck. we dug several of these on the beach in front of the cabin

It was a quiet neighborhood. The one thing that I learned by living on the water is that you have to have money to have a nice place on the water (we were the exception because we lived in a two-room summer cabin and the bathroom was an afterthought built on the outside of the house with no insulation so when it got cold everything froze including the two of us) but you don't have to be a boater or even own a boat. I learned after several years of boating that when you live on the beach you can have a magnificent view of one piece of the water but when you boat you can have almost any view that you want. If you do not like the view that you have today than move to a different anchorage and you will have an entirely different view. We have been fortunate enough to have some outstanding views, from sunset to magnificent waterfalls while at anchor. It helps make the memories lasting and adds to the desire to get back out on the water again. One of the larger boats that I built at Delta was heading to Alaska for a shakedown cruise. Almost all of the big yachts head to the East Coast to cruise the Bahamas and the Caribbean islands. Since they are built on the West Coast, the alure of Alaska usually heads them north before heading east. As soon as I delivered the boat, we got on our 43' and headed to the Broughton Islands in Canada. We pulled into a Village, Sullivan Bay (which is a floating community complete with a general store, fuel dock and a restaurant). We saw the 110' yacht that I just delivered sitting at the guest dock. I went to the owner to say hello and ask how the boat was doing. He said the if he sees another eagle or green tree he will puke. I guess they do not have any of that in Florida.

The floating community of Sullivan Bay during the off season, normally it is packed with boats.

The view from an anchorage in the Canadian Gulf Islands

We had a neighbor, Bob, who was the wood shop teacher for the local high school. He watched as we took our eight-foot pram and would row out to our twenty-seven-foot sailboat and head off into the unknown, or at least out of sight. Bob came to me one day and asked about boating. Being an avid boater, I could not suppress my enthusiasm for boating and somehow sold him on the idea that he needed a boat. He went and bought himself a used twenty-foot outboard boat that was built from plywood. The motor was shot so he could get the boat with the trailer real cheap. He came to me, knowing that I was a boat builder, with the thought of stretching the boat to twenty-four feet. He came to me after he had already cut off the aft end of the boat. Being a schoolteacher teaching wood working, I believe that he thought that his knowledge would be able to take him through this project. He did know what the basic tools were used for, but that was about the extent of his knowledge on that subject. I came up with a straightforward way to extend the boat. He then wanted to make the boat an inboard powered boat. I had a spare engine that I bought for my sailboat boat when I was looking to by engines, so I sold him the engine with the reverse gear, so he would not have to go through what I had to go through when I was coming up through the boat building process. I told him about all my "low budget Bud ideas" such as the steering and the exhaust system with its cooling. The engine that I sold him had cooled exhaust manifolds and a heat exchanger, so it made it a lot easier. He did not need my keel cooling system for this engine. That was the big advantage that was designed from the factory to be used as a marine engine. It had the heat exchanger to keep the engine cool, a water-cooled exhaust manifold to keep the engine room cooler as well as the sea water pump that cooled both items as well as the exhaust pipe going through the hull of the boat. Bob installed the engine, built the shaft strut, and had a shaft machined to the proper length and to fit a standard inboard propeller. My shafts were fitted with outboard propellers and not inboard propellers which was simpler for me to make. The inboard propellers required a tapered shaft that had to be made using a lathe and a person that knew how to run the lathe. My propellers only required a straight shaft of the correct diameter and had a sheer pin going through the propeller and shaft. The sheer pin was designed so that if you hit something with the propeller the pin would sheer, or break, protecting the shaft and propeller. The boat had an outboard motor, so it had the start of the low budget Bud steering system. It had the steering wheel and all the cables that ran to the motor, which had a tiller arm (the attachment for the cables that would turn the engine). I drew up the system including all the details to make sure that it would work. Bob would need his own dingy to go from the beach to the boat with. I showed him my eight-foot pram, which I am sure that he had drooled over for weeks now. I gave him the jig to build one on and he proceeded to build his pram. Bob was also going to need a mooring buoy to tie the boat up when he was finished boating for the day. I told him to place the pram just below the high tide line as soon as the tide started to go out, and then take a thirty-gallon drum, cut in in half so he had about a 15-gallon drum, and place it on planks that are laid across the bow of the boat. Fill the drum with concrete and place a short section of anchor chain into the cement with a couple of bolts sticking out of it so that it was secured into the cement. Then he would need to secure a section of galvanized cable to the chain and run the cable to a float that would be on the surface of the water. I told him to make the cable at least twice as long as the depth that he was going to put the anchor. I told him that he could use my new "Craftsman" depth sounder if he did not have one. Being a carpenter, I was sure that he had his own. It was a beautiful Sunday morning when Sherrie, my parents and I went out for a sail on our boat. Bob had already placed his pram on the beach in preparation for his mooring buoy anchor project. the tide was high and was just starting to go out when we all left in our pram and headed for the sailboat on our mooring buoy. We had a beautiful sail that day. We were coming back to our mooring buoy when we saw Bob sitting all the way back in his pram with the bow of the pram almost under water. Bob was one of these people that if fifteen gallons of concrete were good just think how good full thirty gallons would be. He had all the weight sitting on the bow of his eight-foot pram and was stretched out in the back with his foot against the barrel. He had the cable and buoy in the pram with him. We hurried so we could be a better witness to this disaster. He continued to push until the barrel finally went overboard. The pram went from almost sunk in the bow to almost vertical. The radical motion almost thru him over the stern of the pram which possibly saved his life. It kept him from getting tangled in the cable as the barrel was rocketing to the bottom. Bob now had his mooring buoy, and possibly a messed-up set of shorts.

Bob eventually launched his twenty-four-foot motor yacht. He would take it on small trips to get used to coming back to the mooring buoy without having any problems. Not sure, but I believe that this was the second boat that Bob had operated, the first being the eight-foot pram. He would pick up the mooring line and we would watch as he would tie his complicated knots to make sure that the boat was secured. The first few times that he tied the boat up he would than get into the pram and start to row towards shore. His twenty-four would follow him in. I gave him a couple of lessons as to how to tie a proper knot to keep that from happening. In the marine business there is a saying, "if you can't tie a knot, tie a lot".

One beautiful Sunday afternoon we saw Bob and his wife head out to their yacht. They were all dressed up in their finest clothes. He was taking her to the new Anthony's Restaurant in Des Moines Marina. They departed with no issues and took a nice slow cruise the four miles to the marina. Later that evening I see a set of running lights coming our way. They acted a bit weird; they would be coming at us and then the boat would do a complete circle and then continue coming at us. I watched for a while and then as it got closer, I realized that it was Bob and his wife returning from dinner. I watched as they approached and then picked up the mooring buoy and tied the yacht up and rowed back to the beach. The next day after Bob came home from work, I asked what the problem was. He said that they were having a great cruise, but the engine was not getting any gas, so he had the squeeze bulb for the fuel line under his foot and keep depressing the bulb to keep the engine running. When he built the boat, he did not install any fuel tank. The original boat only used portable six-gallon tanks so that is what he continued to use. It was only about a fifty-horsepower motor, so it did not use a lot of fuel to cruise. Going over was not any issue because they were going slow to see the sights. Coming home it was a bit colder, so Bob's wife wanted to go a bit faster to get home quicker. Bob knew that he could keep up with the fuel demands so that was not an issue. As the boat started to speed up, he had to swerve to miss a log and that is when the rudder system failed. When I gave the design to Bob, there was an upper and lower set of flanges with pipe tees that the rudder shaft would go through. Being a teacher, he couldn't understand the redundancy, so he only installed one set so when he made the course correction, the torque on the rudder when he turned back to the left, caused the pipe threads to loosen up and the rudder came out of the water. He now had to stand at the stern with an oar in his hand while depressing the fuel bulb with his foot, so he could make it home. An inboard powered boat with a single propeller will back to the left and steer to the right when underway. The rudder and a good keel will help keep the boat going straight, neither of which his boat now had. When he got tired of holding the oar in the water to keep the boat straight on course, he would take the oar out of the water which caused the boat to make a slow circle. This was the first and the last time that his wife ever went boating on their yacht.

We had another neighbor down the beach that bought a new Ranger dingy. It had an outboard motor on it and could be fitted with the optional mast with a centerboard and a sail. They were one of the finest dinghies of the time. Early one Saturday morning Sherrie and I headed to the beach and started dragging our pram down to the water, so we could row out to the sailboat and get away. The only way we could be alone was to just leave early. One of the strange facts of life is the people that live on the beach and especially the ones that have a boat moored in their front yard will have more friends than the ones that live in a crowed neighborhood. Just before we got the pram to the water, we heard this loud commotion down the beach, so we looked just in time to see our neighbor with the new dingy step into the dingy while in about two feet of water and flip the boat over. I mentioned that this was a real nice dingy. It was great for rowing as well as sailing, the only disadvantage that the dingy had was it had a rounded shape to the bottom which would allow it to capsize easy if the weight is not kept low and centered. Stepping into the boat and not knowing this was the formula for disaster, which is what happened. We later learned that the reason that he was out that early was so that nobody would see him attempt to get into the boat. This was not the first time he had the same results. He did eventually learn how to get into the boat without tipping it over.

One windy afternoon after work, Sherrie and I wanted to go for an evening sail. The wind was brisk, so we thought that we would have fun challenging the wind and would see what kind of speed we could get out of this old girl. We rowed the pram out to the boat. I will mention that when I built the pram, I built the bow angle of the pram to the same angle as the forward rake of the stern of the sailboat. That way I could hang a cushion on the transom of the sailboat and just come straight up behind the boat. Somebody could tie up the bow line and the pram would be securely attached to the sailboat allowing people to walk from one boat to the other safely. There was one occasion where my friend (who was my best man at the wedding) didn't get the pram tied to the cleat on the back of the sailboat before he tried to board the sail boat and ended out horizontal with his hands holding onto the back stay of the sail boat and his feet inside the pram. He could not hold on long enough for somebody to come to his rescue and ended up falling into the bay. If anybody has been in Puget Sound, they will know that it is cold. Luckily, he was able to get into the pram and get it back to the sailboat, so we did not have to go rescue the pram. I put a bridle in the back stay for the mast, so it would not be in the way to access the boat but would give a good solid handhold. Sherrie and I get on the sailboat and get untied from the mooring. I pull up the sails and we are off. The boat was in fact fast in this stiff breeze. As we headed into the bay, we noticed that the wind was swirling. It continued to pick up speed and started to swirl even more making it difficult to keep the sails full or not overfull to the point the equipment was put beyond limits. We decided to just turn around and head back to the moorage when a big gust hit the sails and severely bent the wooden mast. The bend was in the shape of an S with the center of the mast where the spreaders (which helped to hold the mast straight from side to side) were the center of the S. It straightened out as soon as the wind let off. We were hit by several random gusts each one bowing the mast into an S to a point that Sherrie had to just turn her back and not look at it. We were about one hundred yards from the mooring when a huge gust came over the hill and hit the sails which put the mast into a huge S and then finally breaking the mast. At this point, all of the mast and rigging as well as the sails are lying alongside in the saltwater. The single largest expense that I had in this boat was the sails. I would always take them into the house if I were not going to use them for a few days or if I thought that the weather was going to be wet. Now they are all lying in the saltwater and they may be damaged. We had a lot of time because we were being blown away from the beach, so I wanted to take our time in getting the sails up and the rigging secured to not cause any more damage. As we are carefully working on this, we notice two separate boats coming out to rescue us. Bob in his pram with his outboard motor and the new Ranger with his small outboard motor, the two most unlikely people that one would want help from especially on a rough and windy day on the water. I now have a real problem trying to convince them that I am OK and to just stay away. One is trying to get a line on the boat, so he can tow us to the mooring while the other is running over the rigging. The one running over the rigging, the Ranger, finally caught a line in his prop so thankfully he was out of commission. The other, Bob, gave up on trying to get a line on the bow (being a flush deck boat it has a high bow). The last I saw of them Bob was towing the other dingy back to the beach.

Sherrie and I finished securing the rigging and started the Scripps engine and headed back to the mooring ball and back to home where I could wash the sails and hang them in the cabin to dry. The only thing damaged, besides a small halyard that was run over and had to be cut, was my ego. Now I had the opportunity to design and build a new mast.

THE NEW MAST

After working with the original wood mast, I realized that it just was not strong enough for the loads that can be placed on it by the tri hulled design boat. The boat does not heel, or lean, as much as a mono-hull vessel. When a big gust of wind hits the sails on a mono hull, the boat heels over spilling a lot of the wind out of the sails reliving the strain on the mast. With a tri-hulled vessel the downwind hull will help keep the vessel upright and the weight of the upwind hull will also have a righting force on the boat, putting more strain on the rigging. This is also why the multi-hulls are a lot faster. I contacted the mast manufactures to see what it would cost for a new sailboat mast. I could do all the work so all that I really needed was the aluminum piece without all of the attachments. Even with a bare stick of aluminum it was more than what "Low Budget Bud" was willing to pay. I thought about it for a while and decided that all I really needed was a round tube that was about forty feet long. I learned what the stresses were on the mast and looked up in the metal catalogue to find a tube with the strengths that I needed. I went to a higher authority to make sure that my idea made sense and my dad said that it would work with no issues. At one point, I thought of having the round tube pressed to make it an oval, so it looked like the rest of the sailboat masts but decided that there was no gain for the cost. The tube was sized for the fore and aft forces so the side to side was not going to be an issue. The tube that I purchased only came in twenty-one-foot lengths, so I had to splice the two sections together. I cut two feet from one of the sections and then took a small lengthwise section of metal out of the two-foot section so that when I compressed it, it would fit inside the tube with a tight fit. I applied a coat of epoxy to one section and half of my slice and pounded it into the lower section. After the epoxy dried I than applied the epoxy to the remaining section of the splice and then to the upper section of the mast and pounded the two sections together. I now had a one-piece tube forty feet long. I used some flat aluminum to build the mast head, which is the top of the mast where the four upper mast stays are attached and the blocks for the halyards for raising and lowering the sails are attached. After the mast head was built and attached, the last step was to attach the spreaders which gives the mast stiffness in the side to side direction. I made the attachments and fastened them to the section where the two sections were joined together. That was the stiffest point with plenty of thickness for attaching the fasteners to hold the brackets for the spreaders. The rigging was typical for a sailboat of this size. It had a fore stay that ran from the top of the mast to the bow of the boat. There were two upper stays, one port and one starboard, which went from the top of the mast to the deck and went over the spreaders creating a lot of force on the center of the mast to keep the mast straight. With opposing forces from both sides this made the mast extremely strong in a side force direction. There was also an aft stay that went from the top of the mast to the stern. I put a bridle in the aft stay so that it did not come to the center but had a space that people could board the boat from the stern. There were also four lower stays, two on the port side and two on the starboard side that were attached to the mast just below the spreaders and ran a bit fore and aft to help support the mast in all directions. Now that the mast was built, I had to get it installed. I built the mast in the yard so all we had to do is to slide it over the hill and onto the beach. We could than support it on two prams, mine and neighbor Bob's, and row it out to the boat. We hoisted it up onto the deck in preparation for hoisting it upright. Learning my lesson from the first time I just went to the marina where they had an elevator lift and used that to lift the mast, complete with all of the stays attached, off the deck and hold it in position while we hooked up the stays. Now that the mast is up and secured, we are ready to go boating again.

On evening after work one of my neighbors, Si, called and asked if we could go sailing. It was another windy afternoon, so I said yes. We rowed the pram out to the boat and cut loose from the mooring. I pulled the sails up, still remembering the last time it was windy and gusty like this. I believe that Si wanted to test my invention. He had been a boater for a long time and had never seen a round aluminum mast before. I am sure that he thought that it would fail, and he wanted to be there for the wreck. The wind was gusty, but the mast stood up to it. We had a great fast sail proving the mast in tough conditions.

A GREAT SAIL

One weekend Sherrie and I invited my parents for a sail to South Sound. We went to a place called Harstine Island. It was beautiful weekend weather wise. We anchored by the island where there happened to be several Sea Lions feeding. They are big and mean but interesting to watch. We had a great meal as mom and Sherrie went out of their way to prepare a special meal for the occasion. Sunday morning, we picked anchor and headed for home. As we passed McNeil Island, which used to be a penitentiary, the wind started to pick up. The wind was in our face, so we had to tack, sail back and forth pointing the boat as close to an upwind direction but still have enough wind in the sails from the side to fill the sails and push the boat forward, to continue with our trip. We could have pulled the sails down and started the motor, but we were enjoying the day, so we continued to sail. At one point, I looked up just in time to see a seagull about to give us a present. I yelled duck to make sure that nobody got bombed. As I watched the seagull, I noticed that it was not trying to bomb us, it was trying to land on my oversized mast head plate. We watched as it would fly alongside and then drop his landing gear and try to touch down on the mast head. This went on for a good ten minutes before the seagull finally decided that this was not going to work.

We continued our sail towards the Tacoma Narrows Bridge, which is a short cut from Tacoma to the Olympic Peninsula across south Puget Sound. As we were heading towards the bridge by tacking from shore to shore, we passed a 27' monohulled sailboat in about the middle of our tack. The first tack they were about one hundred yards ahead of us (in the direction that we were heading) and the second tack, they were about one hundred yards behind us. They knew that trimarans would not point into the wind well, so they just pulled their sails down in frustration and motored past us by about half a mile and put their sails back up to continue their sail. They were not going to be out sailed by one of these goofy looking three hulled vessels. We went under the bridge and headed towards Point Defiance where we could make a course correction that would be a bit more favorable for sailing. After we rounded Point Defiance, we headed towards Browns Point. At that point, we could make our turn and head towards home at Redondo. Once we made the turn near Browns Point, we had the wind mostly on our port beam. This direction gave us the best speed for sailing. The wind increased a bit which also increased the size of the waves. The boat was very stable, so the waves were not an issue, but the wind made for the best sail that we ever had. At one point, I let Dad steer the boat while Sherrie and I went to the bow and hanging onto the handrail we let our legs dangle over the bow. Our feet would almost touch the water as the boat rose and fell over the waves. My mom, dad, Sherrie and I always talked about that magical time on the water.

WINTER STORAGE

I did not want to keep the boat in the water during the stormy winter months, so I had to devise a way to get the boat out of the water without having a monthly expense. One day while sitting on the beach I started looking at the four-foot diameter log that had been washed up onto the beach during a massive storm. As I looked at it my mind, as twisted as it was, started to vision a platform that I could sit the boat onto in the winter. I pulled out the old boat plans and using the line drawings, I laid out the locations at the two main bulkheads and built the exact shape of the hull with an added space for a layer of half inch rubber. I built the two frames out of several sections of some scrap lumber. The frames were six inches wide when finished. I had to glue up some boards to make the main stringers that would form the bottom of this boat cradle. I knew that it would have to be very well built because of what I was about to attempt to do with it. Once all the pieces were built, I slid them down the bank onto the beach on Saturday afternoon where I assembled them. I borrowed my Brother in laws big chainsaw to remove the top third of the log to create a flat spot for the cradle to rest on. I did it by cutting down to a marked depth and then taking a splitting wedge and a large sledgehammer I removed the sections of the log. The log was a large old growth fir tree with straight grain and no knots, so it split off easily. The tide was coming in Sunday morning and the weather was calm, so I decided to make my move. I got my dad and brother-in-law to come and help. They thought that this was just another half-baked hair brained idea, but they were always in for watching a good wreck at somebody else's expense. We brought the sailboat in closer to the beach where I had placed the cradle and then pushed the cradle down the beach on three round six-inch logs that we had set the cradle on. We worked the cradle under the boat and secured the cradle to the boat with several lines. The next part was the hair brained, half-baked design. I positioned my Jeep with the big military Braden power take off winch (power take off uses direct power from the engine through a device behind the transmission, so it did not require battery power and would also have lots of power in low gear). We run the cable down the hill and attached it to a chain bridle that we had attached to the front of the cradle. We started winching and to everybody's amazement the boat came up the beach very smoothly without much effort. I had cut four logs, so we would have an extra all the time. Sherrie's brother ran the Jeep while Sherrie relayed instructions. By now there was a fairly good crowd forming so we had a lot of good volunteer help. When we had a log come to the end of the cradle, we would have already placed the extra one at the front of the cradle so all we had to do was to leapfrog the logs. When we got to the big log with the flattened top, things got a bit more interesting. We made some ramps out of some heavy planks to help slide the cradle up onto the log. The thing that helped the most was that the Jeep was about thirty feet above the cradle on the top of the bank so that when we pulled hard it would lift the front of the cradle off the ground. The log had been washed up onto the beach several years ago and was partially buried into the sand which also helped. The cradle came up onto the log and we were able to pull it up with less problems than anybody on the beach would have thought, including me. When we got the cradle with the boat in it as far up as we wanted, which had to be past the balance point by a little bit so that it wouldn't tip back towards the beach but towards the bank instead, we relaxed the strain on the winch and set the front of the cradle onto some blocking that I had sitting there. This entire process worked out better than what I actually thought that it would. I thought that we would be jacking the cradle up onto the log.

The boat sat in the cradle on the log with no issues all winter long. It survived the big winter storms with no issues. I had run a power cord down over the bank to keep some heat in the boat all winter long to help prevent any freezing or mildew. Before summer came, we would want to get the boat back into the water. I had several months to dream up the plan. My plan that I finally came up with was to place an anchor down the beach and put a pulley at that point so when I ran the winch on the Jeep through it and back up the beach to the aft end of the cradle, it would pull the cradle back down the planks and off the log. The boat was built light so it could make speed, which helped make this process easier. We winched the boat and cradle back off the log and onto the rollers and down the beach. I had a heavy line tied to the front of the cradle and had it hooked to a pulley that I had put on the trailer hitch of my brother-in-law's truck to keep the boat from taking off down the log or the beach too fast. The process was a lot easier than I dreamed that it would be. I had a few contingent plans so if one did not work maybe one of my backup plans would. I believe that if Murphy's Law knows that you have several contingent plans, they will allow the original plan to work. We used this process a couple of times with good success.

THE BOAT IS GONE

Every morning when I woke up, I would look outside at the relaxing view on the water. There was always some activity on the water whether it is somebody out fishing, the West Seattle Ferry running back and forth, a large container ship heading to or from Tacoma or just birds looking for their morning meal. One morning I looked out and saw the beautiful view and turned to go to the kitchen to make my morning breakfast, usually a nice bowl of cereal, when I turned back and looked and realized that the boat was gone. There was no storm and the mooring buoy was still there. I woke Sherrie up during my panic. I called the United States Coast Guard and they said that there was nothing that they could do so just call the Police for a stolen boat problem. I called the police about the stolen boat and they said to call the call the Coast Guard because it was on the water not the land. I forgot breakfast and headed north towards work. I figured that I would travel the roads as close to the water as I could, so I could see the boat if it were out there someplace. I did not get far before I saw the boat. It was floating in front of Saltwater State Park. I went to the park entrance, which was closed, parked my car, and ran to the Park Ranger's office. He was already awake, and I told him that my boat was stolen and that it was sitting out in front of the park. He helped me launch his Ranger rowboat, not unlike the round bottom boat that the neighbor had, and I rowed out to the boat. I stepped on the side of his boat to get onto my boat and learned what happened that morning down the beach when our neighbor tried to get into his Ranger dingy. The boat rolled up on one side and started to take on water. I thought that it was going to sink so I lowered my body back into the boat and hooked my toes under the seat to keep it floating while I figured out my next move. To my surprise the boat did not sink. It had enough buoyancy to just barely keep it afloat. I already had the bow line in my hand, so I pulled myself the rest of the way onto my boat and tied off the dingy. I quickly went through my boat to assess the damage. The people who stole the boat must have just wanted to go for a bit of a joy ride. They must have rowed out to the boat and went for a bit of an excursion. They threw out the anchor to keep it from drifting onto the beach. When they swung the anchor, they did a bit of damage to the hull but nothing a good boat builder could not fix. I was happy to get my boat back. I started the engine and powered the boat back to the mooring buoy. On the way, I pulled up the small Ranger dingy and drained most of the water out of it. I told the Park Ranger that I would get his boat back to him that evening and he said that there was not any hurry. I got cleaned up and had Sherrie, who waited at home for my news, take me to my car so I could go to work. That evening we towed the dingy back to the Park Ranger and thanked him with a bit of cash for saving the day. To this day the last people I think of calling in an emergency is the Coast Guard or the Police. Not because I do not have any respect or trust in them it is just not my way of thinking. I have learned over the years that if you need something done, especially in a crisis, then you have to jump in with both feet and do it yourself.

BUILDING A HOUSE

In 1975, Sherrie decided, as women often do, that we needed a better house to live in. The single bedroom cabin was great in the summer when it was warm but not so good in the winter when it got cold. I liked it because we had plenty to do on the water or the beach in the summer with the long days and during the winter we would come home and eat dinner, sit by the fire for a bit and then go to bed and watch TV where it would be warm and cuddly. I especially liked the cuddly part. We looked at open houses to get ideas and she found some books with house plans in them. I understood that women need their nest, so this did not come as a total surprise to me. A man can live in a cabin for extended periods and with all the "chores" he would never get bored. We decided that we wanted a house with a view of the water because living in the cabin on the water spoiled us a bit.

There was always some activity on the water to look at, from the ships coming and going from Tacoma, to the fishermen out trying to catch a salmon to the different sea birds, the view always changed. Sherrie found the perfect house only about five blocks away. It was up the hill from the cabin and had a splendid view of the water. She talked to the real-estate people about it and they told her that it could be bought for about thirty-two thousand dollars which was within our decided budget. We made an appointment to look the house over and decided to "go for it". We contacted the broker only to learn that he gave us the wrong price. Instead of thirty-two thousand it was fifty-six thousand, which was out of our price range. This was a blow to Sherrie, so I decided to make her dream come true and build her the house that she wanted. She picked out a house plan that she liked, and we drove around until we found the building lot that worked for us. We found a lot that was only one house off the beach but on high bank, so it had an unobstructed view. We bought the lot and got the permit process started so we could build the house. We went to get a bank loan but found out that the banks do not loan to people with no money and are building their own house. The bank put us through a lengthy exercise to get all of the bids to build the house. When we were finished getting all of the bids, we sat down with the banker to finalize our loan. The bids showed that it would cost about $32,000.00 to have the house built using subcontractors. We were going to build the house ourselves, so I told the banker that I wanted to borrow $22,000.00 to build the house. This would pay for all of the materials as well as some of the labor for some of the areas that I thought that an expert could do better than us. The bank's loan manager told us that he would give us the $22,000.00 of their money when I show him my $10,000.00. We had $1,000.00 in the bank, which he knew, but he would not understand that we would be able to make up the difference during the construction period. I told Sherrie to go to the teller's window and pull all of our money out of their bank if this is how they want to treat us, the entire thousand dollars. I also told the bank manager that I would invite him to the house-warming party when we finished the house.

We got the building permits and started the house project. We both had jobs, so we would cash our pay checks and go to the lumber yard and buy the materials that we would need to use over the weekend. We saved every penny we could and put it towards the house. We would eat soup for dinner and had no expensive tastes to deal with. We did treat ourselves to one night out every week. I would take my beautiful bride to the Golden Arches Restaurant every Friday night for her special meal. We did the entire build ourselves except for the times that dad was bored and needed something to do on the weekend. Sherrie not only got her dream house she got to drive almost every nail in it. The only part that we did not do was the taping and texturing of the sheetrock and the concrete slab work. We did everything else from digging and pouring the foundation to the finish trim. While we were building the house, we totally focused on the project.

When we got the house all framed up and ready for the roofing material, I did not have the seven hundred dollars that it would take to buy the roofing, so I again went to the bank. We now have a different bank because the last bank made us go out and get bids for the entire house leading us on about giving us the loan to just say no. This time they just said right out front that they do not loan to people building their own house. I asked if they would at least do a drive by to see what I had before they made their decision. The house was all framed up and ready to install the roofing material, so it looked like a real house not just a pile of wood on the ground. I received a call from the bank manager the next day. To my surprise, they actually drove by the house and looked at it. The house was a thirty-six hundred square foot house on a nice corner lot with a view of Puget Sound. The manager called me and asked if we needed more than the seven hundred dollars and I said no, and they loaned the money with no issues. Now that the roof was on the house before the wet season we could concentrate on the inside. We needed more money to keep the project going on a fast pace, so Sherrie talked about selling the boat. She did not push the issue because she knew that this was something that I built with my own two hands before we were married and that I enjoyed my time on it. One day I come home from work to find my precious sails stretched out on the grass with Sherrie and two other people looking at them. I took her aside to see what was going on and she informed me that she just sold the boat. Not wanting to make a scene I had to play along with it. The money came at about the right time, so we could buy the windows and the doors, so the house could be totally enclosed before the winter. I was going to give her a big spanking for selling the boat without getting real approval for it. I bent her over my knee, pulled down her britches and just at that moment I forgot why I was going to spank her.

This was the back of the house which faced the water.
It had windows from end to end to take advantage of the view.

We continued building the house and then finished all the landscape, so princess could have her "dream house".

ANOTHER NEW ROAD

In 1981 we also decided to start a family. After being married for 9 years we figured that the marriage would last, even thought there was good money bet on it not working. We had our first child, a daughter Michelle. We were fortunate that she was a great kid. Started to sleep all night at an early age and did not require a lot of discipline to keep in line. She was smart enough to realize that if she was good, she got rewarded, which she liked better than the spanking she got for being bad. This road seemed to be working out great so after six years we decided to have a second child. We were not as lucky with the second one. She was born on December 23rd and was an un-happy baby. On the 24th Sherrie asked the nurse what that strange noise was in the nursery and she said that it is your baby. In fact, the baby was so loud that they said that Sherrie was doing fine, and she could in fact go home that day, as long as she took Danielle with her. We did go home that day and placed the swaddled baby under the Christmas tree for all to enjoy! Danielle was not the happy baby that Michelle was. She was great if we had strangers over to the house. They could not understand why we were always complaining about this sweet little baby girl. Danielle was always a great little girl as long as the company was there but as soon as they would leave, she would be her old self again. Danielle did grow out of her crying problem and became a great person.

By now, I was missing boating, so I was going to borrow a hull mold for a 37' boat that Delta had sitting in storage and build my own boat. By then I had worked every discipline of boat building and was not concerned with the building process. I went on a road trip with Jack, the VP of Delta Marine, and I told him of my plans. He asked if I wanted to build the boat or wanted to use the boat. I said that I wanted to use the boat. I was basically boat less at the time. I ran all of the boats built so I was getting some boating but was not "going boating". Jack said that I should just go buy a boat. I went to the Tacoma Boat Show and saw the 32' Bayliner. I was impressed with the volume inside, so I bought the boat. Both of the girls loved boating. We bought a bigger boat in 1991 so we could extend our range to Desolation Sound in Canada. We had some great trips on the boat. We would do boating trips to Port Orchard and Gig Harbor on the nice weekends in the winter.

When the two daughters got married and started to have children of their own, we had to get an even bigger boat. The new boat had to have accommodations for both daughters, both sons-in-law, both pairs of grandchildren and their two dogs. And keeping to the pattern as before it is a Bayliner. The worst part is that I bought the first two Bayliner boats from John Ripley, who I went to school with. I tried hard to by my bigger boat from somebody else. The first two boats were new boats, mostly because Sherrie "didn't want to buy somebody else's problem". This new boat was going to be a used boat, since I am in fact a boat builder, so I spent time talking with the boat brokers that I knew in Seattle as well as attending the boat shows for almost two years looking for the right deal. All of the yacht brokers know my background in boatbuilding, which really surprised me when they tried to BS me about a boat. I was not looking at the Bayliner that much at first but then started to add it to the list to consider. The boat that I ended out buying was in fact a Bayliner and I did buy it from a Ripley. John Ripley's daughter has a successful used boat sale business in Anacortes called Banana Belt Boats that John had started and turned over to his daughter Amy, who was honest and great to work with.

Mon Chere at anchor in Desolation Sound with an 80" Northern Marine in the background.

The Career

BEFORE BOAT BUILDING

After washing cars, building casket liners, and trying to sell Kirby vacuum cleaners, I went to work for Boeing Airplane Company as a wind tunnel test model maker. In about 1969 Boeing had a set back and the Model Shop was considered a non-essential part and the shop had a huge layoff. I was given the option of going to their Everett facility to work on the 747 projects, which was really busy, or take a layoff. I liked working so I took the position at Boeing Everett plant building 747's. I worked with a small group of people fixing all of the cargo and entry doors for the first 68 planes. The engineers made a design change, so all the doors had to be retrofitted. Most of the doors were done in a small open section of the plant, but some were on airplanes that had been delivered so we had to go to Seattle's Boeing Field and fix the doors on the flight line. After the refit was completed, I was transferred to a crew in production that finished the doors in the body sections. It was really interesting at first. With a production job, I would challenge myself as to how fast I could complete the work. All of the tasks were inspected by one of the inspectors, so you had to do the job perfectly every time. You could not take any shortcuts, you just had to work fast and efficiently. After I got to my best time, than the job became boring. Same rivet in the same hole every 3 days. The company was delivering a finished 747 every 3 days. After a short while the Model Shop started back up. I was told by my friends at the Model Shop that they were trying to get me back but that I had changed my status, so it had become impossible. I got this notice on a Friday after work from my best friend at the model shop, who happened to be the shop Union Steward. I was scheduled to work on Saturday, so I went in as scheduled. I was only going to work until noon as was agreed by my supervisor. As I was leaving, being the nice guy that I am, I waved goodbye to the man at the supervisor's desk who was sitting in for my regular supervisor who did take the day off. He got up and walked over to intercept me as I was clocking out to leave. He asked me where I was going, and I told him that I worked out a deal with my normal supervisor the day before that I would only work a half day. He asked what I was going to do the rest of the day and I told him that I was going to work on my boat. This is the part I will never forget. He, being a tall man dressed in a nice suite, stood there, and thumped me on the chest and said, "this is your boat, without this job you don't have a boat". I asked him who he was, and he told me that he was the general manager of the entire plant. I said that "you must be the guy that is keeping me from going back to the model shop". He changed his demeanor instantly and said, "you must be Mr. LeMieux". At that point, he said how I could go a long way in production and pretty much write my own ticket (whatever that meant). We exchanged a few niceties and I went home with no objections. The next pay day my check was stupid money, they had to pay me the back pay from the time that they told the model shop that I got a raise as well as the higher pay going forward. They paid the retroactive pay overtime, so my checks were really big for a period. I was making more than supervisors that had been there for more than twenty-five years. I know this because I heard the complaints.

Now that I knew that I lost any chance of getting back to the model shop, don't you just love those unions, I decided that I had to make a career choice. I was bored in production. You can only challenge your own time so much and then you reach a plateau that is close to impossible to beat. At the same time my parents received the letter from the King County Building Department that they had built an extension on the side of their house without a building permit. By now I had a bit of money saved up, so I would be able to survive so I gave my notice at Boeing so I could stay at home and get the boat finished. I got the boat to a point where I could remove the temporary shed so that would take that potential monkey off my back. As a side note I never invited any of my parent's neighbors on a boat trip not knowing which one complained. I did not want to have somebody that made my life miserable and cost me some money get a chance to go out onto Puget Sound and have fun at my expense.

This was when the other road started beckoning me to head down the different path, so I quit the job at Boeing with the hope that I could get a more fulfilling job. This was a huge gamble but one that my innermost thoughts could not ignore. Something in me would beckon me to head down these less traveled roads. The roads had many bends, so you could not stand at the start of the road and see very far down the road. It was always a bit of a gamble as to what may be around that next corner, would it be another fork in the road or would the road get easier or tougher to travel down. Unlike the main road that most the people were going down, these roads looked dark and stormy when standing at the crossroads.

Professional Boat Building Starts
R&H Marine

YARD WORK

It was the spring of 1971 when I decided that production work was not for me. I quit Boeing so I could concentrate on getting the temporary shed removed and sailboat all assembled. After the sailboat was nearing completion, I made a trip to Lake Union in the Seattle area, where there were several boatyards. It was a Sunday afternoon, and nobody was around, so I would look in the windows of the different yards until I saw a set of blueprints hanging on a wall. The boat was well proportioned and looked like a magnificent sport fishing yacht.

The next day I went to the yard and applied for a job building boats. I learned that my seven years of building boats in my dad's backyard was no recommendation at this boatyard, or probably any other boatyard, but they did give me a job offer. I was making top dollar and had all the benefits that came with working at the Boeing 747 plant because of my model-making background and its pay scale being higher than the production workers' pay scale. I left all of that to *sweep* floors in a boat shop. Besides, when would be a better time to switch to a low-paying job without a lot of benefits than just before one is planning to get married? Yes, I was still perusing my hobbies and mating instincts. I always considered myself a multi-tasker.

My first task was to clean up the outside yard. By the end of the week, the owner, Jack Rodgers, came to me and said I was the first helper who had broken two brooms in one week by not just leaning on them. I had removed all of the blackberry vines along the edge of the property and picked up and organized all of the wood blocking materials. I would ask where they wanted the materials and would get them all organized. After the first week, they came to me and promoted me to helping the crane operator with hauling and launching the boats. I also got to scrub the bottoms and roll on the protective bottom paint. Today, they use a power washer to wash the bottom of the boats. If the boat has been sitting for an extended period of time, than it would have a good crop of barnacles that had to be manually scraped off the bottom. Back then, it was all done with a bucket of Zep soap and a brush. I was happy now that I was working on boats.

The yard did a lot of launching boats that came in on boat moving trailers from across the country. All the sailboats had to have their masts stepped (stood up and put in place) on the boats. The yard had a large crane that would allow the hauling and off-loading of the boats for bottom painting as well as other repairs. The crane was rigged with a special strap system to make it easy to install the masts. It was tradition to place a silver dollar under the mast when it was stepped onto the boat. If the owner of the boat did not have one, I would provide it. It was good luck for the boat, so I wanted to have the boat have all the good luck that it could have. The silver dollar that I used was minted that year, so it was the year that the mast was stepped. I was not a superstitious person, but why take a chance. One dollar was cheap insurance if it worked. Some people said that the only luck that the silver dollar would bring was that when the mast blew over the owner could at least make a phone call when he got to the dock.

REPAIR PROJECTS

R&H did several repair projects and also hauled and, because they had one of the biggest haul-out cranes on the lake, launched several boats for customers that would do some of their own work. They would also launch boats that came in on the boat moving companies' trucks. One boat that we were going to launch was a 40' home-made cruiser that somebody built. The keel was an actual telephone pole and the rest was plywood with a layer of fiberglass over it for additional strength as well as to preserve the wood. There was no attempt to make the boat "yacht-like". The workers that were building custom yachts inside the shed would come out and make fun of the boat. The owner of R&H sat the entire crew down and told them to never make fun of another person's boat. "this is their yacht and you will treat it as such". That was a great lesson for me. When somebody takes all the time and effort to build something with their own hands and skill level, they are proud of it and that should be respected. Back during that time period, a lot of people were building boats in their backyards. A lot were made using ferro cement, which was really cheap to do.

Some of the repair projects were interesting and helped expand my knowledge. The ones that stand out the most, and I still talk about today, were three of the repair projects. There were several projects that I learned some valuable lessons on. One was when I had to slither upside down into a tight place to help one of the workers install a piece of equipment. I had to get under the stateroom deck to bolt something up while he held the other end of the bolts above the deck. After fighting my way into the tight space and performing the task, I could not get back out. I got stuck and the more I tried the tighter I got stuck. The worker went to the Owner of the boatyard and told him my problem so the owner, Jack Rogers, came to see what was happening and how he could help. The two of them pulled on my feet to try to get me unstuck but it did not work. Jack said for me to just relax, but with a bit of adrenalin running through my body that was not going to happen. Jack went to his office and returned with a bottle of alcohol that he had for special occasions. Jack worked out a method using a small hose to get the alcohol down my throat. Once I could get the hose into my mouth, he then slowly poured the alcohol into my mouth. It was not the most pleasant stuff to be going down my throat. Jack continued to have me just calm down. After a bit of time the alcohol started to do its job and I started to relax. Once relaxed they could pull me out of the hole. They allowed me to stay on the job washing the bottom of boats the rest of the day to help get the alcohol out of my system so I could drive home safely.

Another project was a boat called the *KELT* that was trucked in from the Great Lakes area. It was a wooden powerboat that had been out of the water for period of time. If you have ever seen a wooden boat that was built from solid planks instead of plywood you would know that the wood swells up when in the water and will shrink up when out of the water and the wood dries out. It takes a while for the wood to dry out. When building a wooden planked boat, you have to leave a space between the planks for the wood to swell up. The gap is filled with a caulking material called Oakum. The Oakum will seal the water from leaking into the hull and be flexible enough to be compressed between the planks as they swell up. This boat was totally dried out, so we did not want to spend a lot of time and money totally re-caulking the hull. Upon inspection, the caulking was still between the planks. We launched the boat and placed a large pump with a float switch on it to keep the water pumped out as it came in. Every night we would move the boat back to the dock where the crane was and place the boat back into the straps and "hang" the boat in the water. Being in the lake there was no tide, so we did not have to worry about the tide coming up or down. This was a safety measure in case the pump failed. After about a week the boat swelled up and almost completely stopped leaking. We hauled the boat out of the water and had Wolfgang, the company's shipwright that did all the caulking on the wooden boats, come out and caulk the few seams that did not dry up. We re-launched the boat and then had to do an oil change on the engine before the new Owner came to pick up the boat for the weekend. To access the engine all that you had to do was to lift a large hatch in the center of the saloon and you had a lot of access. This was not a large boat, so the engine barely fit under the main deck. Being a quality repair yard, we took the necessary precautions to place large drop cloths on the nice white carpeted floors and out the back door just in case we drop something or have something on our shoes or coveralls. There was no way to get to the bottom of the oil pan to drain the oil out and it would take forever to suck the oil out through the dip stick hole, so I came up with the brilliant idea of letting the engine pump its own oil out. The yard manager was doing the job and he thought that it was a great idea. I added a pressure gauge to the hose that we were using to pump the oil out of the engine. This engine was a six -cylinder Detroit engine that my dad had a lot of experience with so with a simple call to him I quickly learned where to place the fitting on the engine to get the oil pressure to pump the oil out and not starve the engine for oil during the operation.. There were several plugs on the engine that had oil pressure, so it was easy to locate one. We connected one end of the hose to the engine port and the other end to the gauge and had a separate hose from the gauge to be able to go into the bucket. We were using one quarter inch hose, so it would be able to have some restriction which would keep some oil pressure in the engine. We got two empty five-gallon buckets to pump the old oil into. Some of these engines had more than five gallons of oil in them so we wanted to be ready. We started the engine and held the hose into the bucket. We watched the oil pressure gauge to make sure that we were not "steeling" all the oil pressure from the engine. Jack H. the yard boss decided to put his thumb over the end of the hose that was going into the bucket to make sure the engine had pressure. At that moment, the hose that he blocked blew off the end of the input side of the gauge line. We now had a loose hose that looked like a loose fire hose spraying dirty black oil all over the inside of the cabin. We shut the engine down as fast as possible but by then the damage was done. We had sprayed the oil all over the curtains, the furniture and everyplace. The only thing that was spared from the disaster was the white carpet that we protected with the drop cloth. If you have ever drained the engine oil out of a diesel engine the oil is jet black in color. It goes in brown but comes out black, unlike the gas engines. The floor was protected with our drop clothes, so it was not a total disaster. We quickly, now that panic had set in, removed all the material that got oil soaked and had the yard owner run it all down to a local dry cleaner to see if they could salvage it. To our surprise, they did get it all cleaned up. In fact, it looked better than when we started. We finished the oil change and the next day put everything back together. The Owner came to pick up his boat and was pleased to see how nice it all looked. I do not know if they ever told him about the little trouble that we had but again it was a real lesson. Always put hose clamps on the hose and never put your thumb over the end of the hose. This method of removing the oil was used several times after that first learning experience.

Another project was a real nice sailboat that was owned by one of the friends of the yard owner. Who better to have as a friend than a boat repairman if you are going to own a boat? The sailboat came in on a Friday afternoon to be hauled out, have the bottom scrubbed and then blocked up. The yard, not unlike most of the other yards, had a policy that you could work on your own boat in the yard as long as you didn't do anything that could cause the boat to sink after it left the yard. That usually meant that if you were going to add a depth transducer or any other thru hull penetration the yards would do it for you, at a nominal cost. This owner wanted to get the exterior of his boat all cleaned up and apply a fresh coat of bottom paint. Bottom painting was not my most favorite job, so I would not have an objection to him doing it himself. When we arrived to work on Monday the first thing on the list was to launch the sailboat. It would be in the way to haul out and block the list of boats for the day. I placed the straps under the boat in the proper location while the yard boss, Jack H. ran the stiff leg crane. We lowered the boat into the water and removed the straps. Jack was the boat operator, so it was his job to move the boats to one of the open slips where the boat would stay until the owner came and picked it up. The moorage was nothing more than a single pier that started from the shore and went out into the Lake and it had fingers about forty feet long sticking out ninety degrees from the pier on one side only. That made it possible to put a boat of about one hundred feet long on one side and several smaller boats on the other side in the slips. Once the boat was launched and Jack had the straps moved out of the way he came to the boat and started the small diesel engine, so we could move the boat. I untied the boat and Jack slowly headed out into lake Union. Being a past tugboat captain, Jack was a knowledgeable and cautious boat operator. As he started going around the end of the pier and heading to the slip, which was next to the furthest slip in on the dock, the furthest slip in (closest to the beach) had a new sixty-foot Marlineer sport fisher that the yard was just finishing, Jack picked up a bit of speed. Once heading towards the slip Jack reached down into the cockpit and took the boat out of gear so it was in neutral. A sailboat will glide through the water very smoothly, so Jack knew that he did not require any more power until he had to stop the boat to make the turn into the slip. The boat was not slowing down as fast as Jack would have expected so he reached down and put the boat into reverse. Jack knew that the boat had a folding propeller, which was common for a lot of the racing sailboats because when under sail the propeller would fold together eliminating a lot of the drag from the blades of the propeller.

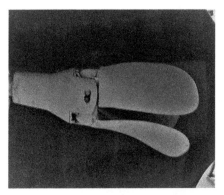 

This was the type of propeller that was attached to the shaft on the sailboat. you can see how the blades fold aft to reduce drag when sailing. it requires some prop speed for the centrifugal force to return the blades to their proper position. This is a lot more difficult when in reverse, as the prop blades are moving aft when the prop is trying to pull the boat aft

Jack concluded that the forward sliding motion was more than the slight reverse thrust, and the propeller never opened so he reached down and gave the boat more throttle. We were getting close to the pier and needed to stop so Jack ran the engine RPM up quite a bit to make sure that the prop would do its job and stop the boats forward progress. He failed to realize that he had put the boat into forward gear and not reverse. Sailboats do not have typical engine controls on the boats dash. It was like they were a secondary thought and a thought by somebody who did not like engines in boats. This boat had the controls mounted on the aft portion of the cockpit down about your ankles. The lever did not move forward and aft it moved side to side. When the propeller received that sudden boost of power it did exactly what it was designed to do and that was to propel the boat forward as fast as it could. We were now heading for the slip and were going to hit it hard. Across the narrow pier from the section that we were heading into was the pilothouse door of the sixty-foot Marlineer with Bud M. standing alongside it doing some final trim work. We yelled, Bud turned just in time to see the sailboat hit the pier, slide up the pier (the sailboat has a long sloping bow section) and up the front of his body. By now Jack had the boat in full reverse so the boat slid back down the dock where Jack got the boat under control and got it to stop. Bud had a wet spot up the front of his shirt where the keel slid up and back down. I must also assume that he had a stained spot on the back of his shorts, I know we did. We got the boat put into the slip and tied up. We looked for damage and luckily saw none except a rub in the bottom paint. The next morning when we came to work, we looked over and saw the sailboat sitting lower in the water than when we saw it the night before. Jack ran over to the office to get the keys while I headed to the shop for the portable high capacity bilge pump. Jack got to the boat and had it opened about the time I arrived with the pump. When the hatch that leads from the cockpit down to the inside portion of the boat was slid open all we saw was water with a layer of oil on top and all the cushions floating on it. I pumped the boat out while Jack went over to start the crane. The crane was powered with a diesel engine, so he had to get it started and warmed up. By the time he came back to the boat it was mostly pumped out. Before we even moved the boat to the crane, we removed all the soft goods and got them sent off to the dry cleaners. We hauled the boat and then continued to get it pumped out and cleaned. We did not know what we broke the day before, but it must not have been good. It did not take long to get things on the inside wiped down. The next thing was to drain all the lake water out of the engine. When the water filled the engine, it floated all the oil out of the engine. It was easy to get most of the water out of the engine. We put in new oil and a new filter and started the engine, so we could warm it up and try to get the rest of the water evaporated or mixed into the oil. To run the engine on the shore all we had to do was to place a homemade device that looked like a toilet plunger connected to a garden hose up against the engine intake thru hull fitting. That would provide the water cooling, so the engine could be run for a period. After running the engine and draining the oil and changing the filter a couple of times the engine was fine. Luckily, it was in fresh water of Lake Union and not the saltwater of Puget Sound. After all was cleaned and put back together, we had the owner of the boatyard call his friend to let him know that we had a bit of a mishap. The Owner was there by the end of the day to inspect the damage. This was a nice sailboat and we were really concentrating on getting it cleaned up and back together. We could attend to the damage when the panic level slowed down so we could think more clearly. When the Owner arrived one of the first things that he did was to come over to Jack and me to apologize to the both of us. The boat had a retractable keel so that it could travel in shallow water. He was going to re-pack the penetration where the lowering mechanism penetrated the hull. He had removed the old packing and then got distracted and forgot to install the new packing, which is what caused the boat to leak and sink at the dock. He thanked us for the oil change and the newly cleaned cushions and all the soft goods in the boat. Whether he paid anything or not was not up to me, but it sure got the adrenalin going. Within six months, after scrubbing and painting a lot of hull bottoms, stepping a lot of masts as well as working on some boat-repair projects, I was promoted to working on the new builds.

NEW CONSTRUCTION

R&H Marine in Seattle was building *Marlineer Custom Sport Fishing Yachts* for a customer in California, Mr. Ted Tate. In late 1971 I was given the opportunity to start a new build on a sixty-foot Sport Fisher for the president of PSA Airlines.

I went from helping with the lofting of the hull lines to sawing oak frames, laying the keel, planking the hull, through to the entire superstructure. It was a vast experience and a lot more fun than installing the same doors on airplanes every three days. The craftsmen I was fortunate to work with were some of the best in the industry. Eddy Olsen taught me all about lofting and cutting frames with the proper bevels as taken from the "loft floor" (which was a full-size layout of all the frames/stations overlaid from middle to forward and middle to aft) which was like what I had to do to build my back-yard boats. Eddy taught me a lot more details about creating the loft floor and how to get even more information off the loft floor which would take more of the guess work out of the build process. He also taught me how to determine the "fore hood" of the planking so the planks are basically parallel down the side of the hull. Since the bow is taller than the stern, the planking must have a wider section as the plank goes forward. The planks must be shaped so that the planks will be consistent from plank to plank as they are installed on the side of the hull. If not shaped properly you would end up with long tapered planks towards the bow of the boat which, besides looking bad, would not have the required strength in one of the more stressful areas of the hull.

Wolfgang was another talent who did a lot of the structure. Bud M worked on the interior and exterior details. Harry did the painting and interior finish to a highest standard. I will treasure the memories as well as all the training and knowledge that was passed along to me from the crew from R&H Marine.

The shop was a union shop, so once I started working in the new-construction projects instead of just being a yard boy, I had to join the union. I had to sit in front of a panel of three boat people, so they could determine where I ranked in the boat-building trade. I learned that the one place I lacked experience, in their minds, was in welding, so I had to take a course in welding to become a journeyman boat builder. A "journeyman boat builder" by definition back in those days was a "Jack of all trades" you had to have experience in all aspects of boat building from the carpentry, to cabinet making, electrical, mechanical, plumbing as well as welding. Building my own boats taught me a lot about these trades. I only welded a few trailers and that was using an arc welder, now I had to learn how to weld using a gas torch. I went to South Seattle College where they had a trade school to learn the welding that was required to get my "journeyman card". This gas welding did come in handy later in life as I wanted to silver braze the bonding studs onto the sea water valves that were installed into all the boats that were built.

One day a long black limousine pulled into the yard, which was always a bit dirty, and three men got out to go look at two of the boats being worked on in the yard. One was the owner of the new Marlineer being constructed in the shop and the other was the owner of a big repair boat in the water. They brought a friend along to see their boats. The group was up in Canada with John Wayne on the boat Wild Goose when they decided to come and see the boats, I happened to be walking across the yard when they came in. The limo driver opened the doors for Bill Boeing Junior, The President of PSA Airlines and Dan Blocker (Hoss Cartwright). I introduced myself to him and he shook my hand. He was my height (not what he looked like in the movies) and had a huge smile and was as nice a man as you could meet. After they got out of the car and headed to the boats, the limo driver took a towel out of the trunk and tried to keep any dust that was stirred up off the shiny black car. The yard was converting a seventy-foot Hatteras shrimp boat into a full displacement yacht for Bill Boeing Junior.

I learned a lot working with this incredibly talented group of people. They all knew that my mind was like a sponge and I wanted to learn anything and everything that they could teach me. They did have their moments that they would take advantage of my willingness to do anything for them. Bud sent me to the parts room one day to get one-hundred feet of flight line so they could get ready to hoist some equipment onto the boat. When I asked for the flight line, I was given a funny look and sent back to the shop to tell them we were out of stock. Eddy just laughed and said that flight line is what is used to land an airplane on, that I was just sent on a wild goose chase to mess with me. I tried to learn quickly and caught most of their little tricks. I did miss the one when I was sent to the supply room to get a gallon of foamy prop wash because we were getting ready to launch a boat. I told myself that I would not take advantage of any young worker that was trying his or her hardest to do everything possible to learn the trade, and for the most part I did not, maybe except for a couple of times. I may have sent people to the supply room to get the foamy prop wash a time or two.

R&H Marine was a major steppingstone for my boat building career. I was fortunate to be able to work alongside some of the best Boat Builders in the area. Not only did the job teach me a lot about boat building, it also taught me to venture out into other areas that I may not be as comfortable with. I stuck my foot into the water on most aspects of boat building while working there. That job opened my eyes as well as my mind to the "bigger picture" of boat building. I wanted to touch it all. That is what I did on my own builds, but nothing to this scale or complexity.

Delta Marine

THE INTERVIEW

In mid-October of 1973, R&H boatyard had a major fire on Sunday and burned to the ground. Now that we were married and watching our expenses I carpooled with Sherrie. We were sitting in the car at her place of work in South Seattle just about ready to let her out of the car when we heard the news about a boat yard in Seattle on Lake Union that burnt to the ground. Once they mentioned the fact that there were three yachts under construction at the time of the fire, I knew exactly who it was. R&H Marine had more work than any other boat builder on the lake at the time. I said my goodbyes to Sherrie and hurried off to work. When we all came to work on Monday, we had no place to go, so we all lost our jobs as well as all of our tools. I was hired by another boatyard on the lake that morning, so I went to work there. On the way home, I stopped by R&H to see how the owners were doing, and they said a boat builder from South Seattle area had stopped by to see if there was anybody who might want to go to their yard for work. I got the name and address, and since I commuted from south Seattle, I thought I would stop by and check it out. I had heard of the builder, in fact, R&H had purchased a forty-three-foot fiberglass hull from them that they had built a charter boat on.

The next morning on the way to work, I stopped at Delta Marine, where I met the Owners for an interview. It was a strange interview. After walking through their facility where they had some forty-two-foot fish boats under various stages of completion, we went to the front reception area, where there was a tall counter. They stood on one side of the counter, and I was on the other side. While they were asking some nontechnical questions, I could see that they were somewhat distracted by something on their side of the counter. Finally, they asked me if I wanted to come to work for them doing some special projects, and I accepted the job. What they were doing was trying to find my name on the piece of paper that the owner of R&H gave them as good people to hire. Once they found my name, they hired me. I never even went back to the boatyard I spent one day at to pick up my paycheck. This was to be the start of a twenty-two-year relationship between me and the owners, workers, and customers of Delta Marine.

I went from building high-end custom wooden sport fishing yachts to building commercial fiberglass fishing boats in one easy step. I enjoyed the challenge of building the commercial fishing boats. I remembered the day I came for the interview at Delta Marine. When I walked out of the office and into the shop, which was a new building with heated concrete floors and some nice new equipment, I noticed that the hardwood guards on the boats looked like they were perfect. The wooden plugs that covered the fasteners were laid out with very even spacing and with some good attention to detail that would be expected on a yacht, not what I would expect to see on a fishing boat. The other thing that I noticed was how clean and organized the facility was. There was a balcony behind all of the boats which made it a lot easier to get onboard the boats to work on them. There was little dirt on the floor. R&H Marine had dirt floors in part of the shop, was an old wooden building with years of sawdust accumulated on the wooden rafters and was dimly lighted. Delta, being a new facility, had all smooth concrete floors and metal trusses that were kept clean.

The thought process for building a commercial boat was totally different than that of the yachts. The yachts were all about the looks and details of the carpentry work. The commercial boats were all about the equipment and the systems. I was a carpenter by trade, and per their request, I did some projects they did not have any fixed tooling for. I did a complete superstructure and rough in interior for a thirty-six-foot gillnetter for a customer. I made the entire superstructure out of wood using the same techniques that I used while building the Marlineer at R&H Marine. After I completed all of the structure, Delta had their lamination crew come in and put a layer of fiberglass over all of the wood to both protect it as well as make it stronger. The biggest difference between the two was that Delta were the experts at fiberglass lamination and being a fish boat, they did not need to make it perfect, so it could be painted. At R&H we spent weeks sanding and filling all the imperfections until it could be painted in a high gloss finish.

LIMIT SEINER TOOLING

After a couple of other small projects, Delta started the tooling for their fifty-eight-foot Limit Seiner. The term "Limit Seiner" was from a rule in Alaska that the commercial salmon fishing vessel could not be longer than 58 feet. There were a few quirks in the rule but that was basically the rule. There was no limit on the beam and the draft of the vessel, just the length. I worked with Bob G. and made the setup jig and a lot of the frames for the hull. This was the same process I had to use to build all my home projects, so I was familiar with the process. The hull was built upside-down, so a mold could be taken from the hull shape after completed. This was different from building the boats at R&H Marine. They were built right side up, which made them more difficult to build, but they did not have to be rolled over. When building a hull to take a mold from, the hull is not used for an actual boat and does not have to be as strong as a boat that will be going out to sea. It will not have to be rolled over, just destroyed after the mold is removed. After the jig was set up, Delta had hired two sub-contractors to oversee the build of the hull. Both men had built several fishing boats in the past and were familiar with the boat building process. After Bob and I set up the three longitudinal supports that all the frames would be set on the two "Boat builders" started the process of leveling the jig. The jig was made from six by sixteen beams, so they would not bend between supports. The supports were at about four feet apart and were secured to the concrete using polyester putty (Bondo) which filled any gaps between the floor and the bottom of the post as well as stick them to the ground. Bob and I crossed braced everything, so the jig was not moving. When the two boat builders started, the first thing that they did was to have one man set up a level (this was like a surveyor's transit) and the other would move from station to station across all three of the beams. If the point where the frame was going to sit was a bit high the one man would plane it down with a hand plane to the exact height. If the location were a bit low, he would than go to the bottom of the post and drive in a tapered wedge to bring the beam up to the proper height. After going through all the points, they went back to the start to check out the beginning again and they found that it was off. In fact, it was high. I watched this for two days as Bob and I were building all of the frames on the loft floor. I went up to the man looking through the level, I assumed that since he wasn't doing any of the hard labor he must have been to one in charge, and told him that instead of planning the high points down and wedging the low points up put the jig back solid on the ground and just go find the highest point and call that zero. Than when you set the frames, put the wedge under the frame and wedge it up to the proper height. All of the frames had a waterline that was transferred from the loft floor to the frame. The one man could use the level to let the other man know when the frame was at the proper elevation and then he could secure the frame. He looked at me with his unlit cigar out the side of his mouth and told me that "I was building boats before you were a gleam in your daddy's eye don't tell me how to do my job". My reply was simple "I may not have been building them as long as you sir, but I sure knew what I was doing when I did build them" and I turned and walked away. During lunch, I picked up all my tools and put them back into my Tide soap box, remember I lost all my tools in the fire and I was starting over so the few tools I had acquired would fit into a large Tide soap box, and went in to say goodbye to Jack and Ivor Jones, the owners of Delta Marine. I had several standing offers to work repair jobs on Lake Union, so I was not worried about getting a job. They asked why I was leaving, and I told them what I was watching and told them "I can't watch somebody waste someone else's money". They convinced me to stay and then they went out and had a conversation with the two men. They did end up doing what I said, or they would have been chasing their tail forever.

All the frames got positioned on the setup jig and the next step was to plank the entire surface. The hull was planked using what is called "bead and cove". The material was made from clear cedar planks about one and one-half inch thick and two inches wide. One edge of the plank had a cove and the other edge had a bead so that the planks would almost interlock but because they had a radius you could connect at an angle, so you could make a curve. After the planking was done, the hull was made fair by using hand planes and sanders. After the hull was smooth and fair, the carpenters had to lay out where the water line was going to be. This was information that they could get from the loft floor. After the waterline was routered into the hull, the plank lines were carefully laid out and also routered into the hull to make it look like wooden planks. When the woodwork was completed my job was completed on that project.

One of the 58' seiners we built at Delta pulling a load of salmon over the rail

SEINE SKIFFS

After the hull plug was built and while the toolers and laminators were building the hull mold and the first hull after that, I started a project building seventeen-foot Seine Skiffs. They had different engines as well as other slight differences, but I turned it into a real production. I would receive the finished hulls from the lamination shop and would have to set them up and install all the equipment and test and deliver them to the customer. The first thing was to roll the skiffs upside down, so I could install the bottom skegs. These skegs were designed so that the skiff could be pulled up onto the deck of the seiner while traveling. The skegs protected the rudder and propeller from damage when pulling the skiff onto the back deck of the seiner. The metal fabrication shop made the skegs out of steel and then had them galvanized to protect them from the saltwater. The skegs also had the support for the shaft and rudder built into them. After the skegs were installed I would use a forklift and some straps and turn the skiffs right side up so that they could be finished. We would have to fabricate the engine rails to match the desired engine that the customer wanted. After the engine was installed, we would have to fabricate the fiberglass exhaust piping which, depending on if the engine, were single or dual exhaust pipes. There was some other rigging to do but these were simple to build. I was allowed to set up shop in a separate building at the end of the property down by the waterfront. The property was along the Duwamish River which flowed into Puget Sound at Elliot Bay by Seattle. The shop was an old slaughterhouse and was a well-insulated building, so it was easy to heat in the winter and would stay cool in the summer if you left the doors closed. I was also able to hire my own crew, so I got just what I needed. I got one person to do the lamination work, one to do the mechanical and plumbing, one to do the electrical as well as help bolt equipment in place. It did not take long to build the fifteen skiffs that they had sold. I built one skiff for a special customer that wanted it red, white, and blue. The hull was red with a white stripe and a blue bottom. The engine had chrome valve covers as well as some other fancy stainless-steel hardware just for show. The finished product looked so good that the owners of Delta Marine got a spot on the Seattle Work Boat Show and displayed the boat. They allowed me to work the show, so I had the skiff tipped up on its side so that the people could see inside the skiff as they walked by. It was a popular display with a lot of people stopping to admire the fine workmanship. While working the show, I met several people that wanted new fishing boats. My job was to tell them about the new 58' Seiner and send them to the boat shop to see the Owners.

58' SEINERS

After the fifteen skiffs they sold were finished, I was put into the fifty-eight-foot Seiner with my small crew to build the integral fuel tanks and the fish holds. Integral fuel tanks are fabricated using the hull skin as one side of the tank. We would have to put in a series of baffles, which were designed to keep the fuel from sloshing fore and aft during a rough sea condition. The baffles were spaced about thirty inches apart to meet the U.S.C.G. rules for tank construction. After the baffles were installed, we would fit and install the inboard (towards the center of the boat) panel. The panel was made from one layer of fiberglass with a core material to give it some stiffness. In this case we used four-inch rigid foam core, so it also had a lot of insulation value due to the fact that the fish holds, which were between the two fuel tanks, were going to be refrigerated to keep the fish chilled. Most of this work was just fitting and installing fiberglass panels. The mechanic and electrician did not like it much, so I took them to lunch one day and explained to them that I had a bigger plan and to suck it up for a bit. The mechanic, who was a general handyman, stayed around but the electrician moved on. When everybody went home at the bell, I would stay after work, sit in the engine room, and visualize what the engine room would look like. The engine room was in the process of being designed by the Naval Architect at the time, so nobody was really working on it. The main engine and the generator were placed into the engine room so that they could set the deck on above that. The focus of the yard was the interior details and getting all the major fiberglass pieces designed, built, and installed.

This is where falling out of that tree onto that sharp rock as a child came back as a slightly rearranged brain that gave me an ability to visualize mechanical systems. Being a carpenter who built luxury fishing yachts prior to working at Delta Marine, I had a bit of an eye for detail. One afternoon after the workday ended, I asked Jack, the vice president of Delta, if he had a minute. I took him into the engine room that was bare except for the main engine and one generator and I proceeded to lay out the entire engine room verbally for him. The next day I oversaw the mechanical portion of the fifty-eight-foot project as well as the tanks and fish holds. My mechanical man was now a bit happier. This got him out of the fiberglass a bit more and into the engine room where he could start mounting equipment and start the plumbing of the systems. The fish boats are all about equipment. It must be perfect because if the boat does not work you cannot catch fish which means that you can't make money. I took it on myself to learn as much as I could about the systems so that I could make them work to the best of our ability. I would make weekend field trips to marinas where there were several fish boats tied up, so I could look at them to try to understand the systems better. I would have to imagine what they did since I never actually went out fishing on one until much later in my career. On occasion, I would meet a proud owner of one of the boats that I would be admiring, he would want to show off his boat to some kid on the dock admiring his toy, so I would get invited aboard. I would ask many questions, and most people would be helpful and explain to me how the process worked. This was an extremely valuable learning experience.

HYDRAULICS

A lot of the hydraulic components were supplied in kit form by suppliers/retailers. I would take the components and mount them and do all the piping to the various valves and pumps per the supplier's design. This process seemed to work fine. We had our hands full doing all the piping for the fuel, water, circulated chilled water for the fish holds, potable water and the hydraulics. We had a problem with one of the hydraulic systems on one of the boats that was delivered a year earlier, so I called the manufacturer of the various hydraulic valves and pumps that we were using and learned that the supplier sent the wrong valves for what we were trying to do. I learned that there are different spools (which direct the flow of oil) inside the hydraulic valves. Some of the spools will direct the oil out to some device like a hydraulic cylinder and then when you let the handle go back to the center, or off, position the spool would block the flow of oil from both sides of the spool, this was so that when you were picking a load with a cylinder, or ram, it would hold the load when the valve was in the center position. It would also allow you to lower the load without having a hydraulic pump turned on. The other spools have the ports open to each other in the center position so that all the pressure is released when the valve is in the center position. This is what is required if you have special devices, such as hoists, that have their own brakes in them, they require pressure to release the brakes before the winch can operate. This also works as a "fail safe" so that if a hydraulic line should break the pressure is released and the break is applied. The company that sold us the valve for the cargo winch on a crab boat that we built sold the wrong valve. It worked great until the boat got to Alaska and when he was loading the seven-hundred-pound king crab pots on board his crew put the valve in the center position and one of the pots came down and almost hit the Owner of the boat. That one incident forced me to learn all I could about hydraulics. The more that I learned the more I wanted to learn. I spent a good deal of time with the factory sales engineers, not the salesmen, so I could learn all I could about hydraulics. It became a lot more interesting to build the commercial boats with all their intricate systems than building the fancy sport fishing yachts. I started buying the individual components and designing and putting the systems together myself. This saved a lot of money, and we ended up with a better working more reliable system. My people and I did the work while the real engineers designed the systems. My education on hydraulics lasted for several years, well into the big yacht building phase where the systems became a lot more interesting as well as complicated.

ELECTRICAL

The electrical systems were sub-contracted out on the first nine fifty-eight-foot Seiners. I became real frustrated watching the electricians milk the time and materials job, so I had another meeting with Jack one night after work and said that I could do the electrical also. I was already doing all the electrical on the USCG-inspected charter boats that we were building. I did all the design and made the drawings to be approved by the USCG as well as all of the installation and testing. I convinced Jack to let me wire the larger boats. The next boat, 5810, was to be mine to wire, so I talked to various suppliers of the different equipment as well as the materials such as wire and the connectors. I learned as much as I could from sales engineers. My policy was if you did not know more than me about what you were trying to sell me then do not waste my time. This rumor got out quickly, especially when I would turn people away at the guard shack if they could not answer the first question that I would throw at them. This policy worked out great because I was introduced to the engineers from the different suppliers, not just their traveling salespeople. The salesman's only job was to set up the meetings.

I wired all the small boats that I had built in my dad's garage as well as the house that we built, which was all 120/240-volt ac and 12-volt dc, so I had at least an introduction to the electrical systems onboard a boat. I studied the different systems that would be required as well as made as many "field trips" to the docks on the weekends and BS my way onto somebody's boat so I could see what they were doing. I had a theory early on and that was no matter how bad the boat looked I could usually find an idea that would be helpful. It may require some modifications or fine tuning, but the basic idea was what was important. Several people that I knew in the industry would go on the competitions boat and just make fun of the way things were done. They had already made up their mind as to how they were going to do the job and were not going to be confused by someone else's idea. My job was to learn something new every day or my day was not successful. I came up with what I thought was a good electrical design. I was always changing it as I built more boats continuing to make improvements as I learned more.

I went to a panel shop to have them build the main electric panels in a configuration that would be easy to hook up as well as maintain in the future. The panels had simple stock parts in them that could be purchased off most electrical supply houses shelves. I had meters installed that made it easy for the boat operators to trouble shoot if there was a problem. Since warrantee repair was also one of my hats, I wanted something easy so that when the boat operator called with a problem all that he would have to do is tell me the readings on the panel and I could usually tell them where the problem was.

When it came time to pull the wires on the boat, I put a simple plan together. We purchased the wire on large spools with about two thousand feet on each spool. There were only five standard wires on the boat, the low amperage 24-volt dc, the higher amperage 24-volt dc, the low amperage 120-volt ac, the higher amperage 120-volt ac and the alarm wires All the rest of the wires were special, so they were ordered as needed. The generator feeds were a large wire as well as the big battery wires and the large wires that feed the refrigeration equipment and fish hold circulation pumps. The rest of the wires were basic ships services such as power to receptacles and lighting, both 24-volt dc and 120-volt ac. I had a rack made that would hold the five big spools of wire and craned it up onto the balcony behind the boat. I put a team of four people together and we would pull all the major wire runs in after work when everybody went home. We could pull in hundreds of feet of wire in just two hours. The wires would come in through the fish hold and into the engine room. I would be at the front of the engine with a pile of labels for the circuits that we required in the boat. Don would be at the aft end of the engine room, Chuck would be at the front of the engine room by the electrical panel and the wire chase that would go up to the next deck, and Jim would be on the next deck. We all knew the boat well so there was not a doubt which wire had to go to what location. As the wires came past me, I would attach a label to the end and hand it off to Chuck who would pass it up through the hole to Jim who would route the wire close to its final location. When Jim was at the final location, he would yell something stupid and we would know that he was done at his end. Chuck would take the wire to the panel location and leaving a bit of extra wire would cut the wire and put the second of two labels on it. When we were done with the big wire pull, we would have the regular electrician tidy up the wires and secure them in a very neat and orderly fashion. I was a bit of a stickler for the looks. I told my crew that the difference between a good wiring or plumbing job and a bad job was the looks at the end of the day. They would both probably function the same just that you would be prouder of the better-looking job. The three men that helped me after work were all my leads. This was part of a training exercise to get their minds thinking about getting the job done faster. By this time, my dad taught me to work smarter not harder.

BUILDING GENERATORS

The owners of Delta Marine wanted to save some money on the components, so they went and purchased some four-cylinder John Deere diesel engines and some thirty kW Kato generators. I installed the generators to the engines with the proper adaptors and flexible couplings and fabricated the rails to support the components. The generators were going into the fish boats, so they did not have to look real pretty. We had the painters blow some white paint on them, so they were at least all one color instead of the John Deere mustard yellow and the gray generators. One of the Owners wanted to know why I picked white paint instead of black, which did not show the dirt. I told him that you could not see an oil leak or fuel leak on black paint. After we built the generators, we had to test them. The first thing I did was to go back to my consultant, dad, for some advice. He explained electricity to me a bit more. Dad was a well-read man who was always learning. He told me that the easiest way to test the generators was to start them up and put a load on them and run them for about one hour to make sure that everything is put together properly and that there are no leaks. To test the generator, you need a load bank that is variable. One way is to get a lot of big heaters and then turn them on one at a time until you reach a full load capacity. An ampere meter will let you know when you reach the full rated load. Dad probably saw the concern in my eye as I was doing the mental math as to how many 1,500-watt heaters were needed to load a thirty-thousand-watt generator. To make it worse, I would have to figure out how to load up three hot lines of power because the generators were three phase and not, single phase. (Single phase has two lines of 120-volt power and together they make 240-volt power whereas three phase has 3 lines of 120-volt power, yet the 3 lines make the 208-volt power). Dad than explained another way to load the generator to the exact amount of load that you wanted. He said to take an empty fifty-five-gallon drum and fill it full of fresh water. Place a board across the top and make three heavy copper bars and attach them to the board so that they are immerged about halfway into the barrel with the top ends above the board so that I could bolt the heavy wire leads from the generator onto them. He told me to put the ground line on the metal barrel to form the complete circuit. Than start the generator and turn on the main breaker and watch the ampere meter. He said that it would read almost zero. I told him that we all know that you throw a toaster into the bathtub with you, you are going to die. I have seen that in the movies many times. He then proceeded to remind me of my first electric outboard motor that I built. He said that motor was exposed to the water and it did not short out it just ran perfectly. He said that I would have to add salt to the water to bring up the load. I started the generator, which now drew a crowd. Most people love to stand around to witness the big explosions, which is what they all thought would happen as soon as I turned on the breaker that would send the power from the generator down the lines and into the drum of water. Nobody would even stand close to me in case I needed to be rescued. I flipped on the breaker and the meter did not even wiggle. I was a bit shocked but not as shocked as the crowd was. I than started to pour in some rock salt and the meter started to rise. I poured the salt in a little at a time. I watched the meter continue to rise each time I poured in the salt. I stopped pouring in salt when the meter read almost full rated load. I was as amazed as the rest of the group. The water got hot before the test was completed. Some people go from hero to zero in one quick move, in this case everybody knew that I was a zero, but I went to hero by the end of the test. People were still afraid of this and especially anything with high voltage, so I was the only person that would test the generators that we built. We tested, and installed several sets of generators, and one day an engine salesman from Alaska Diesel in Seattle, who sold us the Volvo engines for the smaller Seiners and charter boats, saw one of the generators being tested and said they could put the package together for us, do a better job of "marinizing" the engine, and give a warranty for the system. I thought that was a great idea, so they did it. In a few years, the process took off great for them, and they started a division for the gen sets that is now still called Northern Lights. Much later I did build and test all the generator sets for the fleet of twenty-two Mexican fishing boats that we built because I could do it a lot cheaper. Their focus became yachts, so they had to develop water cooled manifolds and heat exchangers where the fish boats were all dry exhaust going up in the air through insulated pipes and were cooled with keel coolers, yes actual manufactured one not my galvanized pipes.

SEA TRIALS

While I was working on the seine skiffs and the start of the limit seiners the rest of the shop was still building other boats. One of the boats that they built was a 43' charter yacht for a good friend of theirs. One evening a group of us went on a dinner cruise in Seattle's Lake Union which was downtown Seattle. At the end of the cruise we were heading back to the dock, which consisted of a pier with several finger piers off it where the boats would be tied between the piers. There was room for two boats between each set of finger piers. As we were heading back one of the engines died and would not restart. Everybody was nervous about getting the boat back into the slip without doing damage to the boat in the slip or the boat that they were driving. I said that I could do it, so I took over the controls. I had a twin-engine boat as a kid and had a bit of experience running with two engines and also with just one engine when the other fell off the back and I had to make it back and into a dock with just one engine, and it didn't have real reverse. It was a direct reversing engine, so you had to stop and restart the engine in the other direction, this made it necessary to learn how to dock without a lot of shifting. I would study what the boat would do under different circumstances. I was able to get the boat into the slip without any problems. Luckily, it was a calm night with no wind and there is no current in the lake, so it was easy. This instantly made me the "designated driver" from that point on. I sea trialed all of boats that were delivered by Delta until the day I left except for some of the 58' Mexican fish boats. I hired somebody to help with that portion since I was real busy running the shop and we were delivering a finished boat every two weeks. I would still take every boat on a final sea trial. Each boat had to make no less than three sea trials so having an additional person that was capable of running the boats helped greatly. I enjoyed running the boats on the sea trials. This gave me a terrific opportunity to learn even more about the systems on board the boats. I would test everything to make sure that it functioned as per design. The fish boats had a lot of specialized systems onboard that had to be tested. All of the fish hold circulation and refrigeration systems had to be tested. If they did not work properly, the fish may not be good enough to sell which would become a severe problem for the builder. I took all of the boats on the "delivery" sea trial, where the boat was basically "sold off" to the buyer.

When I started building yachts, I would take the owners out on an overnight sea trial, so they would have time to learn their new boat operations.

CHARTER BOATS

By now I was handling the mechanical, plumbing, electrical, hydraulics, lamination (on the small parts and assembly of all the components after all the big parts were built in the lamination shop), exterior hardware, launching, and sea trials of most of the boats. I would sit at home in the evening and sketch up schematics, design new systems, and plan sequences to simplify the build process. I talked the owners of Delta Marine into building a series of Westport-type fishing charter Boats. While at R&H marine, they would buy a bare hull from Delta Marine and build the complete charter boat for the fleet down at Westport Washington, which is on the ocean. I knew a few of the people down there from the repair work at R&H so they started asking me about having Delta do the boats themselves. At the time, Delta was building both the forty-three-foot and the fifty-foot hulls for several other builders to build the now expanding charter fleet. When I asked Jack about doing the project he was not interested, he only was interested in doing the seiners. I told Jack that he did not have to build the boats I would; all he had to do was to set the price and collect the money. He finally agreed, since there seemed to be a big line of customers that wanted one. Jack went the extra mile and made two pieces of tooling for the two different size hulls that he had molds for. They had the forty-three foot and a fifty-foot hull that were both popular for the charter fleet, in fact most of the builders were buying the Delta hulls and finishing those their selves. Jack stepped up to the plate and made the cabin and deck tooling for both hull sizes. That way it was three pieces that went together to form a great well-built composite.

After I received a hull from the fiberglass shop, I would have to fit the fuel tanks, the engine and running gear, and the batteries into the hull before the deck went on. Most builders would set the engines in and the tanks and be in a big hurry to get the boat stuck together and then the mechanics and electricians would have to crawl around under the decks to get everything installed and hooked up. My theory was to do everything that I could before you put the lid on and had to work on your knees. The engines were bolted in place and then I did something that everybody thought was a bit nuts. I bolted the shaft to the back of the engine and then slid the shaft log (a device that was what the shaft penetrated the hull through and was fitted with a stuffing box that would seal around the shaft to keep the water out while running out at sea), the forward strut and the large aft strut onto the shaft. I would then put a support under the back end of the shaft that would take up the weight of all the stuff hanging on the shaft but also half the weight of the shaft. I would than fit the strut to the hull as close as it could be and then drill the strut bolts through the hull and install the bolts. Sometimes the strut would not quite touch the hull. I would than remove the bolts and put a layer of wax on them and then fill the gap between the hull and the strut with structural filler and let the material cure. After it was cured, I could remove the bolts, because they were waxed, and then apply the marine sealant to the bolts and bolt the strut up tight. The normal way is to install the shaft and struts and then align the engine to the shaft. That process would sometimes be painstakingly difficult. This method the shaft was in perfect alignment every time. The next step was to build and install the exhaust, install and plumb the fuel tanks, and install and wire the batteries. All this was easy because you could do the work standing up.

After the deck and the cabin went on, which would happen the same day, the carpenters could do the interior while the mechanics, plumbers and electricians finished their tasks. The project did not take exceedingly long. The only problem that I had was with one customer from California who was upset because his boat was late. He was reported to be part of the "mob". The boat was finished and pushed off to the side because we still did not have the engines. He wanted a special engine package and they had not been delivered so there was nothing that we could do. When he called he threatened me by saying "I will send one of my boys up there to take care of you if you don't get my boat delivered" my reply was "don't send one that you care for because this isn't California this is the great North West where we have real men not boys" he hung up and I never heard from him again until he came and took delivery of his boat.

I turned the project into a total production build. My time doing production at Boeing came back to me. All the workers at Boeing did was to install components that somebody else built. I created wire harnesses, standard sub parts that could be used on various models, and a process of building that sequenced the boats in a very efficient manner. This was easy to control because the commercial boats were mostly systems with quite simple interiors. We built over one hundred of these boats that Jack did not want to build. They came at an appropriate time because the 58' seiner project was slowing down. As time went on, more and more forks emerged in the road that I was traveling down. I had to constantly choose which road to take. Each road took me farther away from my original path of being a woodworker/cabinetmaker in a boatyard. I could have never imagined or planned the road that I have taken, but that road has in fact made all the difference.

This is one of the 50' charter vessels that we built at Delta Marine.

MEXICAN FLEET

About the time the charter boat industry was getting filled up with boats, the Owners of Delta put a deal together with the bank of Mexico to build some commercial fish boats to train the people of Mexico how to fish. The project consisted of the standard forty-eight-foot seiners, some of the forty-eight-foot modified or whaleback seiners and one of the fifty-eight- foot seiners. The boats were all named UNICAP which stood for something that I never really knew. The boats were fairly standard with all of the usual equipment with the addition of some air-conditioning for the small cabin. We built the boats in a production since they were alike except the exterior changes of the three models. All the boats were launched and sitting at the dock ready for delivery.

The buyers, as the story goes, went into a famous bar, Jussonds, in Ensenada to find a crew to help bring the fleet from Seattle to Mexico. He found his crew for the boats and they all arrived to get a quick lesson and head south with the fleet. I went to the dock with my interpreter a couple of days before the scheduled departure to find smoke billowing out of one of the boats. The boats were built with generators to run the pumps and other gear as well as to run the galley equipment. The boats have standard household three burner stoves with ovens. There were about four people gathered on the boat, which was tied up alongside another boat, so we had to climb onto one boat to get to the one with the possible fire. When we got to the boat, we saw what the smoke was coming from. They were cooking stakes on the stove. We provided all the cooking equipment including the pots and pans. This group of people never cooked on electric stoves but open fires with grates to set the meat on. They set the stakes directly on the red-hot coils of the stove and to make the stakes even better they liked them smothered in onions. The stakes were burning, and the onions were helping to keep the fire down. There was one man standing at the steering station with the window wide open fanning the smoke towards the aft end of the cabin with a piece of cardboard (probably from the box that held the cooking pans) and another man standing just inside the aft door with another piece of cardboard trying to fan the smoke outside. It was working well because there was a lot of smoke coming out of the cabin. We shut the stove off, the stakes were probably done anyway, showed them the pans and left the smelly boat.

When it was time for the boats to leave, I got three volunteers to help them take the boats from Seattle to Westport, which was over halfway down the coast of Washington. It was a large boat basin and, depending on the condition of the bar (the area where the out flow of the river meets the incoming tide, wind, and waves of the ocean. This mixture can cause some big steep waves if the conditions are all stacked up against you) it should be an easy trip. They made it that far without too many issues. The next leg of the trip was to California. Just about San Francisco they had a problem with the gearbox (that drives the shaft and propeller) on one of the forty-eight-foot vessels. They towed the boat into Morrow Bay California to a commercial dock. I was given the call, so I had to pack up and fly to California to see what was wrong and to get it fixed if it was a Delta problem. I took Sherrie with me for companionship and maybe a bit of help. We flew into San Francisco and got a car and drove to Morrow Bay. When we arrived, we both really needed to use the bathroom.

The boats were tied along a tall pier, so we had to climb down a ladder and onto the fifty-eight-footer where Sherrie was going to use the bathroom and I was going to the next boat, which was tied alongside the fifty-eight- footer, and use that bathroom. When I got finished, I left the boat to find Sherrie had already climbed the ladder and was standing on the dock. I went up to ask her how she could possibly beat me, and she said that there was no way she would use that bathroom. The sewer system in certain parts of Mexico is not quite the same as the US. What startled her was that in those certain parts of Mexico they do not flush the toilet paper. There was a big box that the paper towels came in sitting in the shower that was half full of used toilet paper.

I went to the boat with the transmission problem and was a bit surprised as to what I saw. It was about lunch time and everybody was eating the same thing on each boat. Today they were going to be having pork chops for dinner. That was not the issue. They had taken them out of the freezer and set them on the galley counter. They were in the process of thawing out in the warm California heat and the juices were starting to come out of them, which would not have been a problem if they had them sitting on a plate or something that would contain the juices. The juices, including what looked like blood, were going across the counter and down the face of the cabinets. That juice was attracting most of the flies in the county and they were all hovering around the counter waiting their turn for a meal. I looked the transmission problem over quickly and saw that the problem was from the transmission people and nothing that Delta was responsible for so that was OK. As I looked at the boat, I wondered why they ran the boat until it broke. We installed low oil pressure alarms on everything that requires oil pressure to operate; the alarm panel was printed in Spanish so if it went off, they could read what it was. I looked at the alarm panel a bit closer and noticed that the alarm was turned off. I went to the big boat to ask the "fleet captain" what he knew about this and what he said was that he heard from that "driver" that the noise from that panel was bothering him, so he shut the breaker off to make the noise go away. As I continued to inspect the seven boats that were all tied together on both sides of the pier, I noticed one thing on one of the forty-eight footers. Across the dash, across the instruments and on the electrical panel I noticed what looked like white spray paint. It looked like somebody came into the boat and painted some Spanish graffiti all over. Upon further inspection, and a towel with a bit of water I determined that it was insect spray. It looked like if the driver saw a bug, he would spray it until it died or left. The spray was so thick that it looked like paint. You could track a lot of the fly's that were moving around on the boat. One of the other things that I learned that day was that if you need to tow another boat you don't need a tow line, all you need to do is to place the anchor of the disabled boat on your back deck and tie it to something substantial like the drum that holds the net and then have the distressed vessel let out a bunch of chain and then away you go. The only actual damage was that the bow roller was severely bent and the cap rail on the back end of the big boat was chewed up a bit from the chain. I guess that it is great not owning the boat or even having any assets so if for some reason, they want you to fix the damage you can just walk away.

The next group of fishing boats was an order for twenty-two of the fifty-eight footers. They were to be built for the government of Mexico. They were called Fedecoop.

This stood for the Federal Cooprtiva. I went to Ensenada with the Owners of Delta to meet the Buyers. We had a meeting in the Government offices and then went to lunch, which I learned that was the big meal of the day. After the meal, they would have an hour nap, or siesta as they call it, and then go back to work. That was a policy that I wanted to adapt but nobody would even listen to me. The meal was great, they knew how to cook meat. These were the most complex fishing vessels that I ever built. They had systems for several distinct types of fisheries, from long lining, to trawling to simple net fishing. We built all the drums that sat on the back deck, the skiffs that sat on top of the large bait boxes that sat on deck. The boat had nine fish holds instead of the standard two. The refrigeration system had to be able to do several types of systems in the different fish holds depending on the product. Some holds would be re-circulated chilled water where the hold was full of chilled water, while others may have just re-circulated sea water and others would have what they called spray brine where it was just a partial tank of water and the chilled water would spray onto the product. The boats were all finished in high quality. This was a real production with twenty-two all the same to build so we could make it truly a production build. I devised a system of tracks that just sat on the floor that the boat cradles would sit on. There were heavy duty steel rollers that sat under the cradles, so it was easy to move the boats. The boats were all backed into the balcony with a ramp that was between two boats, so the workers had easy access to the boats. I rigged up some cheap boat winches into the support posts, so the ramps could be lifted out of the way when the boats needed to be moved. We got the cycle down to delivering a boat every two weeks. The only crew that had to work two shifts was the lamination crew because we did as much as we could from molds. The engine room stringer system was now tooled and molded so it was a drop-in piece like the small production boats. Everything that could be made from fiberglass was made from fiberglass. The boats came out great.

When it was time to deliver the boats, we had learned from the first fleet that you are required to hire a Pilot to navigate the "foreign flagged vessels" out of the State, or until the vessel gets to Port Angeles which is out towards the open ocean. The owner of Delta worked out a deal with the Pilots association to only have the minimum of Pilots and have the vessels run as a fleet. They only took eleven at a time. The first group to go was not unlike the last fleet of Mexican boats, which was one delivery Captain with a group of helpers. This time at least some of the crew had seen a boat before and had worked on a fishing boat. They left the yard heading towards Mexico. The next day they called the yard to inform us that they had lost an anchor complete with the ninety feet of galvanized chain and the six hundred feet of cable. When asked, they said that while traveling out towards the ocean, some of the crew wanted to see what some of the buttons and switches did. They turned on the hydraulics and went to the foredeck to see how to run the anchor winch, which was a big drum winch that held all the cable and chain. The winches had a release that would allow the anchor to be "freewheeled" so you could get the anchor deployed quickly in an emergency. They turned the control valve and the anchor started to go down. They stopped it from going down and started to bring the anchor back up when one of the crew decided to pull the other lever to see what it did. It happened to be the lever that allows the anchor winch to "free wheel". Remember they are all traveling at about nine knots down the Straights of San Juan De Fuca now. This time they could not stop it and it all went to the bottom of the ocean. With the boat traveling forward at about nine knots and the three-hundred-and-fifty-pound anchor followed by ninety feet of five eights inch stud link chain, which is heavier to help hold the anchor down, and six hundred feet of three-quarter inch galvanized cable, it went fast. Luckily, nobody got hurt because they said that the cable started to whip back and forth so that is why they could not stop it they all jumped back out of the way. I loaded up a complete anchor rode, the anchor, chain, and cable for one of the next boats and took it down to Westport where I would meet the boat and get it installed so that they could continue their trip.

The boats did finally arrive in Mexico. The second batch of eleven got away without an issue and made it to Mexico to start their fishing. After a brief time, we received a call from them to have their "warrantee" list fixed. We still had our translator, who was now helping in the office, take the calls from them and start to organize the list of issues. We decided that the best thing to do was to travel to Ensenada to view the issues firsthand. The two Owners of Delta, the translator and I flew to San Diego, rented a car, and drove to Ensenada. We arrived there and saw a few of the boats sitting in the harbor. We went to the office for the meeting and we decided that, since we already had the list, it would be better to take a skiff and go to the boats that were in the harbor. We would go boat by boat and inspect the boats to see what it would require fixing the problems. When we boarded the first boat and started down the list of problems it became clear that most of the problems were from a lack of knowledge as to how to run the equipment. We put a very extensive manual together for the boats, all written in Spanish by our translator. My first impression was that nobody read the manual. The translator asked one of the crew a couple of questions and turned to me and said that they cannot read much, and the manuals were a bit to technical to understand.

I continued to look at the list of problems and it did not take long to realize one thing. A lot of the fishing equipment did not work at all, mostly because it was gone. It appeared that they sold the gear to US fishermen on the trip down. None of the people on the boats were Owners or would even get a "crew share" like up in the States so there was no motivation to go out fishing when it was a lot more profitable to just get cash for the gear and report it missing after a storm. We went back to the office after the boat tour and sat at a conference table to discuss the problems and what the fix was. While we were sitting there a ship to shore radio communication came into the office. Our interpreter could hear both sides of the conversation since it was on the marine radio and, when we took a quick break, told us that the call was from one of the boats and it was way out at sea and a storm came up and they "lost" their skiff overboard. That was not the only missing skiff, they were real nice skiffs and there were a lot of fisherman out there that would love to get one for cheap money. At the time, the Peso was almost two hundred to one. The boats had all the fishing gear on them complete with the nets, long lines, hooks and whatever was required for the multiple fisheries that they were going to work. Most of the fishing gear was long gone also. We told the government officials that we could not warrantee anything that was not there anymore. We sent two mechanics down to Mexico for a week to "tune" things up a bit and fix what they could. The entire project did not work for the Mexicans, so the boats were sold to some Americans who re-rigged them with the proper fishing gear so that they would work for their fisheries back in the states.

TRACKING SYSTEMS

Early on at delta Marine, they would come to the end of a build and then sit around and discuss how many hours it took to build the boat. This was a bit painstaking. I soon developed a system that would track the labor. Every employee had to punch a timecard when they started work, went to lunch, came back from lunch, and went home. That timecard was how they got paid. I developed what I called the White Card. It was about the same size as the timecard so it could fit in the narrow timecard slot that was next to the time clock. It would have a spot for the boat number, the project number and the hours worked. the one White Card would be big enough for the week unless you worked on several different boats each day, which was not usual. My crew was using these White Cards while the other leads refused to use them. Once it became obvious to the Owners that now it would be easy to track the time on each project, it became mandatory for the entire company.

The other issue not long after I first started at Delta Marine and they started to build the fifty-eight-foot Alaska Limit Seiners, was that all of the shop leads were asked to come to the facility one Saturday so we could go through the boat and make a list of all of the materials that were used to build the boat. They wanted this so that they could cost out the boat. They knew about how many man hours were put into the build, but the materials were purchased in bulk for inventory, so they could be used on more than one boat. After that process, they started a system whereas the purchase agent would have a book that had numbered pages that people could order the materials for a boat. They would have to write down what hey wanted. When it actually got ordered, the purchase agent would assign a purchase order number (PO) to the request. This went along ok until one day I went to see why my parts order had not arrived. He proceeded to tell me that I never ordered it. This was not the first time that this happened. Because of my past bad experience, I started to make notes on the left-hand page, that was always left blank. When he showed me the order book to prove to me that I never ordered the parts, the page was gone. The numbers, which he put on the pages, were out of sequence. He said that his numbering machine skipped a number. I proceeded to ask him why my description of the part that I wanted was still on the left-hand page and the right-hand page had an order for some carpentry item. He had nothing to say, so I was forced to come up with a better plan. I went to a printing company and had them make me some Material Parts Request (MPR) forms. They consisted of a three-page sheet. The top page was white and was where one would make the request, put in the boat/project number, the date required as well as any other information that may be required to make sure the purchase agent knew what to order. Then you would remove the top/white page and send the other two copies to the purchasing department. Once the item got ordered, a PO number was added to the paper along with an actual delivery date as per the supplier. There was room on this document, which was letter size, for the purchase agent to make any other notes. Once it left the buyers desk, the second copy, yellow, was removed and placed in a basket and the third copy, pink, was sent to the receiving department. Every day my leads would go down and pick up their yellow MPS from the basket, take them back to their desk and put them into a binder for the appropriate boat. They would take out the white copy and replace it with the yellow copy. This eliminated all of the trips to the buyer's office to ask when their item may arrive. Once the warehouse received the item, he would mark the item received on the pink copy as well as where he put the item in the warehouse. He would than put the pink copy in a basket. Every day my leads would pick up the pink copy, throw their yellow copy away. An MPR was for one boat only. It could have several items on it, but was only for one project, that way the leads would have a separate notebook for each boat. When they opened up their notebook, they would know at a glance what was sent to the buyer, what was on order and what was received. The other departments would not use this system. The mechanics were the ones that ordered the most items, so they needed a better tracking system. Once the owner saw what I did, he than required the entire company to use this form. The two forms, the white card and the MPR would make it easier once the company went to computers. These documents would become easy for the office people to input the information into the computer which made it really easy to know exactly what he boat cost at the end of the day.

HELPING A FRIEND IN NEED

After a few years passed and I got over Sherrie selling the sailboat out from under me, I was approached by an old friend to advise him on a boat project. He showed up at my dad's house on a weekend, and I just so happened to be there, I guess that he did not know that I now had my own house and was probably just at mom and dads for a free meal. I was asked about a forty-three-foot sailboat hull that they found lying out in a field. After a bit of examination, I told them that the best thing to do was to finish the hull, which was made from strips of cedar, and to make a fiberglass mold off it so they could produce some nice-looking hulls. The hull had beautiful lines. It was a classic looking full keeled double ended sailboat. My friend Kenny did just that. Being a perfectionist, he, with some help and advice from his boat-builder friend, finished the hull upside-down and took a mold off the hull. It was a great-looking vessel with good attention to detail. Kenney hired a naval architect to make sure that the keel was designed properly. The hull did not have a keel when he purchased it since it was never finished as a real boat. After all the woodwork to finish the hull and the keel, the painstaking job of fairing out the hull was next. I showed Kenny the process of sanding and adding coats of fairing compound in the low sections and sanding again and adding more primer and sanding again until the surface was as perfect as you wanted the finished part to be. After all the fairing was completed, we installed plank lines, or grooves, into the hull to simulate wooden planks.

Kenney lived on Star Lake, which is where I used the first boat that I built, and he liked to swim the lake. One day after working on the hull tooling, it was hot, so he wanted to go for a swim. We went down to the lake and jumped in. it was not far to the other side. Kenney being a great swimmer went past me at a rapid pace and made it to the far side before I could make it to the middle. I was not a good swimmer, just a good boater, so by the time I got halfway across I was done. I could not go any further and felt like I was going to drown. I never panicked, so I rolled over onto my back and back paddled for a bit till I could recover some and then headed back to where we started. Kenney was on his way back by then so he stopped to try to help me. All he could really do was to help keep me calm and re-assure me that we were going to make it.

Kenney had a brother John, who also did a lot of swimming. One night after a long hot day, a group of us boys went to the lake to go skinny dipping. This was not that unusual. It was a wooded part of the lake, so it was very private. Later in life, John became a salesman for Bayliner Boats. I was walking through the inside portion of the Seattle Boat Show when somebody standing up on a Bayliner Yacht shouted down and said, "I've seen that guy naked". It drew a lot of attention. That was not the only time that he did that. It happened at several of the boat shows. He would than go on to introduce me as the production manager of Delta Marine. I did buy two Bayliner boats from him over the years, a thirty-two-foot and then a forty-three-foot. He was the best salesman that Bayliner had, in fact he received a large award from the factory for his efforts.

Once the hull shape (the plug) was completed the next step was to build the actual mold. The mold would be made up of several layers of fiberglass laminate with a structural core material sandwiched in the middle of the layers. I helped Kenney get competitive prices on all the materials and supplies since I was now a familiar face in the industry. I had learned about lamination work at the boat shop that I was working at, so I helped Kenny with all the fiberglass work. Mostly being a two-man job, that made it a lot easier. After all the laminates were completed the mold required some additional stiffening so a series of frames were cut and fit to the outside of the mold and laminated to the fiberglass surface. After the frames were set than a series of longitudinal stringers were arranged to the frames, so the mold would have something to rest on weather laying on its side or upright.

After the mold was completed, he built a hull and then built the deck tooling complete with the cockpit. Again, the detail work was great.

I used the mold to build a hull that I took to the backyard of the new house that Sherrie and I just finished. I hauled the empty hull to my back yard on the same trailer that I used to launch the sailboat years before. After placing the boat in the back yard, I built a temporary shed around the hull to keep the weather out of it so I could build it under cover. I located some diesel inboard engines in California at a real cheap price, so Sherrie and I loaded up and drove to southern California to pick up the engines. We bought six of them with the idea to sell the five that we did not want. The deal was better than I thought, and I sold them the week I returned form the trip. I never got to finish the boat because, now that Sherrie had become a self-made boat broker after selling my sailboat and an eighteen-foot Thompson Center Bow Rider that I rebuilt, she sold the hull as an empty hull with an engine. She thought that it would be better to finish the basement than to have a sailboat hull in the back yard taking money out of her shoe budget. This was the last of my backyard projects building boats. Her theory was that now that I was building boats professionally, I did not need to do it as a hobby in my spare time.

FROM FISHING BOATS TO YACHTS IN ONE EASY STEP

As time went on and the fishing industry took a nosedive, I could see that the fishing boat industry was not looking good. In 1985, as luck would have it, a customer came along who had a dream of taking a fishing boat hull and turning it into a long-range expedition yacht. Bruce Kessler had the dream, and I had the enthusiasm to make it happen. Bruce came to Delta Marine with his designer, Steve Seaton, with a concept drawing for his Long-Range Cruiser, LRC as we called it back in those days. Today they are usually called Expedition Yachts. One of Bruce's requirements was to be able to sport fish from the boat while under way. You troll plastic jigs at about seven to eight knots to sport fish on the high seas which is a nice easy cruise speed for one of these full displacement yachts. Bruce's theory was that if he was traveling, he might as well be fishing. Once a fish, like a big marlin, was hooked the boat would have to become the "sports fisher" and be able to back down on the fish so that the angler could play the fish. Before Bruce could make up his mind regarding this type of boat; being a heavy, slow, single engine full displacement ocean going vessel compared to the standard high horsepower fast twin engine sports fisher, he needed to go for a sea trial on one of the fishing boats that

163

we had sitting on the dock. Bruce was told by almost all his fishing friends that this idea of his would not work. To be a true LRC you would have a heavy full displacement hull shape which was usually single engine with a deep keel. That design was great for crossing oceans comfortably and efficiently. All his big sport fishing buddies told Bruce that a heavy, slow single screw (one propeller) boat will not be able to back down on a big fish. A single screw boat with a right-hand propeller will back to port (left) and will not go straight. I took Bruce for a sea trial on one of the fifty-eight-foot limit seiners that was finished and sitting at the dock.

We left the dock and went down the Duwamish River towards Seattle. We must go thru three bridges to get out the river, so it can sometimes be a bit of a long trip waiting for the bridges to open. There is a curfew in the morning and evening during the peak auto traffic periods, so planning is somewhat important to be able to get back in time for dinner. We headed across Puget Sound where I could encounter some ferry boat waves so that Bruce could feel what it is like to be on a "heavy displacement" boat that crushes through the waves instead of bouncing around like a cork on the water. We arrived at Shilshole Marina where they have a breakwater and a long passageway between the breakwater and all the slips. I went into the south end of the breakwater and turned the boat around as if to leave and then proceeded to back the entire length of the marina which was over a quarter of a mile. The marina had a jog in it which added to the difficulty. We started from the south end and backed all the way to the north end.

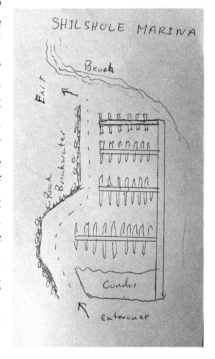

This amazed Bruce and it also put that question out of his mind. The fish boat that we used for the test run doesn't have a fly bridge, or upper steering station with a three-hundred-and-sixty-degree view, it only has a pilot house with limited view aft, especially when there is a seine skiff sitting on the aft deck. I had to open the door and look out to be able to see where I was going which impressed Bruce a bit more because he knew that if he had the fly bridge or even like most sport fishing boats, an aft facing steering station it would even be a lot easier. Backing down this far with no bow thruster or twin propellers for maneuverability was not quite as easy it is sounds. I had to do what is called "back and fill" where I get the heavy boat moving backwards and every time the boat started to head towards the port I would have full port rudder and give the boat a quick blast forward which would push the stern back to starboard. The backwards momentum would keep the boat moving in reverse so to anyone looking we were just backing all the way through the marina. Probably looked a bit weird having this high bowed fish boat with all its commercial salmon fishing gear back full length through a yacht basin.

Bruce signed a contract to start the boat, and the two of us worked together to come up with the ultimate systems for a long-range ocean-going fishing yacht. Bruce was busy directing movies in California, so he only had time on the weekends to come up to discuss the things that he wanted on his boat. We would talk over the phone during the week but there was nothing better than the one on one time together, so we could both get a better idea what the other was talking about. This one on one time would be complete with a lot of my home-grown designs including my crude sketches. I was never a good artist, so the sketches were a bit crude. I was once told by a wise old boat builder, Earl Wakefield who did some teaching in the boat building school in the Seattle area, that when it came to building custom yachts, the buyer, and the builder "must educate and graduate together". I used this process with all the custom boats that I was involved in. As a builder of custom yachts, I had to listen to the customers wishes and then let the customer know if his wishes were doable or not. Bruce knew what he wanted, and it was up to me to understand what he wanted and then do the best I could to put his thoughts into reality.

Like the other boats, I would spend my time at home while watching TV sitting with a notepad designing systems and thinking up innovative ideas, or ways to get to the finished product that the customer is expecting. It was easier to go to Fisherman's Terminal, in Ballard Washington where all the commercial fishing boats sat during the off season and can get onto somebody's boat to look at systems to gather ideas than to get on somebody's private yacht and look at anything. The people that owned the big yachts were very private and wanted to keep it that way, so I had to do a lot more dreaming up systems than taking an existing system and trying to improve on it. I would go to the Seattle Boat Show and look at the boats on display, but they were all smaller production boats and not heavy displacement ocean going vessels.

The relationship between Bruce and I was particularly important to me. I was building his dream boat, so I had to pay a lot of attention to what he wanted. Like the fish boats I needed to know what he wanted it to do and then I could figure out how to make that happen. By this time, I had a lot of "sales engineers" for most of the systems at my disposal. If I had a question or a thought, I could find somebody that could help come up with the answer. I enjoyed designing new hydraulic systems on the fish boats but now I was in heaven because, unknown to me, there were lot more complicated hydraulic systems on a yacht than the fish boats. The fish boats had big hydraulic systems pushing more than one hundred horsepower of hydraulic fluid around to the different pieces of equipment, but the systems were simple. The yachts were a lot more complex. This being the first yacht and my experience building almost one hundred fish boats by than I wanted to simplify the systems. The systems on a yacht, that I barely even knew existed, were the bow thruster, roll stabilizers, anchor drum and the deck cranes. I also designed and installed some hydraulic powered generators, so the boat could have regular household power while traveling without the need to run the generator. The bow thruster was easy, but the controls were a bit more complicated. My hydraulic go to man, Hippie, was an "out of the box" thinker so we got along perfectly. At that time, the bow thrusters were either on or off. I wanted variable speed and Hippie had the answer. He came up with the directional control valve and the controller that would make that happen. The controllers would control the flow proportionately and would spring to center when you let go of the lever. I wanted the lever to stay in the position that I set it so when maneuvering the boat, I could leave it pushing the boat against a wind or current while I ran the engine and steering controls (this is now the standard in the industry on the big boats). The roll stabilizers were a complete system of their own in those days. The deck crane was half of a complete system. It had all its control valves, all we had to do was to give it the required oil. The anchor winch was like that of the fish boats just a bit more yacht looking. The yachts used a lot of stainless steel where the fish boats used galvanized steel. The price was not that different because by the time you truck the steel to the galvanizer, pay them to galvanize the metal and truck it back, you can build it out of stainless. The money in stainless is if the customer wants it polished to a mirror finished. I did a lot of the stainless parts on the first yachts to a "brushed" finish which was easy to do with a piece of sandpaper in just one direction.

Bruce continued to come up with his wish list and I continued to come up with the systems to make it work. The one thing that I designed was to place both generators on one side of the engine room. Yachts have two generators because they do not want to ever lose power, so redundancy is important. When the ice maker for the drinks goes down the trip is over. The owners of Delta, the designers of Delta and the workers of Delta thought I was nuts. I explained my reasoning to Bruce, and he thought that I was right, so he stood on my side. The reason was simple. Everybody was thinking how the engine room was going to look whereas I was thinking how it was going to function. My design was to have both generators on one side of the boat so that the fuel system, all the cooling water system and all the exhaust was going out one side of the boat. This design would also give me more space on the opposite side for equipment as well as a work bench with built in tool storage. I put the generators and the main engine exhaust out the starboard side of the boat. That way there was a "quiet" side so when you pulled up to the dock you did not have the exhaust on the dock. It also made it easier to build. I learned later in life that the starboard side is the side that all "big" yachts dock on, so I switched sides later in life. Servicing the equipment was always big on the list for me. I would always set the generators, which have one side up against a wall, facing whatever direction that would put the service side, the side with the oil filters, fuel system and any main service items, inboard so they could be serviced. I would have the engine manufactures install "remote" oil filters if they were on the opposite side of the fuel system just to make it easy. At Northern Lights, it became known as the "Bud Package".

The other system that I got a lot of heat about was the electrical system. Being a yacht, I wanted something that looked good yet functioned easily. It had to be easy to understand. I had the panel built with two sections. The top section was all the twelve and twenty-four-volt DC battery circuits complete with the meters for monitoring the batteries. The next section had all the 120/240-volt metering and circuit breakers. The side of the panel that faced inboard had all the battery selector switches, so you could turn the main battery off or have emergency battery cross connections for the main engine, generators, and ships services. I thought that this was a great plan until the delivery day when Bruce had a Christening party and invited a lot of his friends and even some of the other boat builders in the area. I went onto the boat to find the competition's electricians in the engine room with the electrical panel opened and when I caught them, they said that this cannot be done, somebody will get hurt. I told them that it will be them if they do not shut the panel and get out. The two electricians were great guys and I sat down with them later that day and explained the reasoning behind my ideas. It did get me thinking so I checked out all the "rules" for electrical on boats and could not find anything against my idea. Again, this has become yet another standard in the industry.

I came up with a simple take-home drive with help from my friend Hippie at the local hydraulic store. My background in designing the fishing boat systems helped greatly when it came to the yachts. I did some things that nobody had attempted in the past. I was fortunate to have convinced Bruce Kessler that I knew what I was doing. If he only knew that I was on the same learning curve that he was, he may have had a different opinion. I learned that the hydraulic powered generator was common on some of the larger yachts, but it had some problems with the biggest one being the control when a large load was put on the generator. The generator would slow down which would affect the frequency of the power output. This would affect some of the more delicate equipment on board, so we had to come up with a solution. I got together with Hippie and he worked on the sensing portion of the controls to make the response time a lot quicker. Than one night while thinking about how to solve this problem I was thinking about the diesel- powered generators and why they worked so well. Than it finally came to me, they have a heavy flywheel which, as I remembered my high school physics class, the mass of the flywheel gave it the inertia to absorb a lot of the instant load that was put onto the generator when a big motor, such as the air-conditioning compressor, started. I had a heavy flywheel made and installed and it work well. Later in life the electric control manufactures invented "soft starts" which keep the load more constant on the generator by starting the electric motor slowly and gradually speeding it up to full speed. Before the "soft starts" the load to start the motor with its compressor, or whatever it was running, could be as much as nine times the load required to run the motor.

I met a guy at the Seattle Boat Show (Dave Medley of Celsius Marine) when I was in the process of learning about air-conditioning systems, which was another new system for me since there were no air-conditioning systems on fish boats heading off to Alaska. We did install simple air conditioning on the fish boats that were going to Mexico, but that was a real small and simple system. There were also a lot of heavy-duty refrigeration systems on the fish boats but that was to keep the fish cold not the people cool. Dave and I ended out having several meetings about design issues, and we came up with a plan. He sold me some chillers, which made the water cold that would be circulated through all of the rooms, and some commercial air handlers with the thermostats and the fan control switches, that would take the chilled water and divert it through a set of coils when the thermostat required cold air. He taught me about the chilled water-circulation requirements and how to size the piping dependent on the flow rate of the water. I installed the system, and it worked better than expected. The only thing I did wrong was I didn't understand what he was talking about when it came to sealing the insulation that covered the chilled water piping. Every place the warm moist air could touch the pipe it would condensate, and all the water in the air would rain out in the overhead. I learned that you had to glue the seams together and then wrap the seams with a foam insulation tape to insure that no air could touch the pipes. The system worked so well that Bruce even removed half of the chillers after his trip around the world, so he could gain more storage space in the engine room. Dave also taught me that, not unlike other systems, there is a set of "rules" to follow. If I followed the rules the system would be designed properly and work great. ASHRAE stands for the American Society of Heating, Refrigerating and Air-Conditioning Engineers, which is the technical body that develops and maintains ventilation standards for the United States. Ventilation codes and energy efficiency programs throughout the U.S. are based on ASHRAE standards. As long as I followed the rules the system would work fine, and they all did.

During the construction of the first two large yachts, we were invited to go to Fort Lauderdale to view some larger vessels. A potential buyer of a third boat arranged to have his Captain meet us there and take us through a few big yachts that he had arranged to show us. We had the two owners of Delta Marine, the naval architect, the lead carpenter, and me. We thought that with the different people representing the different trades that we could absorb more information in a brief period. As we toured the yachts I tried to learn as much about the systems as I could. My goal was to have truly "world class" systems. It was also the goal of the owners of Delta Marine to build the best that they could. The one thing that was repeated on all the big yachts was how complicated some of the systems were. When I looked at the fuel transfer system I was amazed as to the complexity of the system. I took pictures and noted the manufacture's name of a lot of the equipment. After I returned home, I met with some of the sales engineers to discuss what I learned. The valve manifold for the fuel system was available here in the United States by a prominent valve manufacture. I looked at the cost and then I asked what it would require to service this huge all cast manifold and the simple answer was that you would have to remove it and send it to a machine shop to have it fixed. They said that it would last for lots of years before it required any service. I went back to my couch and with my sketch pad in hand and a catalogue from a vale manufacture I designed a totally different system than what I saw. It was simple to understand, and all the parts were easy to repair on site. I used three-piece ball valves that could be unbolted so the working portion with all the seals could be removed. The valve had a safe working load of over one-thousand pounds of pressure so the fifteen pounds of pressure that I was going to use was well within the safe working range of the valve. I have had remarkable success with this design and have used it on boats big and small for more than thirty years.

I continued to take components and put our own system together for several boats until we got into the larger yachts, the 121-foot *Taurus* and 105-foot *Princess Gloria*. I opted to go with marine air-conditioning systems manufactured by large companies instead of the systems that Dave and I put together from random components. The systems did not work as well, mostly because they were noisy inside the rooms, but they had a warranty. The air handlers were a lot smaller than the ones we used, so they were a lot noisier, the noise coming from the air handlers pushing the air too fast. To this day, the manufactured systems are noisier than what Dave Medley and I came up with but they were smaller and so they took up less space. Our system took up more space, but after spending time on these boats, I would opt for the quieter system, so I could sleep at night. Dave's theory was that the boat should be comfortable, but nobody knows why. One of the other differences is that the new systems are "smart," which means you can put the fan controls on auto and the fan speed will change depending on the demand requirements. The problem with the automatic system is that when you are sleeping and pumping out 98.6-degree moist air, the fan will speed up to correct for that condition, which will wake you up. We used three-speed fan switches that were hidden in lockers, so the guests could not mess with them once they were set properly. The only thing they could change was the temperature in the space. On the big yachts, we did not even let them do that; they would have to get the crew to adjust the thermostat. It was always the age-old problem. The guest would turn the thermostat way down to cool the room "quickly" and do just the reverse when it finally got to cold. They could not understand that all you had to do was to make a minor adjustment and the room will get to your set temperature.

As the boats got bigger, the systems became more complex, and the thought process became more intense. The electrical systems were the ones that needed the most work. The air-conditioning systems had been installed on mega yachts for decades, so they had the components pretty much worked out (except for the noise issue). The Detroit Engine manufacturer had stepped up to the demands of the yacht customers by cleaning up their act, so they could compete with Caterpillar Engine. When Rodger Penske purchased Detroit Engine, he sent his Blue-Ribbon Task Force around to all the major boat builders and asked what was required from them to make the product better. The top of the list was to dry up the engine. Anybody who owned a two-cycle Detroit knew that if the engine was running, it was leaking oil into the bilge. Some of the other things on the list were to do a better job of marinizing the engine so the dealer or the boat builder did not have to install a lot of aftermarket items like seawater pumps and isolation mounts. Rodger took all the common concerns and requests to heart and developed a totally new marine engine that went from the bottom of the choices of custom boat builders to one of the best. He also did one of the best paint jobs on the engine package, making it look impressive in the engine room, which became one of the showplaces for a lot of the yacht owners. Detroit had an optional chrome package where they would provide chrome valve covers as well as a few other items that would make the engine a real showpiece sitting in the engine room.

The hydraulic systems, which I used to build up from components, also took a huge leap as the boats become more sophisticated. I learned years ago that hydraulics was a much better source of power to run essential equipment, such as anchor windlasses and deck cranes. Electric motors can self-destruct even with all the circuit protections. Once they start getting hot, they start to fail. The other problem with electrics is the nasty marine environment they are forced to live in. Thrusters, anchor-handling equipment, and deck cranes will have issues if they are electric. The biggest issue with the hydraulic components is the electric controls that are required to make something "more yachty" than a fishing boat. The first time I got involved in this was when I talked American Bow Thruster into building roll stabilizers. I built a boat for a highly intelligent individual while at Delta Marine. The advantage in building for somebody with great intelligence is that you can have a meaningful discussion about systems and designs and by working together, come up with some great solutions for problems.

I had a Seattle-based manufacturer of roll stabilizers for military vessels, who would not build for yachts, wanted to sell me his company. Al built what I thought was the best roll stabilizer system in the world. The biggest secret to his system was an electronic gyro. I took the yacht customer over to show him this system that I just learned about. Al took a quick liking to the customer and agreed to manufacture a roll stabilizer system for his yacht. We installed the system and it performed beyond the customers' expectations. He owned a large European yacht prior to purchasing this vessel and it too had a stabilizer system onboard but did not work as well as this new system worked.

SEA TRIALS

Every boat requires a sea trial to ensure that all the systems worked to the manufactures specifications. The engines had to be run at various speeds while being monitored and checked by the manufacturer's representative. The propeller had to be right for the horsepower of the engine or the propeller had to be resized and retested until it was accepted by the engine manufacture. All the various systems had to be operationally tested in an actual normal working environment, both at anchor as well as underway. I was the one that took most of the boats on their sea trials, especially the trials where the owners were on board.

One of the smaller fish boats had a problem with the engine controls while we were coming back up the Duwamish River from the engine trial. I was on the command bridge steering and the engine representative was in the engine room finishing removing his equipment, so he would be ready to leave as soon as we tied up to the dock. The boats with their masts and rigging installed could not fit under any of the three bridges on the Duwamish River that lead from Elliot Bay by Seattle back to Delta Marine. when approaching the second bridge and after giving the proper long-short-long horn signal, I pulled the boat back into neutral to stop the boat. The boat remained in forward gear and was heading for the bridge. I tried twice to get the gear shift control to work but it remained in forward, so I jumped down into the engine room and over the back of the engine and grabbed the gearshift lever on the transmission and forced it into reverse. I was expecting the boat's mast and rigging to collide with the bridge at any moment. I ran back upstairs to find the boat, which was still in reverse, backing away from the bridge and coming alongside the wall that helps keep logs away from the bridge. I shut the engine down and sat there for a bit while we solved the control problem. My dad always told me that it was always better to have luck than skill, and this was one of those times that Lady Luck was on my side. As with the little forest fire, I did not panic I jumped to action with both feet.

After the "builder trials" were completed and I knew that there were not going to be too many surprises, I would than start taking the owner or his captain out on the sea trials. These were not to check out the boat as much as to prove the boat worked well for the owner. My wife Sherrie would usually come along on the overnight sea trials to help with the cooking. With all the commercial boats, I would have good help handling the lines and fenders, but they were not necessarily great cooks. They would usually hire a good cook as part of their deck crew. I only took a few overnight trips with the commercial boats, usually only if the owner was fun to be on a boat for an extended trip. We took three of the first group of Mexican boats on an overnight sea trial down to south sound past the Narrows Bridge and anchored for the evening at McNeil Island, which used to be a state penitentiary. Sherrie and I were on the fifty-eight-foot mother ship and two of my other leads and their wives were on two of forty-eight-foot vessels. We had several of the Mexican government inspectors to observe the operation of the boats, as well as our interpreter to help explain things. It was a beautiful evening with no wind and a very peaceful setting. After dinner, one of my leads on one of the smaller boats brought out his shotgun and a case of clay pigeons. We took turns standing on the bow while somebody through the clay pigeons and we would try to break them. The Mexicans all got their turn and had a wonderful time. After we were finished, I started wondering if that was a good spot to be doing that, just offshore from the old state penitentiary.

Once we started building the pleasure yachts, the sea trials all became more of a learning tool than on the commercial boats. The fisherman all had several years' experience and have countless hours running boats, so with them it is mostly proving to them that the boat works. Most of the smaller yacht owners only run boats for a few weeks a year, so the sea trial is also a time to teach the operation of all of the systems. It requires several sea trials to fully teach all of the systems to the owners, who are not boat operators as much as they are businessmen. The overnight sea trial is usually the last of all of the trials. I want the owner to actually take control and demonstrate to me that he understands his boat.

One of the overnight sea trials that I took was an overnight sea trial with the owner and his wife. I would take my wife along to help. From Seattle, we would head up to the San Juan Islands where we would spend the night on anchor usually in Roche Harbor mostly because it was quite picturesque. The first of these overnight sea trials was with the first yacht, the ZOPILOTE for Bruce and Joan Kessler. Bruce brought one of his best friends and his wife along so to even up the score I brought one of my top mechanics and his wife along. We left the dock at Delta early Saturday morning and headed down the Duwamish River. After getting through the three bridges that had to be raised and entering Elliot Bay in Seattle, I turned the helm over to Bruce, so he could start getting used to his new boat. Once he was far away from the traffic in the bay I went below to the galley and opened the large Sub Zero refer and looked to see what we would be having for dinner. I take Sherrie along on these overnight trips, so she can cook as well as show the women what their part of boating is. She not only does the cooking she helps with the fenders and the mooring lines. Sherrie normally takes all the food for dinner, but they insisted on buying the food. When I snuck a peek into the refer, I did not see much more than a chicken and some salad fixings. I went and got Sherrie and showed her. When heading north I decided to go to Victoria Canada so that everybody could have a little tour of Canada which, being from California, would be a huge treat for them. Once we docked in Victoria and I cleared customs, we hit the streets. We hit the stores and bought a bunch of snacks, so I would not go hungry. At one point, Bruce and his guests saw us snacking and figured out that we were bulking up, so they went to a store and bought a bit more for dinner. Not realizing that us boat builders from the Pacific

North West can eat a lot. We left Victoria Canada and went to our destination and dropped the anchor in Roche Harbor in the San Juan Islands. It was a beautiful evening and we had a splendid meal. We had a great cruise home the next day. By the time we arrived at the dock at Delta Marine, Bruce had gained a lot of knowledge as well as a great deal of confidence in operating his new yacht. I had him dock the boat which he did expertly. This was different from all his past boats, with only one engine he had to stop and think a bit more. With the help of the bow thruster he had no problems docking the boat even with the current of the river trying to keep him from docking.

As we continued to build these Yachts, I had to take the owners on their "overnight" sea trial. It has now become a tradition with all the Expedition Yachts that I delivered. One of the yachts, *Thunder,* was a "rooster" trip which was just the men. It was the owner, his captain and one of his good friends. As with the other trips, the destination was Roche Harbor. I took this boat to the dock, so we could have easy access to the restaurant and bar. Since we did not bring a cook than we needed to have a place to eat. We had a great dinner and then after dinner we went below to the bar and had a couple of drinks. The captain, who was truly knowledgeable about the area as well as locale customs, introduced me to the locale drink, the Fluffy Duck. It was a great drink and, according to the captain, after three you feel like you can fly. During our after-dinner cocktails, the Owner said that he wanted to do something special for the crew that was responsible for building his boat. He wanted me to pick the top twenty people and he would host them and their wives to a "special" catered dinner on the yacht while taking a cruise around Seattle's waterfront. I looked at him and said, I thought that you said something "special", heck I can do that. He looked back at me with a serious expression and said, "screw you LeMieux, Top of the Columbia Tower". I looked back at him with a serious look and said I cannot do that. The Columbia Tower was an exclusive club for the who's who of Seattle. He took us there and that is when I learned that you must wear a tie to even get in the door. Luckily, they had loaners for people like me.

We had a great meal as well as had a lot of fun. It was just us in the entire club that evening.

When we got into the bigger yachts, I learned that they would all come with a captain and crew. The sea trials were a bit different because we would have to make sure that everything got tested. That included the galley. The owner would be onboard and would have the crew conjure up a great meal. On the first big yacht that we took on a sea trial we headed out of Seattle towards the San Juan Islands. I got the yacht out of the river and turned it over to the captain as soon as we were in open water. I would usually do all the docking and the tight maneuvering because the insurance was still being covered by the Builder and I was the one responsible, besides I liked to do the docking because that was the only real challenge in running the boats. During the trip to the Islands, I went to the galley to see the Owners wife helping the chef work on cooking a turkey. It was early in the day to be starting dinner, but what did I know. I thought that would be great to have a nice turkey dinner. When the turkey came out of the oven, they proceeded to pull all the meat off the bones, so we could have turkey sandwiches for lunch. We went to Friday Harbor in the San Juan's because I knew it had a larger dock than Roche Harbor and that I could tie this one-hundred and twenty-seven-foot yacht to. We ate dinner at a restaurant on the pier and after the usual couple of drinks (I do not drink if I know that I will be running a boat) we went back to the boat and headed back to Seattle. The owners of Delta went along on this sea trial and did not want to spend the night onboard the boat. On the trip back, it got dark before we entered the Straights of San Juan DeFuca. I was impressed by the captain. Every time we got a target on the radar, he would have to find it in the binoculars. It was really early the next morning when we finally arrived at the dock at Delta. The captain said that I could dock the boat since he knew that I enjoyed that part. I docked the boat and we got it all secured and went home.

After all the sea trials were completed and it was time for the Owner to take possession it was now the captains turn to take the boat out alone for the weekend. I got a call from the captain Friday evening at home telling me that there were several problems with the boat and that he would have to cancel the trip for the weekend. I went to the boat that evening to learn that it was just problems of not knowing the systems. I have spent several days with the captain and crew going over all the operations of the vessel, so this problem should not have existed. After convincing the captain that all was good, I went back home. Early Saturday morning I get a call from the captain stating the somebody sabotaged the boat and the trip was off. I took my oldest daughter to the boat with me. As I went through the problems, I realized that it was nothing more than the captain trying to get out of the trip. He was intimidated by the boat and was too nervous to run it. Leaving the dock and coming back, especially when it is in a river that has current can be a bit intimidating. After convincing him that it would be OK, I left the boat. I sat in my car with my daughter watching while the captain tried to leave the dock. The boat had exterior steering stations outside the pilothouse on both sides to make it easier to see the dock while docking. The captain was standing at the steering station, so I could watch what he was doing. He would get the boat off the dock and then it would come back to the dock. As I watched I noticed that he was doing most of the maneuvers backwards. He could get the boat moving in the right direction and then he would make a mistake and it would come back. He did eventually get the boat away from the dock and into the river where he had plenty of room to maneuver. I left for home with the knowledge that most captains really do not know how to run the boats. Of all the large yachts that I have built, only two captains could maneuver the boat in tight places with absolute confidence.

The second big yacht that I built was for an East Coast gentleman that was truly knowledgeable about boats and what he wanted on it. He came to the yard with his Captain, Bob, who helped him team up on me. They proceeded to ask me questions about all the mechanical and plumbing systems, electrical systems as well as hydraulic systems. The meeting lasted most of the week. At the end of the week Gordon purchased the boat. Like all the previous builds, I would work with the Owner or the Owner's representative regarding all the systems that would be used on their yacht. These were totally custom yachts, so it was important for me to learn as much as I could, so the yard could build the yacht that the customer wanted. After the yacht was completed and launched, we took it on all of the required sea trials and then, like the rest of the boats, we went on the overnight sea trial. I took the electrical lead and his wife along to help with any questions and testing. We went up to the San Juan Islands for most of these trips. Most of the customers of the yachts were from the east coast and were not familiar with the San Juan Islands and all of their beauty. This was always a great backdrop for the boats. It made for great pictures for the customers. Knowing that the owner had never cruised the local islands, and also knowing that as soon as the boat was delivered, they were going to head off to the east coast, I thought that I would give them the whole tour. We went to Friday Harbor and as we were making a cruise past the harbor on our route to Roche Harbor, my favorite anchorage in the islands, the owner came to the pilothouse and said to anchor the boat, it was five o'clock, which was cocktail hour. Being a proper Brit, the owner drank gin and tonic, so, being a proper boat builder, I shared in his tradition. We had a great meal that the two women prepared, which was necessary to test the galley. After dark we wanted to try the two spotlights. They were two-million candle power, so they were bright. The lights were on a remote control from the pilothouse. When we turned the first light on it was shining directly into a picture window of a house on the beach about a quarter mile away. We quickly turned the jog lever to get the beam off the house. That light worked great, so it was time to try the other light. What would be the odds that we hit the same window with the second light. I wonder what the people thought when the big white light hit them from out of nowhere. The rest of the sea trial went flawless. We went back to Seattle the next day and Captain Bob docked the boat with no issues at all. He was one of two yacht captains that could handle the boat and not be intimidated by the size, value, or newness of the boat.

Another thing that I would always do on the sea trials was to teach the owner and his crew, usually the wife on the smaller boats, how to operate the boat. On one of the smaller long-range yachts that we built, the owner wanted me to try to teach his wife how to dock the boat in case of an emergency. He told me that it would be a big challenge for me because she could not drive a car with a stick shift. I accepted the challenge but added a bit of a spin on it. I told her that I would teach her how to drive the boat, including docking the boat, if she taught me how to cook a great meal. I was told that she was a great cook, so I figured this would be a wonderful way to get a great meal onboard. The four of us, Dave and his wife and Sherrie and me, got on board and left Delta and headed down the Duwamish River and towards the San Juan Islands, which is about a seventy-mile trip. We did all of the usual testing and demonstrating the functions of the boat while underway. When we got to Roche Harbor, we dropped anchor and enjoyed a cocktail on the aft deck while the women worked in the galley to do their magic. I would make several trips to the galley during the cooking process to "show interest" and "learn" how to make this special meal. We had a wonderful meal in a beautiful location on a beautiful yacht. The next morning it was my turn to do the teaching. We made the eight-hour trip back to Seattle where I was going to finish my lesson on how to run the boat with the final test being docking the boat in their slip in Elliot Bay Marina. The slip was a double slip, meaning that you had to maneuver between another boat and the finger pier. The wind was out of the south which was pushing against the starboard side of the boat. The boat would be tied up along the starboard side which meant that the wind would be pushing the boat away from the dock and towards the boat that was occupying the other half of the slip. I was standing with the wife helping her make the maneuver. The boat had a stern thruster as well as a bow thruster. It was a single engine boat, so it did not have the advantage of twin-engine maneuverability. She was already familiar with the controls from running the boat all day long, so now it was just the final docking. This operation makes a lot of experienced boaters extremely nervous. I knew that the boat had plenty of thrust to combat the wind so all that I had to do was to keep his wife calm. I told her that if she gets nervous, just stop the boat, and re-compose herself. She did an excellent job and did it all by herself. Sherrie and her husband were below ready to tie the boat up when at the dock. The wife never panicked, and all were impressed, especially her husband.

WORKING WITH BOAT OWNERS

When I started working at Delta, they were just building commercial fishing boats with an occasional pleasure boat for a friend. The owners of Delta did some commercial salmon fishing, so they knew some of the local commercial fishermen. When the word got out into the industry that Delta was building the Alaska Limit Seiners and one got delivered into the fishing fleet where people could see firsthand the quality of the boat, people would come to visit the yard and order their new boat. They would discuss their project with the owners of Delta and the specifications were written and the shop would build the boat to match the specs. The only time that I would get involved with the customer was during the sea trials. Since I was in charge of all the systems on board and was the one named on the company's insurance to drive the boats, I would be the one to do all the sea trials. When the company started building the yachts, which they did not want to do but because of the major slowdown in the fishing industry there were no new orders coming in for commercial boats, I was the one that worked with the customer from day one. The owners of Delta did not want to build these boats.

The buyers of the expensive custom-built boats, which cost a lot more than a production boat that anybody could go buy, were usually owners or top executives of large corporations. These were all type-A personalities that had to be in control of the process. The fish boat customer came to the yard, said what he was going to fish for and left. He would come to the yard to show his friends his new boat, or if we had a question about his boat, such as the color he wanted his interior fabrics. The next time you would see the fisherman was when it was time to sea trial and take delivery of his boat. The yacht customer wanted to be involved in every detail of their new yacht. This was a great learning experience for me. I had to come out of my shell from being shy around strangers. There was a lot of discussions about the interior and exterior details along with some discussions about the systems prior to signing a contract. The "look" of the boat was of utmost importance to the yacht buyer. This boat is to impress people not to go catch fish. After the contract was signed, unlike the commercial fisherman, these customers, or their representatives that they hired for the build, would spend a lot of time in the yard "overseeing" the build.

One customer had told us once that "he was the second smartest person in the United States", and he was serious. We had a meeting to discuss his ideas for some of the systems on his new yacht. I knew that one of the systems that he wanted to discuss was the air-conditioning, so I had my expert, Dave, attend the meeting. This meeting was held in the conference room after work so there was not many people or interruptions around. The customer was all about efficiencies. He said that it made no sense to him to run a diesel engine to run a generator to run an electric motor to run a pump. he also did not like the fact that the emergency "take home drive" was run using a hydraulic pump that was run from the generator and went to a hydraulic motor that ran the propeller shaft. He had designed a "new" system that had a diesel engine with a standard marine transmission that was connected to the main propeller shaft with a large drive belt like the ones that drive the large air blowers on the big race cars. The transmission would have forward, neutral and reverse plus the proper gear reduction to run the shaft. The second part of his new plan was to mount the small diesel engine at the aft end of the engine room and then have a long shaft that ran to a generator at the front end of the engine room on the starboard side of the room. The main engine was in the center of the room so that space was already taken up. The next, and most impressive part of his new design was to install pulleys on the shaft at different locations along the shaft to be able to run the other pumps that would normally be run with an electric motor. The pumps would run the equipment such as the water maker and the three air-conditioning pumps. He designed the system with electric clutches that would turn that particular pump on or off. Anybody that has been around for a long time has possibly seen this system design before. In the old days, this is how the big machine shops were run. They had a large shaft that ran through the overhead above all of the machinery. When you wanted to run a particular piece of equipment you would have to put the belt onto the shaft to power your equipment. This was dangerous because the shaft never stopped. A lot of the shafts were driven by large water wheels, so the shaft ran 24/7. When I tried to explain to this customer that that idea went away when they actually invented power, he got a little upset. I went down a different path and told him that the only way to change a belt was to disassemble the entire system so you could slide a new belt over the shaft and past the other belts. He agreed that maybe this idea was not the most practical, so we moved on to the air-conditioning part of the discussion. This is when I let Dave take the lead. The customer was trying to redesign the entire system and it did not take long to realize that it wasn't going to work. At one point he asked where Dave got all his knowledge. Remember this is the second smartest person in the US. Dave made a huge mistake and brought out the ASHREA book, which was the Bible for air-conditioning design. This really upset the customer who slammed his briefcase and stormed out of the meeting. We looked at each other and had a good laugh. He came back in a few minutes after he calmed down and we continued our meeting. Being a negotiator, we did some compromising during the build. The customer, after rethinking the entire process, did come around to a more normal system design. He did want to mount the small generator on top of the large generator. He said that the more weight, or mass, that could be put together and then have the isolation mounts located closer to the center of gravity of the mass, it would be able to eliminate the vibration and could control more noise. Vibration is noise. When you think about it, it requires energy to move your eardrum to create noise, every sound has a vibrating frequency that the eardrum picks up. Eliminating the vibration would help eliminate some of the noise in the boat and I was all for this. My goal was to get the boats as quite as I could. I was already working with the best sound attenuating people that I could find in the industry. I used the owners design and built the mounting system. After the boat was delivered and gone through sea trials the big generator, which is not used much because one of the biggest power consumers is air-conditioning and that is not used much in the Pacific NW, started to have oil pressure issues. The engine was still under warrantee, so the manufacture had to have it inspected to determine the problem. The oil pressure was low, so the engine had to go back to the shop to be fixed. Because of this design with one engine piggy-backed to the other, the engine manufacture would not pay to have the engine removed. I did the work and got the engine to the dealer's shop. When they took the engine apart, they found that the main bearings on the crankshaft were worn out. The engine had very few hours on it, so they went ahead and rebuilt it. We re-installed the engine and I soon, after my curious mind and some discussions with dad, my mentor, I called the owner and told him that this idea was not going to work. My dad explained that the engine that was running was vibrating the engine that was not running and that was "shaking" all the oil out between the bearings and the crankshaft an than beating on the bearings. The term was "berinelling" the bearings (The definition of brinelling is the permanent indentation of a solid surface). I remembered back when I worked detailing cars. The first thing that they would do when a new car was delivered from the factory by railroad car was to remove and replace the wheel bearings of all the cars for that very same reason. The wheels, tires and shock absorbers took up all the vibration, so the engines were ok. In the boat, the engines were connected together with rigid not vibration control mounts. We separated the two engines and then never had a problem again. The other "efficient" system that I installed on his boat was a generator that ran from the main engine. I had built hydraulic driven generators with my friend hippie that were successful. The new "efficient" generator was to hang the generator under the front of the engine and run a large belt that would take the forty-five horsepower that was required to run the generator. The pully size was determined by the speed that you wanted to cruise the boat, about 1500 rpm and the speed that the generator had to run at to create the 60cycle power. The generator had to turn at 1800 rpm to put out the required 60 cycle frequency. This system worked great when cruising. You could run anything onboard without having to run a generator. There is plenty of power in the main engine to run both the propeller as well as the generator at that reduced speed. The main engine was rated at 1800 rpm which is where the propeller demand and the engine horsepower are about the same. Anything below full engine RPM reduces the horsepower demand from the propellor which leaves ample power available to drive the generator. During the sea trial, we were using the engine powered generator. We saw a killer whale so the owner wanted to slow down so his daughter could see the whale. When he pulled the throttle back, I pushed it back where it was and told him that anything less in rpm would severely drop the frequency which would harm some of the more sensitive pieces of equipment like the microwave and computers. He did not argue, and we continued with the sea trial. That generator would be a great idea when on a long trip where you do not need to change the rpm. The hydraulic driven generator was still the best option because it would maintain the same rpm regardless of what the engine rpm was. This particular boat owner, not unlike the others, was at the top of his game in his field of expertise. We would go to lunch together and discuss things all the time. When we talked about his field of expertise, he was remarkably interesting. He worked in the instrument design business. He designed instruments to check the heart. I had a heart attack at age 35 from a condition known as vaso-spasm. I was one of the first patients in the NW to have this actually diagnosed. When we talked about the different tests that can be done on the heart, I became more interested. He was also involved in working with some of the top marathon runners in the country. They could figure out how to nourish the cells but still could not figure out why one would run out of steam. I did a lot or research on the heart when I had my problem, so I had some knowledge about this particular subject. I asked him if he knew that the blood vessels are somewhat elastic. That is how the blood is pushed through the body. The heart pumps and the vessels help by expanding and compressing. This elastic issue is where his problem is. When you start to exercise and you get your blood pressure up, your veins expand, and this creates a volume difference within your body. I told him that we install hydraulic oil reservoirs in our systems to take up for the difference when we extend the cylinders. The human body does not have that expansion tank, so the pump starves for fluid when the blood pressure is up, and the heart rate is also up. He thought about this for a second and said that his next task was to develop a machine that would check the stroke/volume of the heart to prove my theory. This led to what was known as "blood doping" (the injection of oxygenated blood into an athlete before an event in an attempt to enhance athletic performance). They would remove insignificant amounts of blood from their athlete weeks prior to the big race. The body would make new blood to replace what was removed. This is the same as what happens when you severely cut yourself. Just before the race, they would get the heart rate and pressure up and then add the blood back into the runner to "fill" the void. This is now illegal and potentially deadly.

SUPERSTITIONS
We built several hundred boats while at Delta Marine for all those years. One thing that I learned was to not go against tradition or superstitions. We learned the hard way that one of the superstitions in

the boat world is to never launch a boat on Friday. It was the best fifty-eight-foot combination fish boat that we ever built. It was black in color and named *TRADITION*. The owner and his two brothers all purchased a fish boat from Delta. This was the last brother to step up and buy a boat. His theory was that fish boats should be steel and not PLASTIC. After a trip coming up the West coast from California to Washington and being caught in a storm, he decided that the plastic boat may be OK. He was traveling with his brother, who had a new Delta Marine fifty-eight-foot fish boat and he had his new fifty-eight-foot steel fish boat. They both had small video cameras on board, and they took pictures of each other's boats during the storm. Both boats would come clear out of the water when they went over some of the larger waves. The video showed how rough it can get in the ocean with a full storm coming at you producing twenty plus foot waves. Both boats made the trip with no issues but when they returned to their home port in Bellingham Washington, the crew on the steel boat had a lot of work to get the boat ready to be put away for the winter. A lot of scraping rust and painting. His brother only had to rinse the salt off the plastic boat, and they were done. After watching how easy the maintenance was on the "plastic" boat, he then came and ordered the new boat.

Now it is launch day, and a Friday, and all the commercial fisherman from Bellingham are there for the launching. With any launching comes a big launching party. As the crane operator was lifting the boat, he realized that this was the heaviest boat that we had built to date. He was nervous about launching the boat. He got the boat picked up and swung out over the water. We actually had to use a winch on a Jeep to help swing the boat out over the water. The crane's rotation drive mechanism was not strong enough to swing the heavy boat on its own. Once the boat was hanging out over the water parallel with the concrete sea wall, we went to the crane operator and said that just ease the boat into the river, don't let it go and then stop it instantly because the boom of the crane was obviously overloaded, and we didn't want it to have any weird strains on it. The crane operator let the clutch and brake loose and, not wanting to stop the boat during the launch he basically let it go. The boat freewheeled into the river and put out a big wave as well as a huge splash. The boat sunk down into the river and then started to float back up. The only problem was that the crane operator was still letting the cable down. The huge spreader bar that held the straps that picked the boat continued to go down as the boat came up and the two met with a huge bang. The spreader bar hit the top of the big net drum on the aft deck and the top of the pilothouse roof. There were large attachments welded to the bottom of the spreader bar to allow the straps to be adjusted for the various size boats. These pieces were what hit the cabin roof. The boat got launched and the straps removed, and the boat fired up and I moved it to the dock. All the people had to go to the boat to inspect the damage. There was very minor damage which became one of the bigger selling points for the fiberglass boats that we built. Everybody knew what would have happened if a spreader bar weighing several tons was to strike an aluminum roof top.

One of the big yachts that I built went to the East coast after the launch and sea trials. For some strange reason he liked me and invited my wife and I to cruise in the Bahamas and the Caribbean. On year he decided to cruise to London, where he was born, and visit the homelands. When he decided to bring the boat back it was just about hurricane season. The boat was built well so he was not concerned about the safety of the boat or the crew if they got near a hurricane. There is a service called Weather Routing, which will keep the captains informed of all the weather conditions before and during their crossing. The report was favorable for crossing the Atlantic from the Azores to Florida. A big hurricane formed in front of them and they were following it down the Atlantic. The news reports were that this storm was going to hit Bermuda and cause lots of damage. The captain called me from the boat and told me that the sea was totally flat behind this storm. They could just follow it and have a great trip. Anybody that knows anything about the ocean and Poseidon, the God of the seas, knows that he monitors all of these calls. He said watch this and proceeded to create two more hurricanes. He turned the one heading towards Bermuda, which was in front of them, and started the two new ones behind him on both sides. If you remember, this was called the Perfect Storm, and yes, they were in the middle of it. It started hitting them about 7 in the evening. Luckily, it was already getting dark. The captain went below to the galley, which was on the main deck, to get a cup of coffee when he noticed some water leaking through the side door to the side walkway. The normal way to solve a small leak is to open and shut the door which sometimes resets the seal. Something told him to turn on the outside light and see what it looked like. When he turned it on and looked outside the water was up to the cap rail. He thought that the door was doing fine, put a towel down to catch the small amount of water and went back to the pilothouse.

At about 10:00 at night he turned the forward spotlight on to see what it looked like and saw every wave breaking over the bow. At that point he went to the engine room to make a quick check. He saw the engines, which were mounted on "soft" mounts to keep the vibration out of the boat, swaying back and forth. He decided to slow down a bit more to help keep some of the strain off the engines.

At midnight, the boat went up and over a combination of two converging waves and then went nose down and a huge wave went over the boat. He pulled back on the steering wheel, like in an airplane, to get the bow to rise back up. There was no system installed in the boat that would do that, but it did come back up on its own. After the boat leveled out the crew made a quick "ship check" to see what damage they incurred. When they went to the upper deck, they noticed that both of the 18' tenders were filled to the brim with seawater. The drain plugs were out, and the boats were Boston Whalers which had deck drains that allow the water to free itself. This confirmed their thought that the boat totally went submarine. The storms were sending waves from 2 different directions and two large waves stacked up with one on top of the other creating a monster wave that they fell into the trough of.

The boat continued on to Bermuda and all the way back to the Pacific North West. They inspected the boat several times and found no damage from the trip. From the Pacific Northwest they continued their trip to Alaska and returned to Seattle. They learned a lot about superstitions on that crossing.

Later in life, after I owned my own boat building company, I had a customer from the South Pacific that was buying an eighty-foot Long Range Cruiser. We headed to the launch ramp Thursday afternoon and had a problem with the moving dollies so by the time we got to the top of the launch ramp we missed the tide. The tide must be high to be able to successfully launch the bigger boats. It was obvious that we were not going to make it on Thursday. The Owner was there, and we looked at each other and we both new that it was superstitious to launch a boat on Friday. He wanted to postpone the launch until Saturday. I was not in any position to argue with him because of my past remembrances of trying to launch a boat on Friday. We discussed neither one of us being superstitious, but we decided to just not take a chance. We had a successful launch that Saturday.

SPIRITS

Some people believe in spirits, or ghosts while some people have to live with them and all of the consequences. One of my customers that I built one of the first 57' yachts for at Northern Marine had such a spirit, Hank, that he had to deal with on several separate occasions. The first time that I witnessed it was when he was bringing his new 57' yacht down to Poulsbo Washington to display it at the Trawler Fest Boat Show. Sherrie was on his boat as his crew to help with the lines and fenders. The show was an annual event that was well attended by a dedicated group of boat owners that all had the dream of great explorations. They all talked about crossing oceans and visiting remote locations that can only be visited by boat. I was given the usage of a 75' yacht that I had built so I was already there with it along with two of the other boats that I had built that were attending the show. As the 57 was entering the small marina, I was standing in his slip waiting to catch his lines. As he approached, there was a small tender in the water that was running and was about to leave the slip next to his when the owner of the 57, who was driving from the flybridge control station, yelled that he had lost control. The 55-ton vessel was heading towards the end of the short runway at about 4-knots with my wife standing on the bow with a fender to help with the impact. The boat was going to crash into a boat that was tied broadside at the end of the slip. I jumped into the small tender and told him to get me to the back of the boat as it passed by, which he did. I jumped onto the boarding platform of the boat and ran to the cockpit where there was a steering station. I pushed the two buttons required to take control at that station and was able to stop the boat before the big wreck. I backed the boat into the slip where we secured the boat. We were unable to ever make the boat fail again.

The same owner bought a second boat from Northern Marine after I sold the company the first time. He used me as his representative after I left the company. I was there for over 1 year before I left which put the boat at about half built. They finished the boat and it came out great. A few years after it was launched, the owner and his wife wanted Sherrie and I to join them on a trip to Alaska. We said yes and went along. I towed my 21' fishboat so that I could keep them in fresh fish whenever they wanted it, which I did without complaining. On the way north, we stopped in one of his favorite small anchorages, Silva Bay. We anchored and then took the 21' to the dock to do a bit if exploring. We came back to the boat so that the women could make dinner. We all sat down for dinner and just before we started to heat the main engine started up on its own. It requires three separate steps to actually start that particular engine. We jumped up in a panic and ran to the engine room so that we could shut the diesel engine back down. When we returned to the dinner table, the owner proceeded to tell us about Hank, the spirit that has been haunting him for years. He assumed that Hank was also responsible for the incident with the 57 years earlier at the Poulsbo Trawler Fest.

I do not particularly believe in Ghosts or spirits, but I also do not want to say that the do not exist. There is no good reason to tempt fate or do anything that may upset them as the Owner of the two boats obviously has done somewhere during his trip down his road of life.

I am not a super religious person. I do not go preaching to people and do respect them for believing in their religion. Not wanting to have issues with my boats, I made a deal with God when I started my new boat business. I would not pull his weeds and he would not sink my boats. This deal happened about the time I built my home in Anacortes which had a large yard. I knew several boat builders that had some of their boats sink. After careful examination, I learned that they spent a lot of time pulling weeds. To this day none of the boats I built at Northern Marine have sunk. I had one boat hit an island on its trip around the world and another hit a rock breakwater while going into a marine in severe weather and current with either boat receiving only minimal damage. A third boat hit a rock on its first trip and did thirty-three feet of damage to the bottom of the boat. The shipyard where we pulled the boat out to get it repaired said that most boats would have sunk with that much of an impact on the bottom. To this day, I still will not pull any weeds. I do not want to take a chance with the thirty-three boats that I built in the years that I owned the company from 1995 till 2006.

I know that one person that was purchasing my assets, after the first buyer could not make it work, pulled a lot of weeds. He would even be seen pulling weeds outside the office of the boat company. While launching an 80′ vessel that he built, it rolled over and sank at the launch ramp.

The 80' boat after it sank while trying to launch it. Everybody from the boat yard disappeared as soon as they could

The boat before that also had a problem while launching. He took the boat down the ramp at low tide and was going to wait for high tide to launch the boat. He would basically let the water come up and pick the boat off the moving cradle. It was a 95' vessel weighing 200 tons. The owner's wife christened the boat just before the water came up to the keel. The boat was being professionally videotaped. The video operator wanted to re-do the christening shot to get a better "take". By then the water was up onto the hull and we were about one hour away from the actual launch. The crane that held the front dolly from going on down the ramp was still attached. They rigged up a platform that straddled the tow strap that went from the crane to the moving dolly so that she could get up a bit higher for the new video shot. Several of the workers were standing by the bow for the shot as well as to remove the platform when the cameraman was finished. I was standing down on the dock that was parallel to the launch ramp and went to the marina that was 150 feet behind the boat as a precaution. I had the workers put mooring lines from the back of the boat to the docks that were on both side of the launch facility. We were about ready to go to a restaurant to get lunch when a friend of ours, the boat owners and mine, came to the entrance of the marina to see what was happening. He had just taken delivery of his 30′ Boston Whaler sport boat. I motioned him to come on into the dock so we could see his new boat. He came in and we were just holding his boat while talking with him. At that moment, we heard a loud snap and the boat started to come down the ramp. The strap that held the boat from self-launching had broken. It almost hit the wife of the owner while she was getting her new picture taken. There were two electricians on board getting a few items tidied up. I yelled at them to start the boat as I jumped into the Boston Whaler and told Scott to get me to the boat. I jumped onto the boarding platform as fast as I could. The 200-ton boat was heading towards the marina where several boats were moored in their covered moorage slips. The electricians got the main engine started as well as the hydraulics turned on. I arrived at the starboard wing steering station just before the boat was going to hit the marina. The two lines that I had them put on as safety lines helped to slow the boat down. The one on the starboard side tore the cleat out of the dock but the port line held. It started to turn the boat the right direction to aim the boat out of the marina. I got the bow thruster and the stern thrusters going which slowed the boat down. The transom did impact the end of one of the finger piers doing minor damage. Once I got the thrusters and the propeller working, I could gain control of the boat and get it out of the immediate danger and heading out of the marina and headed to the marina where they had a slip awaiting them. After arriving at the marina and getting the boat tied up and secured, I could relax and regain my composure. I thanked the two electricians for stepping up and getting the boat running, which saved the boat as well as the marina. I went to the owner of the boat company as well as the launch crew and asked why in God's Green Earth would they remove the steel cables that held the 200 ton boat from going down the launch ramp and leave a lifting strap rated at less than 10,000 pounds to hold the boat from going down the ramp. This was the same crew that worked for me when I launched over 30 boats down the very same ramp with the same dollies and cradle system. They thought that the strap would hold but had no real explanation as to why they took the steel cables off that went to the aft cradle.

This is a picture of the launch ramp with the marina in line with the ramp. I was standing on the dock to the right when the boat broke loose and headed towards the covered moorage. At 200 tons, it would have done a lot of damage. This is also the same ramp that I launched 30 of the boats that I built

I still refuse to pull weeds because I still have several boats out there traveling the oceans of the world. Still not superstitious and maybe do not totally believe in ghosts or spirits, but I still will not take a chance. A deal is a deal.

Turning Down a Rough Road

IN 1995 I left Delta Marine to start my own company. The day I made the big announcement to the employees (I had already told the owner of the boatyard) was at a launching party for a 132-foot motor yacht. After the party, a few of us went to a karaoke bar to celebrate a bit when somebody sang "My Way" by Frank Sinatra. I sat at the table and belted out my version to what became a standing ovation by my friends. Within a couple of days of me making my announcement that I was leaving Delta, I got a phone call at home one evening. It was my old friend Bruce Kessler. He had an accident with his 70′ Delta that we had built. He had taken the boat from Mexico to Alaska every year for about five years and then took an unplanned trip around the world. He headed to Hawaii and once there he knew that he did not want to head back towards California against the waves that he just saw. While trying to make up his mind as to how to get the boat back to California he thought that as long as he was here in Hawaii he might as well just go see the South Pacific. From there he wanted to go see the Great Barrier Reef where there were some huge sport fish to catch and then on to Australia and New Zeeland. His instinct to discover took over and before he knew it, he had gone around the world. He would call me at the different ports to give me reports on the trip and how the boat was running. This trip made Bruce a legend. He was already a well-known figure in the boating world. He created the *ZOPILOTE* which was the boat to make the biggest impact in the boating world. The seventy-foot Delta was featured in a lot of boating magazines.

The new sixty-four-foot Spirit of Zopilote at chatterbox falls in Canada

After his trip around the world Bruce came back to the Pacific Northwest and was going back to Alaska to start his Mexico/Alaska routine again. On his way to Alaska he struck an unchartered rock and the boat sank. Bruce, being a real boater, needed a new boat. He had already contacted another boat builder and had just finished with the preliminary design for his new boat. He was going to downsize from a seventy foot to a fifty-seven-foot full displacement yacht. Bruce called me and asked that if the rumor that he heard about me leaving Delta was true. When I confirmed the rumor, he said that he was looking for a smaller boat to replace *ZOPILOTE* and he will buy my first boat. This took a lot of the pressure of starting a boat company off my shoulders. There was plenty to worry about but now the first boat sale was not one of them.

To me, leaving the security of working for a big company and starting my own business was a big step down a scary road. Sometimes it was hard to know what side of the saw to stand on while I was out on the limb. I learned that standing next to the trunk was safer. The trunk was all the people I had been associating with during my past twenty-plus years. They were my sounding boards to help keep me safe while standing alone out on the limb. The other side of the saw I would be alone with only me to solve the eventual fall. I knew how to build boats; I did not know what was behind the scenes in the big office.

I started with two other partners to help with the unknowns of running a business. One had accounting skills and the other was going to be the salesman and office manager. I learned early on that I was actually doing most of the tough decision making that was required to run a business. The only thing that I was not doing at Delta was signing checks, I was doing the sales, working with the customers as well as the management of the projects. I grew my new company from virtually nothing but an underfunded start-up business to a multimillion-dollar business in less than five years. I told myself when I started, "I don't have a real boat shop until I sell at least five-million-dollars in boats." I remember the day I broke the five-million mark, which I broke by quite a big margin. I walked through the shop after everybody went home, assessed the shop, equipment, and crew, and told myself, "Bud, now you have a real boat-building company."

Now that I owned the business, I had to make all the decisions in all the areas of boat building, not just the areas that I had control of at Delta Marine. I knew that I had to spend most of my time in the shop helping with the day to day boat building, so I needed somebody to answer the phone when it rang. My oldest daughter, Michelle, did not have much to do since we just relocated to Anacortes and all of her friends lived in South Seattle, so I had her spend part of her day in the office. One day, one of my employees asked me to come to the break room where we displayed our company rules as well as the other state required notices. He pointed to a new sign that was posted that morning, which read "If you are not fired up with enthusiasm, than we will fire you with enthusiasm". After I had my chuckle, I took the sign down and went to the office to ask who put the sign up. Michelle said that she did it and that she thought that it would be a good policy. It was hard to disagree with her thought process, but I had to explain reality to her.

I also had to learn, even though I ran a portion of the fiberglass lamination work, more about lamination, which was one of the first processes in building boats. I knew how to start the wooden hull, which we were going to use to make the fiberglass mold that we could make several boats from. That was no different than when I started in my daddy's garage years before. Now I had to learn the best way to do what I was not doing back at Delta. One thing I learned was that there were several diverse types of resin and that one resin does not necessarily work everywhere. I decided to go with an upgraded resin compared to all my past experiences because it would cure potential problems in the future. Normal lamination resin would not work well for the underwater portion of the hull because it would blister. Anybody who has been around boats for any length of time knows about blisters or osmosis. The proper resin would solve the osmosis issue but costs a good percentage more per pound. You cannot use the good resin on the bottom and switch to the cheaper resin on the above-water section because the bond between the cheap resin and the good resin is not proper. You can put the good resin over the cheap resin with no issues. In fact, it is the best method to solve any secondary bonding issues with the cheap resin. If you put the cheap resin over the good resin, the secondary bonds will fail. What this means is that if you use the good resin on the hull, you must use it on all the secondary attachments. You can use the lesser-quality resin on the bulkheads, decks, and other items, but they must be attached with the better resin or you will have a failure. I also had to learn about the fiberglass materials themselves. Because of my past reputation in the boat building it was easy to get the sales engineers to come to Anacortes, where I set up shop, and help me and my people learn the best materials and the best way to insure top quality work. I told my customers that if I do not build you the best boat it is because I do not know how, not that I am trying to cut corners. I learned early on in owning the company that saving money by buying cheap materials was the wrong way to run the business. The way to succeed was to manage the labor. The difference in cost between the best and second best was not that much. If you had to warrantee a problem because of cheap materials, the extra cost of the material to buy the best would be nothing compared to the labor cost in one warrantee claim.

While I was learning about the latest technology in the different tasks of boatbuilding, from lamination materials to new woodworking techniques, we were building the hull plug and mold just as we did back in the old days. I also had to get the building ready for the boats to be finished. When I rented the building, my dad and I went there to clean the building and get it ready to start the tooling. When we walked into the building, the only thing there was a dead pigeon laying on the floor. The building was a warehouse, not a manufacturing facility. There were not hardly any 120-volt plugins for using power equipment. The three partners all put in equal amounts of money to get the business started. It was a lot less than one-hundred-thousand-dollars. The money had to buy the equipment to get started. I had a lot of wood working as well as mechanical, plumbing, and electrical hand tools as well as some electric power tools. Our first purchase was a used forklift, thirty-six-inch band saw and a large jointer. When I announced my departure from Delta, Jack came to me and said that him and his brother discussed what to present to me for my twenty plus years of service. He said that they talked about a gold watch but then thought that, since I was starting a new boat building business, their old compressor, which I had just replaced with new, state of the art, rotary screw compressors would be a great parting gift. The building that we rented was owned in part by them. I guess they thought that when I fail at this extremely difficult and competitive business, the compressor will already be in their building, which is what happened when I eventually grew out of that building and went to a bigger facility. The building had posts down the center and no door big enough to take a finished boat out of. It was not long before I had rented three of their buildings here in Anacortes, two of which we would build hulls and boats in, neither of which had big enough doors. I designed a system for rolling doors for both buildings. I built the doors and hung the door hardware. After that was completed, I had a concrete cutting service come and saw out both door panels in the two buildings. By then I had a small crane, so I used the crane to push the door panels out and hang the new doors. The very next day, I got a "stop work" letter from the city planning department. I was so involved in the design and the construction of the doors that I totally neglected thinking that we would require a building permit. The planning department would not accept my sketches as the engineering drawings required for approval. I had to than find a structural engineer that could design what I had built. They wanted some additional braces but other than that we were good to go. It was none to soon, because within weeks I had a finished boat to move outside.

Once the tooling was done, I had to start hiring more people to help with the process. I placed an ad in the *Anacortes American* newspaper and was surprised that I never even got one call. I started to panic when somebody came to me after almost one week and told me that the paper only came out once a week and it would not be on the stands until the following day. I did get several responses and was able to hire some incredibly talented people. The work ethic in Anacortes was like taking a twenty-year step back in time. The people worked hard and had great attitudes. It probably did not hurt that I was the only big yacht builder in the area, so I had something to offer the workers, which was a great deal better than working on small used boat repairs or building small production boats.

A couple of years later, I was fighting the posts that went down the center of the building. I bought an eighty foot beam that would span most of the short distance of the building. The beam was not going from wall to wall, which was one-hundred-feet. It was going to rest on a post near one wall and on a second post that was about sixteen feet from the other wall. That sixteen feet was the space where we constructed a balcony that the boats would be backed up against so that the workers could board the boats easily as well as have a lot of the work stations so that the people didn't have to walk up and down stairs all day long. The sixty-four-foot boats could move past the bow of a boat that was sitting at a station because there was just over twenty feet of room to move an eighteen-foot-wide boat past. I built an eighty foot with a twenty-one-foot beam, that was not going to fit, so I had to move the post. I went to lunch with Bob, the owner of a local commercial construction company, to discuss the installation of this beam and the removal of the post. By then, I had a quote from another construction company for ninety-six thousand to do the job. For that kind of money, I would lift it in place myself. I would pick it as high as I could with our crane, and then block it up. Than I would put large hydraulic jacks on both ends and jack it up and add blocking to keep it up. While out to lunch with Bob, I told him my idea and he said that he could do the entire job for twelve-thousand-dollars. I said go for it. Bob hired a two-hundred-ton mobile crane that had another job in Anacortes to come over and pick up the beam. He cut a hole in the roof so that the crane could reach out over the roof, pick up the beam and hold it in place while the workers stood up the two posts and secured them to the beam. The entire process was done on lunch break, so nobody was working in the area nor were near the beam.

THE NEIGHBORS

When I got the company up and running, I was approached by one of the neighboring business owners. Howard, from North Harbor Diesel, came to the shop and introduced himself. He told me that this was a friendly town and we help each other out. He said that he had a lot of equipment and, as he looked around, could see that we lacked bigger equipment. I contacted Howard when we had the large main propulsion engine for the first boat show up so he could bring his big forklift down to take it off the truck. As we grew, we continued to rent more of the empty buildings in town. We built the second seventy-five-foot hull in a different building several blocks down the street. I asked Howard if he could help move the boat down the street and put it into our shop. This hull was built in the third shop that we rented, shop three as we called it. Howard took his travelift to the shop and picked the empty hull up and delivered it to our building. Howard used his big forklift to help take some of the parts out of the molds and flip them over. I was in the market for a crane, but until I got a crane, this was the best solution. The relationship between Northern Marine, me, North Harbor Diesel, and Howard has continued now for twenty years. I sold the company in 2006 but we still help each other out today. Before long I bought one fourteen-ton mobile crane and a couple of years later I acquired a twenty-two-ton mobile crane, which I still own today so I can help out the locals. Once I got a lot more equipment, the favors were returned. Howard never sent me a single bill, nor have I sent him one. After I sold the business and got it back on four separate occasions, I kept some of the equipment that I had duplicates of, and I have given it to North Harbor. If you ask Howard today about helping Northern Marine when I asked to borrow his big forklift, he will tell the story that when he arrived at the shop with his equipment, my crew was not capable of running the fork lift and the project of moving the big boat part was past their ability so he would stay there and help. He will say that I tricked him into coming and taking charge of the project and getting it done. The reality is that Howard is a hard worker and will always rise to any challenge. He will step up, push people out of the way to get the task completed.

In 1998, when I was up and running well and hitting on most cylinders, another boat builder came into town. I went to their office and introduced myself. I explained Anacortes to them, where we all help each other. I told them that I know how difficult it is to get started. By then I had a lot of work and a lot of equipment, so I said that I could loan them what they required to help them get started. The next day the two owners came to my office and proceeded to thank me for my generous offer. The said that, after thinking about it all night, they should build our boats for us. They said that they were better builders and could do a better job. I was involved in the construction decisions of the new buildings back in my Delta days. All of the doors to the production facility swung out so that it would not hit you in the ass on your way out. I told them that and never dealt with them again. They, along with one other new repair yard, would not play good in the sandbox. Most of the other yards still help each other when asked.

THE CONTINUAL LEARNING PROCESS

Technology had come a long way in the twenty-plus years that I had been building boats. The biggest advantage to starting a new business is that you have the chance to start with the latest in technologies if you are willing to learn. All my life has been about learning, so this was not a problem. I wanted to have all the right stuff in the new boats. The suppliers I had been working with in the past were extremely helpful going forward. The hydraulic tubing and hose systems had just made a huge change in the industry. The change was to try to eliminate the constant leaks. The new system, which was a face-seal system, used O rings to make the seal. All the big-equipment manufacturers, such as Caterpillar, made the switch, so without having to replace several thousand dollars of existing parts and equipment, I went directly to the latest in technology. The same thought process went with every system I chose for the boats.

I had a Seattle-based manufacturer of roll stabilizers for military vessels, who would not build for yachts, wanted to sell me his company. Al built what I thought was the best roll stabilizer system in the world. The biggest secret to his system was an electronic gyro. The other system that we were using at the time had a mechanical gyro that required hydraulic oil to run it. The gyro was the part of the stabilizer that would cause the system to react to the roll of the boat. If you have ever held a gyro in your hand you would have noticed how it resisted when you tried to tip it from its normal position. If the gyro, which was nothing more than a disc that was spinning at an extremely high rate of speed, would remain level. We had them as kids. Some you could spin using the stem and others had a string that you could pull that would get them spinning fast. The way the gyro would work in the boats was that as the gyro was spinning and as the boat rolled the gyro would stay level and the bout would move around the gyro which would open a sensor that opened a valve that would send the hydraulic oil to the fins to react to the roll. The system did a decent job of removing the roll from the boat caused by waves. The problem with the gyro is that if the force remained constant such as with a steering or wind induced roll, the gyro would eventually catch up with the new angle of the boat and that would be the new up. The steering of a high-speed boat is different than the big heavy boats.

When you turn a high-speed boat, it leans into the corner. When you turn a big full displacement round bottom boat, it leans out in a corner. As you keep turning the boat keeps the same leaning force on it until the boat is straightened out.

The system had some other design flaws in the mechanical portion. Now that I was spending time learning about higher end hydraulic systems, their system was really outdated. The system would require a lot of cooling to work. When a system requires a lot of cooling that means that it is really inefficient, the excess hydraulic oil is making heat instead of work.

The difference between Al's gyro and the others, was that his knew where up was. All the gyros in the systems would do a decent job in reacting to the varied rate of roll, but none knew where up was, so none would remove a steering- or wind-induced roll. I put a meeting together with Al, the owner of Pac Mar the Seattle-based manufacturer of military systems, with the owner of American Bow Thruster, who I thought put the best bow thruster system and integrated hydraulic system together at that time (I used several systems provided by the various manufacturers, so I had some knowledge of how most of them worked). They never did put a deal together, but Al did share the one secret about the electronic gyro that knew where up was, with them. American Bow Thruster, now TRAC, built the roll stabilizers and in my opinion, is one of the best in the world. They take over ninety percent of the roll out of the boat.

I ordered one of their first systems to install on a small forty-eight-foot Trawler yacht that was built in the Northwest. The boat was tender, which meant it would roll from side to side in small waves, so it was a prime candidate for active stabilizers. I saw the boat one day while returning from a weekend trip on my 43' Bayliner. (Yes, the owner of a yacht manufacturing company owned a Bayliner. It was actually my second one. I bought a 32" in 1985 and the 43 in 1991). When I passed the boat, I looked back and saw how bad my wake made the boat roll. I felt bad, so I waited and followed the boat to the marina where I apologized to the owner. He said that it was OK because it was just how the boat reacted to the waves. The boat had paravanes or fixed stabilizers with all the poles and rigging. The problem was that the system was difficult to deploy and retrieve, especially when island hopping or just taking short trips. You would have to bring them in every time you came to a dock. The other problem with the paravanes is that in real rough water you must bring them in because, as shown in the movie The Perfect Storm, they will come out of the water and smash into the side of the boat. On a yacht, that would usually be the windows, so the boat would become in danger of taking on water and sinking. Because of the difficulty of using them this owner hardly ever deployed them for short trips.

After having met the owner of the boat he learned what I did for a living and wanted to visit my shop, so I set up an appointment to meet him and give him a personal tour of the facility. I had several boats under construction at the time, so it was impressive for a real boater like him to walk the shop and see the boats under construction. After the tour and a bit more conversation with him, he told me his background. He was the commander of the aircraft carrier Constellation. I got his contact information, so I could get back with him. After he left, I contacted the owner of American Bow Thruster, who was just starting to build their roll stabilizers, and told him that I had a great candidate for their first set of roll stabilizers. We contacted Jack, the boat owner, and gave him a proposal that would be hard to pass up. He excepted the proposal and we now had our first customer.

I hauled the boat out, put it into my shop and installed the components. When we launched the boat, the owner of American Bow Thruster and his chief field man came to Anacortes for the sea trial. While we were sitting tied to the dock, they performed their initial tests which required working the fins back and forth hydraulically making sure that there were no leaks and that in fact we had the system plumbed correctly. They had a way to test the fins by placing them in a "reverse" mode which would make them work to increase the roll instead of decreasing the roll of the boat. They turned the system on, and we walked from side to side to get the boat rolling at the dock and we were amazed what the fins did next.

The fins continued to increase the roll on the boat to a point that you had to hang on or you would get thrown off your feet. They quickly shut the system off and we stood there and looked at each other in amazement. The boat was sitting at the dock rolling drastically. We realized the amount of roll they had just put into the boat was the amount that could be removed from the boat while at anchor. This was a great breakthrough in the industry. Up until that point, the manufacturers in the industry would tell me that you could over stabilize a boat (although I had no understanding of how something could be too stable) and that the boat had to be traveling above seven knots to have the stabilizers work. Jack was extremely happy with his new roll stabilizers. The other manufacture was proven wrong as the industry made yet another improvement in making the yachts more comfortable.

The other area I had very little involvement in for twenty-plus years was the carpentry department. Delta Marine had a great carpentry department, so I never got involved in it. Fred, the carpentry lead at Delta, was extremely talented. He had a lot of artistic ability and could figure out how to accomplish almost any task that was required on the large mega-yachts as well as on the fishing boats. I had been a carpenter by trade over twenty years prior, but I was sure technology had effects in this area also. I contacted the wood dealers to learn what was new and what really worked. My personal theory was that people would help you if you asked. The only trick was to ask the right people. The preferred wood for boats in the old days was teak. My fist boats were teak. While at Delta, we built a boat for a gentleman that had a beautiful highly figured teak interior. Dave had purchased ½ of the log to do his boat. The tree was already sliced into veneers and ready to be laminated onto backing materials so that they could be put into the yacht. He was required to purchase the entire half of the log, which was more material then was required to do his boat. When I started the mew business, he approached me about buying the remainder of the log from him, which I did. I also went to the supplier and purchased the other half of this beautiful log. There was enough teak veneer to finish the first five boats that I built.

You can see in this picture the highly figured teak that was installed in the first 5 boats built that wanted a teak interior

This was the interior of the STARR which was the first 75' that I built. This was one of the boats that I built using the special teak veneer that I purchased

The other thing that I did in the carpentry department was to provide the workers with the proper equipment so that they could do the best job that they could. By the time I sold the company in 2006, I had one of the best cabinet shops in the entire north sound area. I was also fortunate that I had some of the best talent in the area to work the tools and create the masterpieces that we built.

As I sold more boats, the price continued to rise as the quality grew. I started building boats that ended up winning international awards. Remember my motto "the quality remains long after the cost is forgotten"

Another area that I needed to learn more about was material selection. While at Delta, we used what we used for years. We would improve when we learned something new in the industry. In my new company, I wanted to be a bit more proactive. I invited the suppliers in to teach us the latest innovations in their industry. The plumbing materials had taken a large leap in the marine industry. I jumped in with both feet, even though the materials were costlier, to get the latest and greatest in materials.

PROJECTS

I started by building the sixty-four-foot Long-Range Expedition Yachts (LRC), and within less than one year, I was approached to build a seventy-five-foot LRC. I expected that this could happen when I built the tooling for the sixty-four-foot hull, so I made it with a joint in the middle, so a section of tooling could be inserted to make the larger vessels. I continued to build the sixty-four-foot and the seventy-five-foot LRCs for several years. I had people interested in smaller vessels as well as larger ones, so I built the tooling for a fifty-five-foot LRC and an eighty-foot model with a three-foot wider beam

Me sitting on a Man engine that was going into a 75' yacht that i was building for a German Buyer that was planning a 1000-day trip around the world

which allowed for substantially more interior space.

I was approached by a few customers to build something we did not have any fixed tooling for, so I developed a system to take parts from our tooling and make some modifications to give the customer what he wanted. I built a couple of boats over eighty feet in length and one fifty-five-foot double ended boat, all using the same sixty-four-foot tooling. What I learned was that once the designers started using the computer to design their boats, they would "steal" their own design to make a new product. The designer that drew the sixty-four-foot for me had a customer that wanted a fifty-five-foot double ender. The thought was to have a "more fuel efficient" boat. They wanted me to bid on the project which I did. When they gave me the set of hull plans, which showed all the "lines" on the boat in one section, I placed them on my newly patented light table, the large window in the office facing the morning sun, and overlaid my sixty-four-foot lines drawings on them. Luckily, all designers work to one quarter inch to the foot scale so both drawings were to the same scale of size. What I quickly noticed was that the designer used the same basic hull shape except for the canoe stern. I kept this little secrete to myself and went ahead and gave my bid for the boat. They signed the contract and then I went into the shop and had them set the two back halves (the mold was in four sections so that I could add a section in the center to make the longer boats) of the sixty-four-foot hull mold upright and next to each other. I had them lay down the loft floor for the original boat so we could add the "new" aft sections. The next step was to cut the new frames that would make the new aft section of the hull and glue the frames into the mold with a hot glue gun. I hired a company that could install spray foam, to come in and fill the gap between the original mold and the top of the new frames thus making a "new" mold for the aft section of the boat. We sanded the foam smooth and fair and added a thin layer of fiberglass to keep it from being dented or damaged while we were starting the hull lamination process. This worked out great. We did not have to spend a lot of money creating a new mold to build the different shaped hull.

I had another gentleman that wanted a larger boat than what I had a mold for. He wanted an eighty-three-foot boat and one that was three feet wider than my "stock" sixty-four/seventy-five-foot model. This was before I had developed a new 76' model with a three-foot wider beam. I had the same designer, "Steve Seaton", do the drawings. Now that I broke his code on stealing his own design to make different models, all I wanted him to do was to design the new hull shape so that all I had to do was to set the hull molds up next to each other but three feet apart. I would have to build frames that would continue the hull shape towards the center. This would require making a new keel section of the mold but that was easy. Knowing that the hull would have to be longer I had the designer locate a line where the existing mold would start getting narrower and the longer boat would continue to grow from. This was not a straight line. I had the line laid out on the old mold and then had the lamination crew build a section of the hull that started from that line where the new bow would be extended and worked aft for about eight feet. After the section was made, I had the carpenters reinforce the section so that it would not lose shape or move when we removed it from the mold. Once we removed it from the mold the section was placed on a simple set up jig just like the old days of backyard boat building. Some temporary frames were cut and setup so that my people could build a "one off" hull section using the bead and cove method. While the new forward section of the hull was being built, the lamination crew was building the aft section in the newly widened mold. They built up to the same line that I had the eight-foot section built to. I knew that the two sections, the aft section, and the forward section, would mate perfectly because they had the exact same point out of the same mold that they referenced. Once the aft section was removed and set on a cradle for support and the forward section was complete, we mated the two sections together. We had a structural engineering company make sure that the connection would be stronger than if it came from a one-piece mold. I look back at the way I tackled these issues and realize that people on the outside looking in must have thought that I was nuts. This boat has been sold twice already and has made several ocean voyages from the east coast to the west coast with no problems.

I even built a sailboat hull for a gentleman that came to me with the design. It was built using the same method that we built the fifty-eight-foot fish boat hull thirty years prior at Delta Marine. It was a bead and cove planking system. The only difference was instead of using wood for the planks we used a high-quality foam board that was an ideal core material for building the hulls. The foam was fiber glassed over and the hull exterior was complete. After the exterior lamination was complete, the hull was made smooth and fair (no bumps or hollow areas) and given a coat of primer. After the hull was made ready for final paint (it is a lot easier while upside down to sand and paint the bottom) we rolled the hull over with the set-up jig still attached to help maintain the hull's shape. We than had to set the hull onto a cradle that we built while the hull was still upside down. The set-up jig was removed, and the inside of the core was laminated. Once the inside was laminated all of the structural stringers and bulk-heads were installed and the hull was ready to be delivered.

The 75 men and women crew in 2001 standing between the 4th 64' and the 4th 75' prior to launch

I had several people approached me to build a smaller boat. We designed a fifty-seven-foot model to fill that need. I had a different thought process for this boat. Instead of building a hull shape to build the mold, I would build a real hull just like we did with the sailboat. The normal hull or plug as it is called, is usually destroyed after the mold is built and removed from it. After building the forward section for the eighty-three-foot boat as well as the one-off sailboat hull, I decided that we would build a one-off hull for the fifty-seven-foot hull. The term "one-off" usually means that you only build one of the models and not a series of them. We built the hull using the same methods as in the old days of boat building except we used the modern technology available today. The hull material was the foam bead and cove system covered with several layers of fiberglass for additional strength. Once the hull was completed and before we removed it from the set-up jig, we faired the hull smooth and applied a coat of gloss paint. The glossy finish would help us find any imperfections in the hull finish. The imperfections were repaired, and a second coat of gloss paint applied. Once we were satisfied with the look of the hull, we waxed the entire surface in preparation to build the mold from the hull. The mold would give us the ability to build several of this model of boat.

Three of the 57' trawlers out on a photo shoot. note that they are all different colors. we made custom boats. none of the boats had the same interior layout.

The fifty-seven-foot project was the first project that I started a new process for the lamination of the hull. I heard about resin infusion, where the yard installs all of the fiberglass materials into the hull mold dry and then puts a "bag" over the entire surface and puts the entire hull under vacuum. I got my fiberglass leads together with the materials supplier and we discussed this new process. As soon as we started to discuss this, I remembered that back when I was building wind tunnel test models for Boeing, we did this very process. We did it on a small scale, but the process was exactly the same. My lamination leads were not only up for the challenge but excited enough to learn more on their own time. They did some research and came back to me with a plan. It was obvious that they had talked amongst themselves and with outside sources and came up with what seemed to be a very workable plan. There was a company out of Canada, that would help design the intricate resin feed system and how all the resin would flow into the hull. Our full displacement hulls were a lot heavier than any of our competition. We had five layers of material on the outside of the hull, a one and a half in core and then five more layers on the above water portion of the hull. We had twelve layers on the underwater portion, and it was doubled at the keel. The hull is laid up in two halves, so the keel was actually tapered back in the lamination and then installed when the two halves were put together. The hull is built this was to allow it to be laid up working horizontal. The mold can be tipped so that the hull sides are down flat not vertical. This first attempt of infusion went fairly well. We had outside design help so we should not have a problem. We started the infusion and quickly learned that their design would work for thinner hulls but did not work well for this hull. My leads had put their own "plan B" together in case there was a problem and they totally solved the problem. I thanked the people that came to help but had no solution when it was going bad and hoped that they would have a nice trip back to Canada. We started doing all of the hulls as well as all of the components using the resin infusion method. It made for a much better part as well as quicker to build. The process also eliminated all of the odor of fiberglass in the shop. Instead of spraying resin into the mold daily for a week or two to lay up a large hull, all the materials would go into the hull dry and then would be infused all at once. We invited the Puget Sound Air Pollution people to the shop for one of their inspections during a day that we would be doing a major infusion. My lead laminator had a chicken BBQ that same day, so the only smell was the BBQ not the resin. The Air Pollution people were impressed. When we started building the one-hundred- and fifty-one-foot yachts, my team came to me with an additional improvement on the process. They wanted to not only build the hull but add all of the stringers and frames in at the same time. All of the hull layers would go into the mold. Now we are building the hull together and upright as one piece, because the resin will not "drain out" of the vertical surfaces because everything is being fed towards the vacuum and the vacuum is in the top edge. The resin starts at the keel and works up towards to upper sections. The stringers are in the way, so the resin has to go over and through them. There are resin feed lines with valves on them at about every foot running full length of the hull. As the resin works its way towards the vacuum, it reaches a new feed line, which is turned on and the process starts over again. I had them set the resin up so that it had a twenty to thirty minuet gel time. That was more than enough time to get past the next feed line before the resin would start to harden. This was an additional fail safe that I added to the design just in case. Not doing this caused a total disaster for the second group of people that bought the business. The same workers that I had, minus my top lead person, did not believe in my theory, so they promoted the resin so that it would take several hours to get hard. They lost the vacuum as the resin was almost all the way to the top and it all slumped back down into the bottom of the hull.

My team did install all of the hull structural members and then built the large bag so that they could have a tight seal when they applied the vacuum. They test the vacuum for a day to make sure that there are no leeks. They started the resin infusion as soon as the workers went home. It took over eight hours to do the infusion. It also took forty-four drums of resin for the infusion. I have been told that this is still the largest single infusion in the boat industry around the world.

The team did that on a several hulls with the same positive results. One of the side benefits to building a hull this was is that everything is as one. The strength was beyond my expectations. The other benefit was that the team could build a one-hundred- and fifty-one-foot hull in five weeks with five workers working one shift.

AWARD WINNING BOATS

We built several award-winning boats out of little old Anacortes Washington. My crew was the best. If a customer could dream it up, they could build it. One such project was the 80' *Meander*. It was the first of a new series of boats that we started. More people were coming to us to have larger custom boats built. The Meander had an interior decorator that was incredibly talented and worked well with the crew. Most of the interior descorators, as I called them, would be stuck on their idea even if it were, what we called, un-attaniaum, or almost impossible to attain. Scott had as much respect for the talent that we had as we had respect for his talent. The end product of the boat proved that it was a talented team project.

The MEANDER out on a photo shoot in the San Juan Islands

The International Superyachts award for MEANDER

Another buyer for an 80' Long Range Trawler Yacht came to the yard to see if we could build him a truly high-end custom yacht. The Buyer was very particular. He wanted to be involved in the design elements of his yacht. He hired an interior decorator that had worked on several larger yachts and was very capable of designing the minute details that would make the yacht an award-winning vessel. Scott, which was the same interior designer that the owner for the *MEANDER* used again worked with my cabinet workers designing the details for all the interior trim. We would have special cutters for our wood shapers to get exactly what he wanted. The boat came out great. The boat ended out winning the ShowBoats International award for its class that year. The owner taught me an important lesson about custom boat building. He said never lessen your quality on the structure and systems of you boats. Not one boat out there has sunk because of flawed interior workmanship. It is the structure and the systems that will keep the boat afloat, not the interior. My company was known for our robust fiberglass hulls as well as the commercial quality systems.

One of the first things that I did when I started the business was to hire a structural laminate engineer to design the hull thickness. The criteria that I used was a steel ship that was American Bureau of Shipping approved. A lot of my competition was steel trawlers and they were telling their potential buyers that steel boats are much stronger than fiberglass. I had the engineering data as well as some test samples to show the customers how much stronger the fiberglass hulls that I built were compared to steel. Pound for pound, the fiberglass is 819% stiffer and 2513% stronger. We didn't need to make the hull the same weight, so I chose to make it closer to the same stiffness as ½" AH32 steel. At the same stiffness, the laminate hull is 497.83% higher strength. That means that it would be able to "bounce off" partially sunken containers floating around in the ocean. That was what the steel boats told the customers was the biggest issue while cruising the oceans of the world. One of my boats has now made its 10 Pacific Ocean crossing and has not found that container yet. He was hit by a rogue wave that went totally over the boat with no damage to the boat on his crossing in 2019.

The 80' Julianne that we built that won number 1 for its class Show Boats Award

The award-winning interior of the Julianne. Note a lot of details such as the wood beams in both directions, the Brazilian Cherry wood floors as well as lots of other design elements that set this project above lots of others built in the world

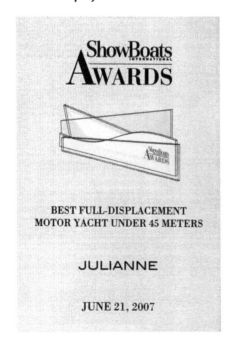

ShowBoats
INTERNATIONAL
AWARDS

BEST FULL-DISPLACEMENT
MOTOR YACHT UNDER 45 METERS

JULIANNE

JUNE 21, 2007

THE NEXT GENERATION
While we are doing all of this work and the company appears to be growing, I was nervous about getting workers as we grew. We were always looking for new talent in all departments. I was told that one of the premier yacht builders in the world would travel to third world countries and scour the villages to try to locate the best talent from each area. They would than move the worker and their families to the manufacturing facility where they had housing set up for them. They built undisputedly the best yachts in the world. I did not have any company housing, nor was I interested in traveling the world, with all the language and cultural barriers, to try to find workers. I went down a different path. I started a training program for boat builders. The first phase was in our facility and started with safety. After that looked to be successful, I was invited to a meeting at EDASC (Economic Development Alliance of Skagit County), where there was a round table discussion about the school system in the county. The discussion started across from me and went all the way around the table. There were representatives from both local as well as State government and the schools. The Dean of Skagit Valley College was sitting next to me. Everybody talked about how great the school system was doing in the County. When the discussion finally got to me, I asked everybody what county or state they lived in. I told them that I was sure that they did not live here. That year the high schools had removed all of the automotive and wood shop classes. I proceeded to tell the group that all people do not need to be computer programmers. They will need people to fix their cars, build their houses and build and fix their boats. I actually think that this came as a bit of a shock to the politicians. I discussed my thoughts of training for the next generation of boatbuilders. They must have taken this to heart because before long I was sitting at the college with a video monitor in front of me having a video tell-a-conference with the Governor's office. The next thing that came out of all that was a six-million-dollar grant to start the boat building school here in Anacortes.

The Marine Technology Center was started and has become an enormous success.

The school has been doing great. The enrollment has increased each year. I am on the advisory board as well as do occasional speeches to the classes to try to inspire them a bit more. The students that go through the class have jobs awaiting them upon graduation. This did not backfire, I did not now that I would be selling the company when we started this school. My HR person, Wes, who was involved with me from the initial inception of this is now a teacher for the High School component of the school. Before the school, Wes and I would "take the show on the road". We would take one of the scale models to the high school and put on a show and tell talk. My goal back then was to try to inspire the kids to become boat builders. The teacher in the school, Mike Beamer, is now the main instructor at the boat building school. He is doing an outstanding job teaching the students how to become great boat builders and boat repair people.

While I was in the process of getting the next generation of boat builders developed, I received a letter from the Governor's office asking if I was interested in attending a trade mission to China. After reading the letter I sat back and assumed that if I got this letter, every business in the state got one, so I ignored it. The day that I was at the college on the video conference with the governor's office regarding the boat building school, I asked a person that was sitting there, who represented a large business in the valley, if she got her letter from the governor about the trip to China. She was very much into politics, which is why she was there, knowing that I would be talking to politicians. Lisa looked at me and said, "what you talking about Bud". I dropped the subject and went back to work. The very next day I received a call from the governor's office. They asked if I was going on the trade mission to China. They said that I do not need to discuss that with other businesses. Lisa had called them the day before and inquired about the trip, which she was not invited to. At that point I said that I would go. I originally assumed that every business in the state was invited, where it was only a small hand full. The only reason that I could assume that I was invited at that time was because of the boat building school. As it turned out that was not the case.

The news story was: *Gov. Gary Locke today released details of the trade mission to China and Vietnam that he will lead Sept. 15-24, to promote two-way trade and tourism.*

We went to China. We started from the top of the country and worked our way south stopping at the major cities along the way. About halfway through the trip, while sitting at the American Consulate for dinner, I proceeded to explain to the governor how big the boat building actually was in his state. He really did not know. After that evening, he made a special point of introducing me to the various mayors of the cities that we visited. When we got to the bottom of the country, the trip was finished. The governor was going on the Vietnam, but I remained in the city of Zhuhai in Southern China, which is considered the "marine district". I was escorted by a businessman that could speak fluent Chinese. We toured several of the boat builders there. It was a very eye-opening experience. There was not a work bench to be seen in any of the yards, they just worked on the floor. The Mayor of Zhuhai had us to lunch at an expensive restaurant. The restaurant looked like a big boat up on the beach. We were directed to what would be the pilothouse. We had a great lunch. I had a beer with my lunch. They would top my beer off every time I took a drink from the glass. I did not want to tell them that It would take a lot more than a few beers to make me a bit drunk. After the lunch, we went to a site along the river where they commenced to describe what they envisioned as a world class boat building company. They told me that my total investment would be thirty-five-thousand dollars and I could be building and repairing boats there. It was an interesting proposition. After I left, I went to Hong Kong for two days to tour, but to mostly consider this opportunity. I made a complete book of notes on this proposal, weighing the good as well as the bad points of this move.

After I arrived back in the USA and went back to work, I was interviewed by the Seattle Times newspaper. When asked about the trip and the proposal, I told the reporter that "I am not going to take what took me thirty years to learn and give it to a foreign country" over the next few days, my phone rang constantly praising my patriotism. I still feel the same way to this day.

CUSTOMERS, THE GOOD AND THE BAD

The custom yacht building business seams to attract all types of customers. While at Delta, I worked with all of the yacht customers. That is where I learned tolerance. Not the tolerance of how tight the wood joints had to be to be acceptable, the tolerance to work with high end type A personalities. These people are entrepreneurs that had become successful. I had to learn how to deal with them in all respects, from the money issues to the humor story of the day. One of the customers was a chemist that perfected a couple of the medicines that he patented. He was a proper Brit, so every day at exactly five o'clock, it was cocktail hour. His drink of choice was Tanqueray and tonic. I was not opposed to that, so I would help him enjoy this tradition. We cruised with him in both the Bahamas as well as the Caribbean after the boat was delivered. That tradition continued. He was an intelligent person, so we would have discussions about all the different systems on board his new yacht. He had several requirements for how he wanted things to operate so I would work out the details to make it happen. One example was that he wanted to be able to start the engines, put the boat in gear and move it even if he was drunk. He was against all of the "fly by wire" systems that were going onto all the boats of that period. The main concern was the engine and transmission controls. They had to be with push pull cables like you would have in your twenty-one-foot boat. It was a bit easier on this boat because the engine and transmission package was the same as was in some of the big commercial vessels. Unlike most boats, you had a lever for the engine to advance the throttle and another one for the transmission to put the boat from neutral into forward or reverse. This had a small lever that ran the engine throttle and a big lever for the gear box. This boat was set up so that all you did was to set the throttle at a particular RPM and then control the transmission from 100% slip to 100% lock up. There were shaft tachometers that showed the speed of the propeller shafts. That way you could creep real slowly coming into a marina. It gave better maneuverability at low speeds but with the engine RPM at a higher speed, that gave more horsepower to the hydraulics for the bow thruster. Thirty years later the new captain still loves the system. The boat works out of Anacortes in the summer months so I can talk to the captain and crew to get updates.

Another one of my customers was a famous author who wrote books that some became movies. I was at three of his houses as well as his business. He was another smart individual. This one I never drank with nor even went on a sea trial with. He tried to mess with me, so the relationship deteriorated quickly. The boat still turned out great, just no Christmas cards.

One of my customers was the astronaut that took the picture of the earth from the other side of the moon. He told me how the picture actually came about. He was the

The signed print of the Earth as they came around the back of the moon

flight engineer. As they were coming around the moon and the earth was starting to show up, he had to turn the space capsule so he could take the picture out his window. He had to engage the side thrust rockets to move the capsule. When he engaged the rocket to get the thrust, the flight commander, who was in the back relieving himself, panicked thinking something was wrong. Bill took the shot and put the capsule back on course.

When it came time for launch day, we had another company come with their Travel lift to the shop and pick the boat up and take it to their launch site about a block away. The boat only weighed 55 tons, which was about as much as they could lift, but it was easier than going down the ramp. As the lift was moving down the street, I asked Bill what the most exciting part of the trip was. When they lit the fuse or when you crashed landed into the ocean. His reply was, 'when I was a little boy, my father took me to the circus. There was a tall tower that looked 500 feet tall. A man walked out onto a platform on the top of the tower and jumped off. He landed into a small pool at the bottom. When we came around the moon is when everything struck me. All of the pre-flight training was that we had a thirty-four square mile target to hit. When I looked down at the earth, I could not pick out a one-thousand square mile target. I knew that if the trajectory were to flat, we would bounce off the earth's atmosphere, and if it were too steep, we would burn up. That was the most intense part of the entire trip". The owner sea trial was an overnight trial with a few of the leads and him. We went out into the San Juan Island to Sucia, which is a popular anchorage. We anchored for the night and tested a lot of the equipment so that he could both learn the systems as well as see that they worked. the following morning, we pulled the anchor and started heading back towards Anacortes. Out of nowhere, he would bark out an order as if in the military. One was "total steering failure" which meant we would have to go down and shut the hydraulic steering off, hook up the emergency tiller, secure it and figure out how to steer the boat. This particular day was windy and had fairly large waves. Steering the boat without an autopilot or even manual steering from the pilothouse would be a bit difficult. I turned the hydraulics on and used the bow thruster to try to turn the bow to a new course. I did not expect it to work, but to my surprise it did. I never told him that this was the first time I ever tried that system, I stayed cool as if this was just a normal operation. We did a few more emergency drills and than we made it back to the dock.

Another customer took advantage of the company by working with the project manager. I would go to the cabinet shop and see some furniture being built that did not coincide with the specifications. When I asked, I was told that the project manager had change orders for all the upgrades. The specifications were really clear. The buyer traded in a sixty-two-foot boat and the interior was to be the exact same style and quality. The interior was a huge upgrade from that simple production boat. The same thing was happening in the mechanical department. They installed a forth diesel engine that had a gear box on the end with a belt going to the main propeller shaft. This was going to be his take home drive system. It also had a big hydraulic pump on the front of the engine for servicing all the hydraulic equipment on board. It was a great idea, just not part of the specifications. I was told by the crew that this was also covered by change orders. One day the buyer was in my office asking questions about anchors. I took him on a field trip to my buddies' shop that built great anchors. He also built a lot of the "yacht jewelry" for the big yachts. The yacht jewelry was the polished stainless custom bow rollers, custom stainless mooring bits as well as almost anything else that you could dream up. He built polished stainless anchors for the big yachts across the country. We went there so my customer could learn more about anchors and order some special anchors for his boat. On the way back to the shop I asked if the project manager had discussed any of his additions with him. He said that nothing has been said so I just dropped the subject. He got to thinking about that conversation, so the next day he came into my office and asked why I asked. I told him that the project manager had told me that all of the interior upgrades, and the extra mechanical systems were all covered on signed change orders. He told me that nothing was ever said. I called my project manager into my office and asked him to bring me all of the change orders for this man's boat. He gave me that deer in the headlights look, so I said that you do not have any do you. He admitted it, even though he had told the shop as well as me that he did have them. I gave him fifteen minutes to leave the facility. It cost the company about one million dollars for all the upgrades that he received for free. It was past the point of stopping the process and just installing what was in the specifications, so we continued. I went to the customer and tried to negotiate with him. We both knew that I had no legal grounds to stand on, it would be a moral gesture on his part if he wanted to pay anything. My contract stated that any change order will have to be pre-approved and paid for by the buyer prior to doing the work. He paid a small percentage. After the boat was completed and he headed out, he went to Alaska and then down to Mexico. He invited my wife and I to visit him and his wife if we wanted to get away during the cold months of the winter in the Pacific Northwest. We accepted his invitation. He asked if I would bring him five-thousand dollars for him in cash so he could pay some workers that he hired to clean and detail the boat. I took a chance that he would not screw me over the second time, so we took the cash down with us. We had a wonderful time in Puerta Vallarta. As we were leaving, he handed my wife a check for the five-thousand dollars. I learned a long time ago to not hold grudges, and I think that my life has been better for it. As the saying goes, keep your friends close, but your enemies closer. The good thing is that I treated my customers fairly. I was tough but fair, and they all appreciated that. Several of my customers told me that the projects managers that "give the farm away" are great to work with because you get a lot for nothing, but they had absolutely no respect for them. I was the one that was tough with all the customers. I was also the one that was invited to go boating with them in exotic locations.

OUTSIDE PROJECT

Now that I have the boat company up and running at a fairly good pace, my wife finally surrendered to the fact that the company might just make it. That would mean that we would be stuck living here in Anacortes for a while. She decided that she would like to get her own house. The only thing that we ever rented was a cabin on the beach until we built a house down south. We were renting a house with a nice water view here in Anacortes. We rented our Redondo house out, so all was even in the game. She figured that she still had one more build in her now that she got over all the pains of the last one. Being not only the navigator on all of our trips, she was also the interior decorator. In about 1992, while we were still living in our house down at Redondo Washington, we visited the Seattle "Street of Dreams" home tour. They were all really high-end custom homes and we both really liked one of them. We kept the brochure and kept looking at it and dreaming about the beautiful house. One day while out driving around the neighborhood we saw a parcel of land for sale it was only about ¼ mile down the beach from us. It was a shy acre and had a magnificent view of Puget Sound looking north. We talked to the Real-estate agent and ended out making an offer that got accepted. We purchased the property. It had to be cleared, which would require some time. While I was clearing the property in my spare time, we took out the brochure and I re-drew the house plans. Every industry has their secrets. The design industry secrete to a nice drafting table was a hollow core door that was smooth. It was light weight and would remain flat. I borrowed a drafting machine, so I could be more accurate. I drew the plans up at ½" to the foot scale instead of the normal ¼" to the foot so that I could get better detail as well as easier to measure with a tape measure. I evaluated every room, sometimes laying it out full scale in our house so it made sense. We got the lot cleared and the floor plans all finished and we went to an architectural firm to start the process of getting the drawings finished so it could be taken for permitting, within a couple of days I woke up in the middle of the night in a cold sweat. There was no way that we could afford the taxes and insurance in that neighborhood working for wages at a boat yard. I stopped the process immediately. Sherrie went to the county to learn how we could get the lot divided in half and we decided to sell half of it. It was a real nice neighborhood and we thought that we may still want to build there, just a simpler, much less expensive house. it took several months to get the City, which just became a city, to go through the process and get the property split. It was actually two lots to begin with, all we had to do was to move the line to make them equal in size. The process was completed, and we put one half on the market. It sold really quickly.

The property sold and we relaxed to ponder our next plan. About the same time, I was contemplating leaving Delta, so it all worked out. Now we have been living in Anacortes for about four years and she starts looking for a house to buy. She, being spoiled a bit, could not find a house in a neighborhood that she would like. She decided that we would probably have to build one. Since the first cabin that we moved into, we had a view of the saltwater. This was going to be almost impossible for her to give up. She looked from Anacortes down as far as forty miles South, mainly so she could be closer to the family. She finally found some property that she liked. We went there with a salesperson and he verbally represented where the property lines were. I put on my heavy hunting gear and went through the brush to locate all of the property stakes. They were nowhere that he said they were. The property, all be it almost one acre, it was all over the hill and useless. We had put a deposit on it, so we got that back and moved on. We located another piece of high bank waterfront (the beach was not accessible from the property) and we were about to make an offer on it. I went to view it one day during lunch when heading back to the shop I noticed a new for sale sign on several lots less than a block away. They too were high bank waterfront but were larger and had a splendid view of Mount Baker. I pulled off the side of the road and called the number. They wanted about thirty-five thousand more than what I could buy the property one block south. I told them that I was accepted on the other lot, but I would buy theirs for the same price. They took my number and would talk to the owner and see what he would say. They called me back that day and accepted my offer. There was three lots there. The one to the south was 250' wide the middle lot was 220' wide and the most northly was 200' wide. We liked the one to the north but because they were treed, we would be at risk with my view if the other two people did not trim or remove trees in my view. We took the southern lot. We cleared the lot and took our drawings to a builder here in Anacortes. His designers could put our design into a cad file and do all the required engineering to get a permit. The only problem with our original design was that it was backwards for this lot. I made the drawings on vellum so you could turn them upside down and still see the lines. The drawings were made, approved, and submitted for a building permit. Two of my requirements for her to get her house was that I would get a shop and the property would be big enough that I could get a riding lawn mower.

The contractor built the house to the point of final framing with the siding installed and the roof sheeting in place. We took over from there and finished the exterior as well as the interior. We hired subcontractors to help with the roofing, plumbing and a lot of the interior trim. The house was tall inside so I brought a scissors lift from the shop that would fit through the front door. The trim guy as well as Sherrie used it to install all the trim and do all of the interior painting. Sherrie did all of the interion painting, Sherrie and I laid all of the hardwood, marble, and tile floors. We hired the carpet install out. The only carpet was the living room, family room and bedrooms. I would have only had carpet installed in the bedrooms, but one can't always win. We installed tubing in all of the floors of all of the rooms, including the garage. Each room had its own thermostat so each room could be set at a different temperature. The house has worked out well for us.

The view from the back patio. remember that when you have a boat you can get almost any view that you want, we are stuck with this one all the time, except for the clouds it never changes.

NOT ALL PROJECTS ARE GREAT

During the ten years that I ran my business, I was fortunate to have some awesome customers. They were always helpful with making decisions on the details that would make their boat more personalized for their particular needs. Some of the customers wanted to go fishing while others never wanted to even see a fish unless it came from a fish market and was already cleaned and ready to place on the BBQ. I also had a couple of builds that were a problem. Those were usually the ones that had a captain or project manager. I believed that they had a plan before they ever signed the contract. The first one was a gentleman from the New York area. He had a captain as well as an owner's representative. The captain I knew from before. He actually worked for me years earlier. He was a nice person and was a capable boat handler, which he should have been because I taught him over several years. We built the boat, made all of the additions that they wanted, and life was good. We launched the boat, made some of the required sea trials. The boats are launched running. I have my crane back them down a launch ramp just like you would launch your trailer boat. Just before the keel touches the salt water, we set up a platform so that the owner could break a champagne over the bow thus christening the boat. After the ceremony, we continue to lower the boat down the launch ramp. Once the back of the boat is deep enough, I stop the launch while I get the engines and generators started. All of the hydraulics worked so I would have the bow and stern thrusters for added security. We would continue to back down the ramp until the boat was floating at which time I back away and maneuver the boat out of the moorage, which is real tight for the big boats, and then head over to Capt Santé Marina where we tie up in a slip. While I am moving the boat, my crew is starting the launching party for the owner and his guests. The day after the launch, which usually on a Sunday, I take the owner and his group of people on a boat ride around San Juan Islands. This actually lets the owner know that that boat is seaworthy and almost ready to go boating. The key issues that had to be finished on the boat, besides all of the carry-on items and the carpet, which I wait till the very end, was the alarm system and a special shore power system that the owner wanted. Both of these items were being provided and installed by the same sub-contractor who was chosen by the captain. We were having an issue getting these two items completed by the sub-contractor. We did all the engine, generator and hydraulic sea trials making sure that all of the systems worked as pre the manufactures requirements. On the following Thursday, I got a gut feeling that something was wrong. I took my camera to the boat and took three rolls of film. I told my lead electrician to remove the computer module from the engine controls. I never told anybody why. On Friday afternoon, the captain went to the electrician and told him to make sure that the boat can run be-cause there may be a storm coming and they may have to move the boat to protect it from the weather. The electrician re-installed the modules. I should have told him to give the modules to me. That night the captain and crew took the boat out of the marine and disap-peared. We noticed it the next morning when I had my crew go to the boat to work on the sub-contractors' problems. The boat is gone, and they owe me about six-hundred-thousand dollars. You cannot hide a big boat like that. My gut feeling came from the fact that the owner's representative was the captain on a 130' that I built at Delta Marine years before. While there he bragged once about "stealing" a 90' sailboat out of the builder's yard that was just being finished. It hap-pened to be for the same client that I was building this boat for. Things worked out OK in the end with us getting some of the money and us not having to do any warranty work. It is still a good boat today.

The very next boat, in fact it was sitting alongside that boat in the marina after being launched just a few weeks earlier, decided that he would do the same thing. One morning we go to the marina and the boat is gone. He took off with the boat owing me twenty thousand dollars. This was a customer from Germany that was head-ing off around the world. The boat had made all of its sea trials and had made a short shakedown cruise. He took off with the boat and headed for California. I told my people to not get upset about it, he was just trying to follow what the other guy did. Before he arrived in California, he must have realized that he would lose any warranty, so he sent the money.

I had one other of the thirty-three boats that I built try to follow suite. This time I had the same gut feeling. The boat had a captain as well as an owner's representative. The owner was a well-known author. He owned houses all over the world. I visited three of them as well as his business office during the construction, mostly to work with his wife to hammer out interior details. Just before we were going to launch the boat, I went to the owner's rep and said that they would have to put the rest of the money that they owed us in an escrow account here in Anacortes, and I will right the escrow instruction. "If the boat is not in Anacortes and I am, the money is mine". The owner's representative would not agree to my terms so I told him that I would just park the boat outside till they do it. I did consult with my lawyer about this and he said that It was legal. He asked if I needed the money, which I said that the company was doing just fine (I never let the boat get behind on payments) so he said that we would just play defense on this. The boat sat on the beach for one year. During that year, the owner's lawyer called me once to have a chat. It was a very friendly conversation. At one point he said that, like all things, this will get resolved and the owner has a lot of really rich boating friends. Neither the owner nor the captain will be able to say anything good about the company and it could cost us some business. My response was that I had built two boats for New York Jews and I would not build for number three anyway. (I need to add that I have built boats for several other Jews and they all were great customers to work with. All were honest to a fault). About a week later, I had to drive to the ferry dock to meet a yacht broker that was coming from Port Townsend to visit my company. He was walking on the ferry, so he needed a ride. I was running a bit late, so I grabbed my daily mail and headed out to meet this person. When I arrived at the ferry dock waiting area, I had a bit of time, so I opened my mail. One letter happened to be from the east Coast Lawyer. He said that I made several bad remarks regarding Jews. I called my lawyer and read the letter to him. He just laughed and said that was nothing more than sabre rattling. He asked if I were honest about not building any more boats for New York Jews, and I said that there was no way I would ever go through that again. Both cases ended up in Arbitration.

The first arbitration took one week, and the argument was weather the boat delivery was early or late. Nothing to do with them stealing the boat without paying the bill. When I signed the contract, I was asked to put in a penalty clause for delivery. They knew that no builder ever delivers on time. The penalty was seven-hundred and fifty dollars for every day that the boat is late. Knowing a bit about the law, I added that I would receive the same incentive clause. I would receive the same seven-hundred and fifty dollars for every day that the boat is delivered early. Every change order would add days of delay. They had to approve every change that was created for the boat, and this boat had a lot. That is another advantage to having a full time representative on the project, he will cost you a lot more money in changes that he, and only he, thinks are important. Each change was documented with a written and signed change order. By the time they took the boat we were just over ninety days early, and that was real upsetting to them. I even told them that I did not care about getting that money, just what they owed us. After arguing for a week as to who was in default, they approached me to settle which I did. I took a lot less money just to get my sanity, and health, back

The second boat, which was still sitting on the beach, finally went into arbitration. The case took about one week. The owner's rep was the worst witness anybody could have. He could not tell the arbitrator who he even worked for. "I don't know, the money just showed up in my bank account". We heard all the arguments on both sides of the fence. The boat was nice, and I wanted to try to get the arbitrator to go to the boat. I knew that if he saw the boat it would defiantly sway him in our favor. Just another rich person trying to take advantage of a poor boat builder. He would not do it because he thought that could be the case, so he did not want anybody to call foul. An arbitrator will usually split the case somewhere. Their job is to see the good and bad in both sides. When the judgement was finally sent to us, it was 100% in our favor, in fact they had to pay 12% interest and put the money in the bank, like I originally wanted, before I would launch the boat. The arbitrator did come to view the boat after the case was finalized, he told me that after viewing the boat with its impressive workmanship, it would have definitely swayed his view.

The owners of both of these boats contacted me after they were out using them and told me how great the boat was. The one that stuck me for the money was very appreciated of the quality. I almost asked if he would pay me what he owed me, but I left it alone. Life has a way of correcting the score. The owner of the first boat got an illness that took him totally out of boating within one year and had to sell the boat. He was a true boater and loved to sport fish. He has traveled all over the world in his past boat and was looking forward to doing it in a boat hat was actually designed to do it. The second boat owner took the boat to Asia where he did a lot of boating. He owned two larger yachts of over 120' I was told that this 64' was the boat he used the most. He could operate the boat and it had plenty of room for his grand kids. It was not long before I was told that the boat was for sale. He got the ultimate disease that ended his boating.

BIGGER IS BETTER?

A designer from the southeast who had a customer for one of his designs approached me. They came to Anacortes to meet me and to discuss their potential new build project. It was a one hundred and thirty-two-foot custom yacht. It became obvious to them after the first meeting that I was not interested in building them a boat because I wouldn't give them a price. They had to visit a few other builders on the West Coast and said to think about it. They were going to return a few days later and wanted me to give them a price, so I sat down with all my leads for all of the different trades and told them that building mega yachts can be rewarding, but it can also be the biggest pain in the ass because it is usually a captain who is the owner's representative. He usually knows nothing about how to build a boat but is the "smartest" man in the world about boats. (As a side note, I had to teach most of the paid captains of the mega yachts I built [yachts over one hundred feet] how to dock the boat without crashing when there was a wind and current to deal with.) The leads all took a vote and decided they were up for the challenge. When the customer and his team returned a few days later, I met with them and gave them a good sales pitch and sold him the boat. My sales tactics were simple. I never really concerned myself with the competition, but it is hard not to know their products since we all attend the same big boat shows. I may not know some of the details on the interior, but I can see all the exterior details. When this customer came to me, I knew who the competition was going to be. There were three other yards bidding on the same boat. One had no chance because they could not control their costs and would be out of the running just on price. One of the others was a production boat company that would not allow you to "personalize" your boat, it was going to be their boat and the third had a shot at this. I knew that my detail work on the exterior was much better than theirs so, without pointing out their defects, I just pointed out what we did that I knew they did not. All I did was educate the customer as to what to look for. If the discussion every came to the interior quality I would just look back to them and say that we had the talent to build to any level that they had the money to pay for. The customer, along with his captain and designer, made their comparison. They

had two pages of bullet points that they rated each builder on. I got the project under one condition. The Owner insisted that his boat had to make the cover of Show Boat magazine. We built the boat to their design. I paid careful attention to the intricate details which I knew were important to a quality minded customer. The boat did make the magazine but never made the cover. He allowed me to use his boat in the big Fort Lauderdale Boat Show as a model of what we could do. Although it never made the cover it did get nominated by the International Super Yacht Society. Most boats over eighty feet in length get nominated for one of the four categories. The categories are by size, 80' – 124', 125' – 150', 150' – nuts and sailboats. In fact, I had two boats nominated that year, the eighty-foot *MEANDER* and the one-hundred- and thirty-two-foot *MAGIC*. Just like the Oscars, they take the list down to the top five in each category. This is a European event so it is difficult for the Americans to win but just getting into the top five would be a big achievement. Both of my boats made the top five that year. We did not win but we did get a nice plaque. I went to the owner of the *MAGIC* and had to apologize for not making it onto the cover of Show Boats magazine, but I believe that the plaque trumped that. He was in fact incredibly happy and proud of his boat.

The Magic was the first Mega Yacht that we built at Northern Marine and one of the fist award winning boats that we built

Before I was even half finished with the one-hundred and thirty-two-foot yacht, I sold a one-hundred and fifty-two-foot yacht from the same designer. This owner built the boat as a project and was going to market it once it was complete. The owner, along with the design team, did an excellent job of coming up with a stately design both from the exterior look, as with the one-hundred and thirty-two-foot, as well as the interior details. The team at the yard did an outstanding job of building the boat to the high-level design, and it was another boat that received top honors. After it was completed, the owner took the boat to Fort Lauderdale to sell it. All the top brokers in town came to me after getting a tour of the boat and told me the boat was worth $4 to $5 million more than what he was asking. The quality was apparent throughout the boat. The boat sold at the show at a good profit for the owner.

The one-hundred and fifty-two Lia Fail during a sea trial in the San Juan Islands

The owner of the *Magic* allowed me to show the boat at the boat show. It was docked alongside the *Lia Fail* on the main dock where all the big yachts are tied up. The boats are all stern tied, so they are sitting side by side with just the stern of the boat at the dock. The designer, Ward Setzer, came to me onboard the *Magic* and pointed to a yacht that was tied up about four boats down the dock. He said that he also designed that boat to be the same as the *Magic*. As I looked at the boat it did not look like a "sister ship" or even a close cousin. Ward pointed out to me that the same details were in that design as he put in the *Magic*. The yard decided not to put the intricate details in the construction since they were a bit time-consuming which would cost more. It was the intricate details that made the significant difference in the looks of the boat. This was a big lesson for me that we can build a pretty boat, but an important part of the team was a good designer. One that would help on both the interior as well as the exterior. When it came to the interior, we had the talent to build whatever you could design but we were not good interior designers. The owner would hire their interior designers to put the finishing touches on the boat. I would tell the owners that we can build the pretty lady, they must put the lipstick on her.

THE START OF THE END

Northern Marine continued to build boats and continued to grow. A customer approached me about a mega yacht. He wanted to buy a 144-foot yacht with the option to buy nine more. He wanted to build the boats and market them himself. We put a deal together and started to build the boats. Not unlike all projects, especially those where you get designers involved, the project grew from 144' to 151' before we actually started the boat. The difference in boatbuilding in the twenty first century was the invent of computer modeling. The hull could be designed, and the design sent to a company here locally that could cut the female mold in several tuckable sections, and it would be perfect when completed. It was considered a "temporary" mold capable of producing only about 10 boats. I had used this method when I started to build the eighty-foot series. The tooling cost more but the accuracy was great, and the timing was quick. It would take weeks instead of months to build a usable tool and I did not have to tie up my talented workers building the tool. All of the boats were going to be painted with a high-quality marine paint, so I was not as concerned about the surface condition as I was about the accuracy and fairness of the finished part. Being that we were possibly going to build ten of these the same, we even had the superstructure tooled so it almost became a kit boat.

The construction was the same. We used a structural engineer for all of the structural components. The hull was infused complete with the stringers and frames installed which eliminated all secondary bonds. The same for all the decks and superstructure. We would place the entire superstructure on in one piece and then laminate it to the hull. This piece did not go onto the hull until all of the tanks, engines, generators, all major equipment as well as the entire lower decks with all of the walls and cabinetry installed.

This was the first of the 151's built. Note the anchor pocket where the bottom of the anchor "seals" the hole. My friend that built the yacht jewelry came up with the design after I told him I wanted the hole plugged so the anchor did not rattle in the pocket when bucking into big seas. I also wanted to stop the spray of water on deck that was coming through the chain pipe when pounding into the waves.

Before the third boat was started, the buyer approached me to buy the company, and I agreed. The company was not for sale, but I believed that if he purchased the company, he could help take the company to a better level. He had the ability to get the money to build the boats first and then sell them. That takes a lot of the pressure off the builder. He does not have to try to please a client all the time while building the boat.

An article came out in the publications regarding this buyer:

Doug Mergenthaler's recent foray into building superyachts started one sunny day about four years ago on the Caribbean island of St. Thomas.

He decided it would be "good to have a boat" to explore the region, and also decided the boat should be large enough to need a crew, so he and his family would be able to arrive and set off exploring without a lot of prep time.

"I ended up ordering a 150-foot boat," said Mergenthaler, CEO of Ashton Capital Corp. of Renton.

Mergenthaler ordered his new yacht, named after his wife, Irene, from Northern Marine Co. LLC of Anacortes. He was so impressed with the shipyard, and its products, that he bought up the company's entire large-yacht production into the future.

"I said, 'If I'm ordering one, why don't I order 10, because yachts are a pretty good market,'" Mergenthaler said.

Then he bought the entire company on Sept. 8, with plans to expand Northern's production and facilities to build even larger luxury yachts, up to 180 feet.

As he mentioned to the press, he had great thoughts for taking the boat building business to the next level. I was excited for the future of the company. This also got me out of a difficult partnership. The deal was done. I remained at the yard to help, but it was obvious that my help was not wanted so I moved on after about a year and a half after selling the business. This is also when I learned about loyalty of some people. Some of my top people were, or appeared to be loyal, dedicated workers. Once I sold the company, a group of them turned against me and, behind my back, told the new owners that I did not know how to build the boats and to listen to them and not to me. This was also when I learned that I spent most of my time out in the shop supervising the build of the boats and not just sit around the office wasting time. The owners of both of the boat yards that I worked at prior to starting my own company very seldom came into the shop to see the day to day operation and its progress. They only came when there was a problem that required their attention. The people that bought my company (I sold it 5 times) also never spent any time out overseeing the projects. It was not till I left and looked back that I realized that I was involved in almost all aspects of the day to day build of the boats. I worked with the leads on systems and processes to make the project go smoother. Ten years after I sold my business, I was told by one of my leads that I was a "micro-manager". It caught me a bit off guard, but my quick response was that if he knew what to do I wouldn't' have to be telling him what to do every day. I could build my custom boats in about half the hours of my competition. I was building them for about the same hours as the production boat builders. I was also selling my boats for a lot less money than my competition.

This is when it really came to me how important it is to have a boat builder when it comes to having a boat built. The naval architects and marine engineers, although necessary, lack the ability to make something work. I have countless stories about designers and engineers who have been taught more by somebody from the working side of the industry than the academic side of the industry. I think they believe the sheepskin instantly makes them much more knowledgeable than the people doing the work. I have a great deal of respect for people that take the time and money to go off to school to learn. It is after they come out of school and do not continue to learn is when I start losing respect for them. My dad had several sayings about people from the academic side. About teachers, he always said that "those who can do them who can't teach". He also taught me that the best thing that you can learn from school is how to teach yourself. I tried school but being a shy person, I listened to the counselors and took subjects that I had no interest in like Ancient History and English. I wanted to further my math and physics classes. I dropped out early and just went to work instead.

My dad ended his career working for an oil company. That was the reason we moved when I was still a young lad. Towards the end of his career he was tasked with helping to re-design their underground piping system that transferred all of the crude oil, diesel and gas from the ships and put it into the various storage tanks. He worked with the contractors laying everything out including all of the piping and the pumps. He designed the system with reversing pumps so he could move the product to or from the tanks and be able to direct the product to its location with a valve manifold system. He would get frustrated with the workers because they could not understand that the fluid really did not care which way it moved through the pipe. The workers wanted a pipe going to the tank as well as a separate one coming back from the tank. That would require twice the pipe in the ground as well as more pumps. One day he received a call from one of the top executives from British Petroleum who asked him where he went to college. When my dad told him that he never went to college he became real concerned about this huge project that was under construction in the Seattle storage yard. After a bit of explaining they finally believed my dad and the project was finished. It worked so efficiently that after my dad retired, the competition contacted him about redesigning their new facility that was going to be built on the coast. My dad said that he would do it. When it came time to discuss his pay, he said that since the oil companies had such a great benefit program, he would do the job if they paid for his and mom's insurance until they die. They agreed and they put the deal together. Before the project got started, the environmentalist killed the project and it never got built. The company did continue my parent's insurance till their final days.

DESIGNERS AND ENGINEERS

Designers and engineers are a strange breed. I do believe that going to school and working with the instructors makes them believe that they know everything. Learning from some of the teachers, and I can speak from experience, is not a great recommendation for getting a job in a custom boat shop. The industry changes rapidly. If you are not in the industry day to day and trying to keep up with all the changes, it will pass you by and it will be hard to catch up. The reason "that's how we did it on the last boat" was never a good reason for me to do it on this boat. Everything needs to be evaluated. It looked like a good idea, but after going through the sea trials, you may realize that it requires some improvement. I told my people to always look at the project and see if you can improve on it. They had to run the idea past me first and if it looked like an improvement, we would go with it. I would also make sure that the worker got full credit for his idea. I would point it out to the customer in front of the worker so that the worker would feel good about his idea, which would usually get him to do better. Most of the innovative ideas came from the shop not the engineering department. In my company, I would not allow the engineers to talk directly with the workers., they had to go through me and the leads before anything got built. To this day I have people that cannot understand how a liquid can travel either direction down a pipe. I stole my dad's design and put it into the first yacht fuel transfer system that I built. I saw what the competition was doing and did not like that direction. My system had two manifolds, one for the fuel suction and the other for fuel discharge each manifold had a valve attached to it so that you could select the fuel tank that you wanted to take fuel from and which one you wanted to discharge to. The transfer pump was connected to the two manifolds. The two valves were tied together with a "T" fitting that had a single line going to the bottom of the fuel tank. All that you had to do to transfer fuel was to turn on the tank, or tanks (it didn't matter how many you turned on) that you wanted to take the fuel from and turn on the valve for the tank that you wanted to send the fuel to. Turn on the transfer pump and transfer fuel. Typically, you would be transferring fuel from the forward tanks to the aft tanks which were in the engine room. There are sight glasses in the engine room that show the level in those tanks so you cannot make a mistake and overfill them.

I met a scientist after I retired, that taught me about the Dunning-Kreuger Effect that was developed in 1999. It was designed by two people who did a comprehensive study of lots of people. It was basically the relationship of knowledge and confidence on a given subject. We all have met the person that "knows all" but cannot really figure it out. I had one worker that fit perfectly into this chart. Actually, everybody fits somewhere in the chart, this guy was at the highest point of the chart. I had him layout the underwater gear on a 64' trawler yacht. I instructed him to git a big piece of cardboard or a door skin, which ever he preferred, and place it behind the keel from the bottom steel all the way to the back of the boat. I told him to carefully lay out where the shaft will come out of the keel, where the propeller will be as well as the location for the rudder shaft. He came and got me when finished. He was so proud of his layout. He was always telling me, as well as everybody else, that he was a marine engineer. I went over to see his layout and I pointed out what was wrong. The propeller did not have the proper tip clearance from the bottom of the hull and the rudder was too close to the propeller so you could not remove the propeller without removing the rudder. I than asked him why he just did not turn around and look at the boat that was next to the boat he was working on and just copy it. I wish I had this when I ran the boat shop. I used to have my leads do a "self-evaluation" once a year. I would have them place themselves on the chart.

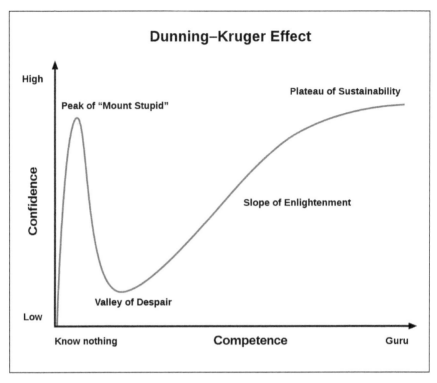

This is a copy of the Dunning-Kreuger Effect. I could put the names of my people all the way down the curve.

There are certain areas that the engineers are greatly appreciated. The hull shape is best designed by a Naval Architect that has the experience and the knowledge to crunch the numbers and come up with the most efficient under water hull shape. There are a lot of the details of construction that should be left to a good boat builder. When I was at work, I lived in the boats on a daily basis. I had an instinct for coming up with ideas that would improve the design. When I tried to talk to engineers or designers about these ideas, I would learn that they would not like the new idea because they could not understand it. I was fortunate that the people that I worked for believed in me and my ability to do the right thing. When I owned the company, I did not have to worry about the designers not liking my ideas, they did not have a choice. I was the person who sea trialed every boat I worked on. I was also the guy who took the owners out on their sea trials to teach them how to operate the boat. This is something that is invaluable in the learning process. The owners and operators of the vessels all have some good input that will help grow the knowledge of the boat-building company and its people. Listening has always been an important part of the learning process.

Some of the examples that rated high on the list of the engineers not knowing the little details of the boat and therefore making mistakes is when I came into the engine room of a one-hundred-and-ten-foot yacht that I was in charge of and the lead mechanic had directed the worker to move the battery bank from the port side of the boat to the starboard side of the boat. The engineering department did a calculation and decided the boat was going to have a two thousand–pound list, or lean to port, so the battery move would solve the problem. I told the workers to stop and to never make a change because somebody told them to without talking to me first. My lead had an interest in working in the design department, so he went running to the designer and told him I would not let him move the batteries. The designer went to the owner of the company, and the owner came to me with the complaint. I walked the owner through the boat and tried to convince him I was right. On the way to the boat I tore a piece of cardboard from a box that was lying behind the boat. We entered the boat from the stern and went into the lazerette (the aft lower section of the boat where the steering mechanism is located). I made a simple sketch of the boat on the cardboard and asked if that area had a port or starboard list and he said it was balanced, so I put a zero on that section. We went into the engine room where there were two main engines, two generators and a lot of other equipment. He looked around and saw all the batteries clear over on the port side and said with a big smile, port side by about one thousand pounds so I marked that down. We continued into the lower staterooms where there were four rooms all balanced both sides of centerline, so that area got a zero on my score card. Next were the forward crew's quarters. The way that the laundry room with its equipment was placed it was a bit heavier to starboard, so he gave that five hundred pounds back towards starboard. We then went up to the main lever where there was the main saloon aft, a formal dining area and the galley with the owner's stateroom all the way forward. As we walked through from aft to forward, he would point out the slight port to starboard differences and I would mark them down. The biggest difference on that level was the galley with all its heavy commercial appliances was all on the port side. He gave that another five hundred pounds to port. We went to the upper deck, which was not yet complete, and he said that was about even. He looked at me and asked what my tally showed, and I said that we had a two-thousand-pound list to the port. He started to beam a bit because he was there at the request of the design department to prove me wrong. I than mentioned that the large tender (shore boat) on the upper deck will be on the starboard side as well as the grand piano that the owner was going to put in the main saloon. I said that the boat will have a starboard list when it is completed especially when all the supplies that will be stowed in the pantry on the starboard side are added. He was not convinced because the design department, which he was paying a lot of money to do a complete weight study on the boat, said I was dead wrong, but he did not make me move the batteries as if I would have moved them anyway. He knew that the time would be the same now or later, so it would not cost any more. The day came to launch the boat, and the designer could not let it go, so he and the owner of the company came to me to bet me I was wrong. My standard answer was, "Put your money where your mouth is," so we bet the standard hundred dollars on which way the boat would list. I am on the boats when they launch them and must drive the boat to the dock, so I did not have a real opportunity to see which way the boat was listing. When I got the boat secured to the dock, the owner walked up to me, handed me the hundred dollars, and walked away not saying a word. I became a bit of an ass towards the design department because it was always left to me to fix their mistakes.

This was from the same designer who called me to the office one day to complain to me that I was not doing a proper job in the shop. He, or his design team, would send a drawing out to the shop, and sometimes my people would not do what was on the drawing because I told them to do it a different way. After he was finished chastising me and showing his authority because he worked in the "big" office where the owners as well as the salesman and all the designers work and I only worked in the shop, I told him a couple of facts. I asked him where he worked prior to this job. He said he was a structural designer for a large boat builder in Tacoma Washington where they built some large steel commercial vessels. I asked him if he had to have a man sitting behind a big oak desk in a nice suit approve and sign his drawings before they went to the shop to be built, and he agreed that he, as well as all the designers, in fact did have to have all drawings approved and signed before the shop could receive them for construction. I then told him that I was the man behind the desk, and just because I did not wear a suit or sit behind a big oak desk all day long, it did not change the facts. I told him, "If you don't want to run your designs by me for an approval then don't get upset when I don't use them." Then I stood up and walked out of the conference room. He never did like me, but he could not argue with my success ratio fixing all his mistakes. There were a lot of examples that make for great reading, but out of courtesy, I will not go into them here. Suffice it to say that I had a great reputation for fixing their mistakes.

I always enjoyed working with people, from the owners of the boats to the workers installing the systems. Everybody can add something to the project. When somebody came to me with a problem, I would usually ask them how they would solve the problem. If they had a workable solution, even if it were not the way I would solve the problem, I would go with their idea. That would give them ownership in the solution and build up their confidence so they could become better workers. When a big mistake did happen, my rule was that you could not go fix it without coming and talking about it first. I did not want somebody that was a bit in a panic because of the mistake, making the problem bigger. If I had any success at all, it was from having a talented team of people around me. We all worked together as one. I let every different team of workers know that every part of the boat was just as important as all the other parts. The cabinet makers thought that their part was the most important because that is what everybody saw when they came onboard. I explained to everybody that without a good hull and good mechanical and electrical systems the best cabinet work in the world will not go anywhere because these boats were bought to go places, and that is just what they did. Several of the boats that I built have traveled around the world. Most have traveled to the east coast and back and some are still in faraway lands enjoying the beauty that the boat was able to take them to.

After I sold the business and retired from the day-to-day business of building the boats, I had the opportunity to go out and see firsthand other boat-building businesses. Not just here in America but in Canada and all the way to China. The new generations of boat builders do not appear to have the passion for building the boats as in the old days. This could be nothing more than the thoughts from a retired boat builder who started his career by falling out of a tree and landing headfirst onto a sharp rock. It could also be from a boat builder that started a boat building company with no financial support from a bank or even a friend. I had to pay close attention to the day to day operations of the business. As the business grew, much to fast, I had to hire and put more trust into other people. That worked great except for a couple of the project managers. I grew to just over three-hundred employees for a while. I slowed it back down to about one-hundred and eighty, which was a good workable size. Getting and keeping enough work was not a problem. I always had at least five boats under construction at one time. Sometimes there would be two of the one-hundred and fifty-foot yachts as well as some of the sixty-four and eighty-foot yachts all in various stages of completion.

I have had a distinguished career meeting some of the best people in the industry. The buyers of the bigger boats all become explorers when they get onboard their boats. I have been fortunate to become friends with several of the buyers of the boats I made. This friendship has allowed me to become part of the journey in the boating experiences of these individuals.

I remember getting a satellite call one Friday afternoon from a customer while he was on his seventy-five-foot Northern Marine sitting on the East Coast. These are scary calls to take because if somebody is going to pick up their satellite phone at over one dollar a minute and call the builder, it usually must be to complain about something. The owner of the boat was sitting in a nice harbor in Florida and told me that he and his wife were reflecting on their life and said I had become an important part of their journey because of the quality of the boat I built for them. They said that if I wanted to, they would allow me to put their boat into the Fort Lauderdale Boat Show and show their boat as an example of the quality that we build. I accepted their offer but on one condition, and that was only if they remained on the boat during the show. They agreed, and we went to the show. They were helpful, but the most important part was that we all had a wonderful time. To me it was not as much about showing the boat as it was showing my appreciation for them both for allowing us to show the boat but mostly for being another great customer.

The boat eventually came back to the west coast to make a trip to Alaska. On the way up the coast from California, the captain hit a large log off the Columbia river bar. The log damaged the stainless-steel stem band, which was a two-inch boat shaft cut in half, polished, and bolted to the stem of the boat. With the bulbous bow, the logs usually get hit and get pushed down the side of the boat and not pushed under the hull where they can do substantial damage to the roll stabilizer fins and the propeller. The boat arrived in Anacortes and we had the boat pulled out of the water so the owner could have a fresh coat of bottom paint applied. When the boat was out of the water, I sent two people down to the boat to repair the stainless-steel stem band. After the boat was launched, the owner had us do a couple of small additions to the interior of the boat. When he was ready to leave, he came into my office with his captain to go over the bill. We were discussing his future trip to Alaska when I noticed that the owner was looking really agitated. I asked him what was wrong. He asked what his bill was for the work that was done. I told him that when the boat was on the east coast, the captain had to fix a couple of problems with the boat that would be considered warrantee so with what we did here I think we are now even. He slumped back into his chair and said that he was ready for an argument and that was why he brought his captain to the meeting. He thought that was more than fair.

I have been invited by several past customers, both from Delta Marine as well as my own company Northern Marine, to cruise in various parts of the world. After spending the better part of two years building somebody their "dream boat" you get to know them really well. There were some people that I chose not to go boating with while others I would jump at the chance.

One such customer was the Owner of the second large yacht that I built at Delta. The yacht was one-hundred and thirty-feet long. As with the other vessels that I built, I took this on an overnight sea trial with the owner and his captain. We usually just head up to the San Juan Islands where it is like being in a different world, especially if you are from a different part of the country. We would work all the systems and, on this vessel, especially the commercial ice maker for making the gin and tonics. We had a wonderful time on the sea trial, and he must have liked our company enough to invite me and my wife to the Virgin Islands for a ten-day cruise. That was the first time I had ever been on an extended cruise on a big yacht let along in a place like the Virgin Islands. We had so much fun that he invited me back the next year to cruise the Bahamas.

My wife of forty-plus years never did take up fishing, but she is my navigator in all our yachting around the Pacific Northwest. As I would say to mixed groups of people in different venues like Trawler Fest, there are only three reasons to take a woman on board a boat. After the shocked expression on most of the ladies' faces would lessen, I would proceed by telling them the three reasons. They are obvious when you stop and think about it. First and fairly important is to cook, second and less important is to clean, and the third and most important reason to take a woman on board a cruise is to *navigate*. We men just want to be on the boat and point it somewhere. That may be part of our Christopher Columbus coming out. Columbus went for the adventure. He had to have a navigator to make sure he got somewhere or at least could find the way back.

While at one of the Trawler Feast events, I attended a seminar held by my competition. During the question and answer portion of the speech they were asked the difference between a Northern Marine and their boats. They knew that I was in the audience, so I believe that they wanted to be a bit careful with their answer. They knew that I would never say anything derogatory about them. They told the audience that the biggest difference was DNA. My DNA came from building robust fishing boats that fished in most of the oceans of the world whereas their DNA was from building smaller yachts and growing them in size. I had the robust systems that one would find on the commercial boat where they had the fancy interiors. They did know at the time that I was no longer just building the simple boats but was in fact building the larger mega-yachts with very up-scaled interiors. To this day they are still a good builder of the long-range yachts and I am just a washed-up boat builder that started making boats in his daddy's garage.

Aftermath

THE ROAD OF boat building has been a great road for me. I have been able to use my creative juices to design and build several hundred vessels. I have also met a lot of interesting and knowledgeable people during my forty-plus years of building these boats. One example of meeting somebody I built a vessel for was when I was going into the hospital to have a hernia fixed. (I got the hernia by showing a group of people who were trying to put a large propeller onto the shaft of a fifty-eight-foot fishing boat how to do it. After I lifted the 350-pound propeller and put it on the shaft, I started having some pains in my leg, which turned out to be the hernia.) I scheduled my operation for a Friday so I could recover over the weekend so I would not miss much work. As I lay on the operating table that Friday morning, an elderly gentleman walked up to me and said to me, "Today is my last day of work, and, by the way, you built me a boat in the past." He was the anesthesiologist for the process, so, being concerned, I looked at him and said, "I sure hope it was a good boat." He told me the name of the boat, *White Cap*, which was a fifty-foot charter boat I built several years earlier. He said it was still a great boat and not to worry; I would be wakening back up.

It is very seldom that I do not meet some old acquaintance while out boating. Usually it will be in some secluded anchorage someplace where there are a several yachts enjoying the serenity of the water and the surrounding landscape. That is what boating has brought to me. Besides the birth of my two lovely daughters, boating has brought some of the best memories of my life. My wife does not like the fact that boating or boat building is the usual conversation when we are out with friends. She does not realize that the discussions are nothing more the memories of an old man coming out of his mouth.

There is an old saying in the boat building business. "how do you make $5million dollars building boats? Start with 10". When I started my boat building company in 1995, it was underfunded. The three partners put in less than a total of one-hundred-thousand dollars into the account. I had a contract to build a boat and it did not take long to get more business. The company never had a bank note to worry about. I learned how to "cash flow" the business. The company purchased over eight million dollars of equipment and tooling while I owned the company, all with cash flow. I did not have the money to build production boats and then sell them when finished, which would have been a more profitable business plan. To this day I have very few regrets as to how I operated the business. The people that purchased the company have worked hard to destroy the name and reputation of the company. The second buyer rolled a boat over and sank it during the launch because he would not listen to anybody about the ballast required to maintain stability.

I feel I have one more boat in me. Now that I am not employed, I have the time, as I did before I started a career, to build one more boat in the garage. I must admit that my garage is a bit bigger than Dad's small two-car garage that I built my first seven boats out of, and I also must admit that I have lot better tools than I had to work with back then. The rest will be about the same except that I no longer have Dad, my mentor, to bounce ideas off and help when it becomes a two-man job. I do have a handful of volunteers that, also being retired from a great life, want to help. I sometimes wonder if it is to help build the boat or, like my Dad in the early days, to be able to go out on the water and enjoy the bounty that is waiting for people like me to harvest.

My knowledge and technology have both come a long way since those days in junior and senior high school. It will be a lot like the old days except I will not have any seventy-five-cent plans to work from. The boat will be a continuation of what I started way back then. As all my builds grew in size and complexity back then, this new boat will be bigger and a bit more complex than the last one built in my dad's garage. It, as most of my other builds, will be used for fishing as well as exploring. I will be able to tow this one behind our small yacht when my wife and I head out onto the water for a month or so each summer. As when I was younger, I have the idea in my head and will make it become a reality in the winter months. And like all my earlier builds, it will be a light, strong, and fast boat. This will be a great boat to take people out fishing and crabbing on sunny weekends, much like I used to do in the early days. The biggest difference will be that I will have my own vehicle and a driver's license, so I do not have to depend on somebody else to get the boat to the water, or at least until I get a bit older.

I, unlike most boat builders, have spent a great deal of my life on the water. I have endless stories of storms, near disasters, and just plain fun. Like the old saying, "Nobody talks about the thousand great dockings I made over the decades but make one mistake, and they tell the world." The mistakes I made are all memorable, possibly because there was always some adrenaline involved, which helps to imprint the moment in one's brain.

I have never sunk a boat or seriously damaged a boat, which has defied the odds based on the number of hours on the water and the number of dockings made, especially those in very adverse conditions. Remember, I was the one who sea trialed almost every boat I built during my working career. It consisted of several sea trials as well as a final sea trial where I took the owner and taught him about his new boat. On the larger yachts, I would make the owners sea trial an overnight event so we could use the entire boat. We would have a fantastic dinner on board to try out the galley. The sea trial would be in a location that was away from the big city. Most of the people were not from the Pacific Northwest, so it was like the beginning of their journey. My wife would usually come along, especially if there was a couple involved. Sherrie was invaluable in teaching the women how to manage while onboard. From handling the lines and fenders before and after docking to cooking incredible meals, she made the women on board feel at ease while on board.

If I can get around safely, I will continue to spend my time on the water. When the weather is good, the water sirens call out to me. I can enjoy sitting and just drifting while my shrimp or crab traps are doing their jobs. I can sit back and enjoy the vessel traffic as it passes by. I am fortunate to live in the Pacific Northwest by the San Juan Islands, where we enjoy boating. The weather is usually nice in the summer. We spend a month up north in Desolation Sound in Canada or venture even farther, where fewer boats go. The fishing is a lot better farther north, so it is a wonderful place to be able to fill the freezers with the winter's supply of seafood. I have been fortunate enough to make great friendships while going down this road. I have had several of my past customers offer me their boat to use for the summer or to take an extended cruise with them

I will always be a boater, it has been a major portion of my life and the boating bug has bitten me hard in my early formative years. As hard as it tried to scare me off the water with storms and tough weather conditions, I always return to the water. My body is seventy percent saltwater and the world is seventy percent saltwater. It is only natural that I try to spend seventy percent of my free time on the saltwater.

As one goes through life, one starts to realize that you cannot get any more out of life than what you put into it. One of the things I can attribute much of my success to is my 100 percent dedication to my work. I lived and breathed my work. That dedication to work cost me two special opportunities. The first was an opportunity to fly with the Blue Angles one year when they came to town for Sea Fair week. I went to a party that was set up to invite them into Seattle and by the end of the night I had convinced the commander to let me sit in the second seat on one of their test runs. I used the excuse that I was too busy to go so I never did it. I did make that up later in life when I got to sit in the second seat of an Alfa Jet behind one of the aircraft carrier fighter pilots. We made two trips around Mount Baker, did a couple of wing overs, one "Top Gun" move and a couple of other maneuvers that had my equilibrium messed up for about four hours.

Another dumb decision to stay working and not take up a once in a lifetime offer is when the owner of Todd Shipyard in Seattle invited me to go out to sea with them for a day on a high-speed military boat to "shoot down drones". Again, I was too busy.

I was constantly learning how to improve at whatever I was do-ing, whether it was when I worked for somebody else or was working on my own. This dedication became a way of life, whether it was at work or at home. We built two houses and finished both, which is not the norm with most people building their own houses. Most people lose interest and start a new project before the house is 100 percent complete. This follow-through is what I believe separates the differ-ent success levels of people. I have never considered myself a smart person, just a dedicated hard worker. If I can pass one thing on to the people who want to be successful, it is that focus, and dedication are all it will take to get to the top of your game. There are always some obstacles in the road. There are things I wish I had not done and things I should have done, but indeed, there are many things I am happy to have done. It is all in a lifetime. Life is a gift to you. The way you live your life is your gift to those who come after. Make it a fantastic gift. My wife of 40 plus years told me one intelligent thing one day a few years ago. The reason that you get married is to have a witness to your life. All your accomplishments, no matter how big or small, if you are married to a special person, as I am, you will have that witness to your life. It is also a two-way street. I have witnessed all her accomplishments along the way also. Some were as simple as just keeping me out of trouble and others were as astonishing as giv-ing birth to my two lovely daughters. The only thing that you leave on this earth when you pass is your reputation. Any accumulated wealth will disappear, but your reputation will live on. That is what people will remember you by.

Remember that the road less traveled will not be as smooth as the well-traveled roads, but the road less traveled will make all the difference.

THE END

Dedication

THIS BOOK IS dedicated to Odin, Landon Oscar, our three grand-sons, and Elaina, our cute little granddaughter. I just hope that I live long enough to help all of them like my grandpa helped me. I was fortunate to have great, as well as intelligent, parents as do Odin and Oscar, Landon and Elaina have. With an engineer for a dad and a doctor/professor for a mom, Odin and Oscar may just have a chance. Landon and Elaina have two very smart, hard-working and dedicated parents who will be able to pass on a lot of knowledge as well as other traits that should help them with any road that they may choose to travel down. Hopefully, I also may be able to add a bit of my knowledge and work ethic to the four of them.

I also want to dedicate this book to all the people that helped direct, guide or push me down the road of life. Without them I would have had an easy normal life but because of them I had an interesting full life with many adventures along the way. These were the people that brought me into this life as well as a lot of the people I met while traveling down my chosen road of life. The suppliers were a great asset to me. They were the ones that were always there to help whenever I needed it. Keith Mahler is still a close friend today. He still helps out the past customers of my boats when they need advice or parts to fix one of the systems that he was a representative for. Steve made sure that he was always there if my people needed any hydraulic tube and hose supplies, equipment, or training. There were several others. Like in the Oscars, it is hard to mention the countless people that made it all possible. All of these suppliers. And there was a lot of them, were considered as part of my crew. They were invited to the parties as well as other company functions.

My dad was a great friend as well as my mentor throughout most of my life. If I had a problem, he would help me work it out. He did not get to see any of my boats that I built at my own company. I am sure that he would have been proud of my accomplishments. He had several great sayings that I use even to this day. One was "life is a crap sandwich. The more bread that you have, the less crap that you have to eat". Another one was "if I ever need a brain transplant, I will want yours, because I don't think it has ever been used". I have used both of those throughout the years. He taught me to not try to re-invent the mouse trap, just try to improve on it. Another saying that I learned to late in life was "there is no I in team but there are three U's in shut the f--- up" I did get to use that just before I sold the business, so my leads did get to hear it once during a production meeting when I had to address one of my mechanical leads that wasn't a long way down the curve on the Dunning Kruger graph.

I ran an honest business and my wife was honest and fair to a fault. It was not about the dollars as much about the customer and the boat that motivated me. My crew was like extended family and were always an important part of my life. I still help some of them with any questions that may have. Neither I nor my wife were ever greedy but just the opposite. Hard work and dedication to the job would always pay off. And it did.

The road to a great future is not easy and will require a lot of dedication to the job. The people that succeed are the ones that can stay focused, ditch your ego so that you can learn and listen more than you talk. You will have plenty of time to talk when you retire, trust me, just ask my wife.

Richard "Bud" LeMieux

CPSIA information can be obtained
at www.ICGtesting.com
Printed in the USA
BVHW091055011220
594381BV00003B/8